Captain Hook

Captain Hook

A Pilot's Tragedy and Triumph in the Vietnam War

CAPTAIN WYNN F. FOSTER, U.S. NAVY (RET.)

Naval Institute Press
Annapolis, Maryland

© 1992
by the United States Naval Institute
Annapolis, Maryland

LIBRARY OF CONGRESS CATALOGING-IN-PUBLICATION DATA
Foster, Wynn F.
Captain Hook : a pilot's tragedy and triumph in the Vietnam War /
    Wynn F. Foster.
        p.   cm.
    Includes index.
    ISBN 1-55750-256-0 (alk. paper)
    1. Vietnamese Conflict, 1961–1975—Aerial operations, American.
    2. Vietnamese Conflict, 1961–1975—Personal narratives, American.
    3. Foster, Wynn F.   I. Title.
DS558.8.F67   1992
959.704' 348—dc20 92-5089

Printed in the United States of America on acid-free paper ∞

9   8   7   6   5   4   3   2

First printing

My work is war. I don't hate it and I don't love it. I didn't invent it and I don't preach it, but somebody has to take care of it when it comes along.

Martin Dibner, THE ADMIRAL

Our belief at the beginning of a doubtful undertaking is the one thing that ensures its successful outcome.

William James, PSYCHOLOGIST

Contents

Foreword

This is the gripping story of a man with a tremendous sense of purpose and uncommon tenacity. I knew that before I read this book because I flew with then-Commander Wynn Foster repeatedly in Vietnam, when he was one of my top strike leaders in the aircraft carrier *Oriskany*'s air wing. In fact, Wynn and I were a flight of two A-4 Skyhawks, I an Alfa-strike coordinator and he my backup, when I was shot down as the air wing's commander.

Wynn Foster represents a determined generation of naval aviators who caught the flying bug early in World War Two as high school kids, entered the service as soon as they had the diploma required to enter the Navy's pilot-training pipeline, missed the war because of timing, got out and finished college and reentered flight training as officers, and got their wings in time for the Korean War. Wynn was an F9F jock with seventy-five combat missions in that conflict, and continued his cockpit life as a tailhook pilot thereafter. But it was the carrier skipper for whom he worked in his ship's-company tour who made sure that Wynn, soon to be a lieutenant commander, got in on the ground floor of the new, popular A-4 Skyhawk program.

Wynn was soon qualified and certified across the board, and his top performance as an A-4 squadron operations officer, throughout two Mediterranean cruises and the Cuban Missile Crisis aboard the nuclear-powered carrier *Enterprise*, ensured his selection for an A-4 squadron command. And that squadron was to be VA-163, the Saints, whose battle accomplishments on the first three *Oriskany* cruises of the Vietnam War are the stuff of legends.

But it was on the second, with Wynn in command, that the unforgettable part of this autobiography of this highly adaptive man's *courage* will be indelibly burned into the reader's consciousness. What's it like to take a hit in the cockpit and some moments later rather casually discover that you are already part way down the track on a trip through the valley of the shadow of death? What's it like, as the trip through the valley develops twists and turns upon twists and turns—in a shattered cockpit, then in midair, gushing blood and waiting for your chute to blossom, then in a destroyer's whaleboat, totally woozy, unable to find a part of yourself you thought you had brought along, then on operating tables and in helicopters and then on more operating tables as the surrealistic story unfolds from the pen of this singularly observant and composed man, this talented writer.

This story is not a tragedy as Aristotle defined the term: a good man with a flaw who comes to an unjustified bad end. It is not a tragedy because nothing bad happened as a result of a flaw, and also because the striving will of Wynn Foster would not let the end *occur* when things were still bad. He fought back, necessarily against the system, to finish a proud naval career as a captain at sea, working in the field he knew best: directing tactical naval air operations in a hostile environment.

The Foster story is also not a tragedy because his loyal family wouldn't let it be one. They supported one another. And now Wynn and his wife, Marilyn, support the community in which we all live. This is the story of real people seeing real problems through to a successful ending. And along the way, the reader learns something about the resilience of the human body, and the resilience of the human spirit.

James B. Stockdale, *Vice Admiral, USN (Ret.)*
Senior Research Fellow
THE HOOVER INSTITUTION

Acknowledgments

Since no man is an island, there are people who deserve recognition for the encouragement and assistance, intentional or otherwise, that resulted in the publication of this story:

Marilyn, my wife, lover, and companion of forty-three years, agonized through the events recounted herein, tolerating me through it all while providing immeasurable moral support. And she had the good sense to save every letter I wrote to her during our wartime separations, letters that subsequently proved invaluable as memory-joggers.

Barrett Tillman, author of numerous historical books on naval aircraft and, recently, of several successful novels, was instrumental in bringing the manuscript to the attention of the Naval Institute. It was Barrett, by genealogical happenstance a distant (tenth) cousin, who suggested the format of the story.

Several people read the manuscript and encouragingly said, "Good story; you ought to have it published" (as if the idea hadn't occurred to me!); but "Mac" Greely, a retired U.S. Marine Corps aviator and former A-4 Skyhawk driver, provided the first objective analysis and critical opinion of the manuscript and helped it on the way to eventual publication.

"Zip" Rausa, a retired naval aviator and currently the editor of *Wings of Gold,* the magazine of the Association of Naval Aviation, volunteered many long hours from his own busy employment to the detailed editing that polished the story into a form acceptable to the Naval Institute Press.

Jim Stockdale, Vice Admiral, U.S. Navy (Retired), recipient of the Congressional Medal of Honor for his superhuman conduct, personal integrity, and leadership as the senior Navy prisoner of war during the Vietnam War, was both an integral part of my story and an indelible influence in the later telling of it. Most call him Admiral, but I still call him CAG, the title he held as my air-wing commander during our professional bonding, before he became a long-term "guest" at the "Hanoi Hilton."

Finally, I acknowledge the contributions of all the Saints of VA-163 and the men of USS *Oriskany* who were part of this story.

Captain Hook

1 A Mild Sting

 Its engines screaming, the C-141 "Liftmaster" noisily thumped and lumbered down the runway. It was uncomfortably warm in the medical evacuation aircraft. I lay wrapped in a cotton blanket, strapped to an aluminum pipe–frame bunk in the belly of the plane. I was a patient, but because I had been a naval aviator for sixteen years, my mind was up front in the cockpit of the huge transport, "helping" the pilot. I "held" the throttles forward, eyeing the airspeed needle, ready to ease back on the control yoke to coax the plane safely off the ground and into the sky. Seconds seemed like hours as the Liftmaster gathered momentum in the hot, sultry air.

Finally, the pilot and I were successful. The wings bit into the air, and the vibrations that accompanied our roll down the strip dissipated as the wheels of the Liftmaster left the ground. The roar of the jet engines sounded less frantic. A dull thump announced the retraction of the landing gear. We were airborne from Clark Air Base, north of Manila in the Philippines, climbing northeast toward Japan. It was 1 August 1966, and I was going home, a casualty of the Vietnam War.

Surgery would be performed when I reached the naval hospital in Oakland, California. In the meantime, the stump of my right arm was "packed open," encased in a monstrous, almost immovable wad of bandages. Cooler air began wafting through the fuselage as the plane climbed to a higher altitude, and I became more comfortable. My arm throbbed dully, but thanks to the shot of Demerol that the flight nurse had given me a few minutes earlier, I was on a high and felt no pain. Phantom sensation was strong, however. My nonexistent right hand was still gripping the control stick of my A-4E "Skyhawk," just as it had that morning a week earlier when a fragment of a North Vietnamese antiaircraft shell ripped through the right side of the cockpit and dramatically changed whatever plans I had for a continued career in the Navy.

It was hard to pin down exactly when the United States got involved in the Vietnam War. The war itself had been going on since the end of World War II. Only the players had changed. U.S. military "advisors" were in South Vietnam during the Eisenhower administration in the 1950s, and President Kennedy authorized a buildup of ground forces. By 1964 President Johnson had authorized more troops, and U.S. military involvement in Southeast Asia's ground war was stepped up significantly. Simultaneously, American photo-reconnaissance planes, alone at first but later with armed escorts, were flying secret intelligence-gathering missions over Laos and North Vietnam. Primarily, they were spying on North Vietnam's use of the "Ho Chi Minh Trail," a collection of trails and small roads that formed the main route for supplying the insurgent forces—the Vietcong and Pathet Lao—in the south. The "trail" wound its way from North to South Vietnam via Laos, across the spine of Indochina's 5,000–6,000-foot Annam Mountains. Flying from the carrier *Kitty Hawk,* two U.S. Navy photo-reconnaissance pilots were shot down. Fortunately, both were rescued.

Then, in a fateful seventy-two hours on 2–5 August 1964, came the Gulf of Tonkin "incident," and the shit hit the fan for naval aviation. North Vietnamese PT boats allegedly attacked the U.S. destroyers *Maddox* and *Turner Joy* in the Tonkin Gulf, and President Johnson used the incident to order retaliatory strikes from Seventh Fleet carriers. Aircraft from *Constellation* and *Ticonderoga* bombed the PT boats' bases and a petroleum-storage facility in North Vietnam. A variety of low-key offensive air operations against North Vietnam and Laos followed in late 1964. Operation Rolling Thunder, the sustained interdiction bombing of North Vietnam's LOCs (lines of communication), began in mid-February 1965, and the air war over North Vietnam was on in earnest.

My first combat deployment to Southeast Asia as a carrier strike pilot came in mid-1965. If President Johnson had allowed U.S. air power to pull out all the stops that year, we could have decimated Vietnam's ability to conduct war in short order. But the leadership in Washington decreed otherwise.

My 238th combat mission, scheduled for the morning of 23 July 1966, was to be relatively easy. I was the CO, the commanding officer of Attack Squadron 163 (VA-163)—the "Saints"—operating from the deck of the carrier *Oriskany* on Yankee Station in the Tonkin Gulf. I would lead three other A-4 Skyhawks in a mini-strike on a POL (petroleum, oil, lubricant) -storage depot seven miles north of Vinh, North Vietnam. Located in the central "panhandle" of North Vietnam, Vinh had a reputation as a hot spot. There were numerous antiaircraft and surface-to-air missile (SAM) sites in the area. It was high on the list of places to avoid, if possible.

In the business of naval aviation I had the best job in the world—skipper of a "tailhook" squadron flying from a carrier. The prize assignment was an honor and a challenge accorded to but a select few who wore Navy wings. The frosting on the cake was our aircraft, the Skyhawk, the world's finest light-attack jet. Known by many names—Bantam Bomber, Scooter, Heinemann's Hot Rod (after Douglas Aircraft's Ed Heinemann, its designer), and Tinker Toy—the "Hawk" was an immensely popular and capable warplane. Small, powerful, and highly maneuverable, the single-engine, single-pilot A-4 carried large bomb loads and was ideally suited to the kind of air war we were fighting over North Vietnam. The Saints were one of five squadrons that composed Air Wing 16, *Oriskany*'s main battery. My squadron was assigned 21 pilots, 4 ground or nonflying officers, 123 enlisted men, and 14 Skyhawks.

The basic tactical element used when flying combat missions from a carrier was the section—two pilots, two planes, operating as a team. My wingman, the pilot who would be flying with me, was LTJG Tom Spitzer, a good-looking, sandy-blond young man with an easy manner and a pleasant smile. Of German-American stock, hailing from Baldwin, North Dakota, Tom was a twenty-six-year-old farm-kid-turned-aviator. He'd recently completed his training in the Skyhawk at Cecil Field near Jacksonville, Florida, and was a squadron "newboy," with the Saints for only a week. Tom hadn't flown in the four weeks it had taken him to wend his way around the world to the Gulf of Tonkin. During his first week on board *Oriskany* he'd flown several noncombat warm-up flights. With the kinks and cobwebs worked out, and his carrier-landing skills rehoned, Tom was as ready for combat as he could get. The Vinh mission would be his first time "over the beach."

I began the preflight briefing earlier than normal that day and went into considerable detail about the mission. Tom wasn't the experienced, comfortable, "old shoe" flying partner that my previous wingman, John Shore, had become during our eleven months of flying together in the past year.

For Tom's first combat mission, I tried to be reassuring yet candid. In particular, I stressed the probability of our encountering antiaircraft fire and reviewed the procedures for jinking—flying a sinuous course while randomly changing heading and altitude. Jinking complicated the enemy gunner's aim.

"Gimme a cigarette," I said absently and was not surprised when Tom produced a package of my brand without hesitation. He didn't smoke, but other junior pilots had already cautioned him: "The Skipper smokes like a steam engine but *never* carries his own. *Always* have a pack of menthols stashed in your flight-suit pocket!"

I lit up and continued the briefing, stressing the possibility of encountering flak, hoping that my words would reduce Tom's "pucker factor." I vividly remembered my first air-combat mission during the Korean War thirteen years earlier. My flight leader had been casual about antiaircraft artillery and had provided little information about what to expect. I was surprised when, over the beach, I rolled my F9F Panther into my first combat attack run, against a North Korean railroad tunnel. Tracers streamed up at me, filling the sky with angry black puffs. They didn't look at all like the antiaircraft bursts I had seen in war movies. The North Korean flak was real, mean, three-dimensional, and personal. I grew up suddenly as a combat pilot that day, absorbing forever the knowledge that the enemy was an authentic threat, shooting at me in anger with live ammunition, with the express purpose of blowing *me* out of the sky.

Getting shot at for the umpteenth time over North Vietnam was just as scary as the first time over that North Korean railroad tunnel. In the air war over North Vietnam, conventional AAA (antiaircraft artillery) fire was expected on virtually every combat sortie. Coupled with the hazards of supersonic SAMs, AAA made combat flying an always unnerving experience.

Tom would have plenty of opportunity later to experience the sleepless nights and stomach-churning emotions that accompanied the preparations for "Alfa" strikes deep into North Vietnam's heartland. There would be moments of stark terror over the target as flak and SAMs whistled toward him in the sky. But for that mission on 23 July, we'd be a "mini"-strike group—only four planes. I hoped that only light antiaircraft fire would greet us. Nevertheless, I assumed the worst and went into detail on the subject of flak.

The "yellow shirts," the flight-deck aircraft directors, gingerly signaled my Skyhawk forward and into position on *Oriskany*'s port catapult. Crewmen tensioned my bird snugly between the catapult bridle and the hold-back cable. The catapult petty officer rotated two fingers rapidly above his head, and I responded by shoving the throttle forward with my left hand. The tension compressed the nosewheel strut. The plane "drew down" on the cat, as if squatting to spring. The J-52 engine wound up, and the RPM steadied at 100 percent. Ten thousand pounds of thrust made my Skyhawk strain against the mechanical restraints of the cat. I scanned the engine instruments, rapidly ensuring that my machine was ready to go, then I nodded my readiness to the petty officer in the yellow shirt. He returned the nod and passed me off to the catapult officer standing at deck center. The catapult officer repeated the turn-up signal. Unconsciously, my body tensed. I was strapped securely in the tiny cockpit with my left elbow locked in a straight-arm position, holding the throttle full forward. My thumb was hooked under the throttle handle. My fingers were curled over the top of the throttle grip, a fold-down aluminum rod just forward of the throttle. The grip was simple but effective insurance, designed to prevent a pilot from inadvertently pulling back the throttle during the catapult stroke. Quickly, I scanned the cockpit again and double-checked the engine gauges. With my right hand I tossed a salute to the catapult officer, signaling that my aircraft and I were ready. As I lowered my arm, I pushed the start button of the elapsed-time clock and dropped my hand to my lap, my thumb and fingers forming a horizontal "V" behind the control stick. I snuggled my helmeted head against the seat's headrest and waited. The catapult officer acknowledged my salute with a nod. From the corner of my eye I could see him twirling his fingers over his head. He glanced at his catapult-control dials in the small steel-lidded recess in the flight deck between the catapults. Then he looked forward to the bow of the ship. He crouched, sweeping his arm in an arc in that direction until the fingers of his extended hand touched the deck. Out of my sight in the deck-edge catwalk, a technician jammed the heel of his hand against the red firing button of a catapult-control panel. Precisely at 0730 I was shoved against the seat as my Skyhawk was hurled along *Oriskany*'s port catapult track. Two seconds later I was airborne.

"Yahoo!" I shouted my habitual reaction into my oxygen mask as the aircraft accelerated. The "G" force of the catapult shot forced the control stick smartly backward into my waiting right hand, and I closed my fingers around the handle. That was called the "hands-off" technique. The theory was that, because of the programmed acceleration of the steam-powered catapult and the proper trim-tab settings of the plane, the aircraft knew better than the pilot how to transition smoothly to flight once the "cat" let go at the end of the stroke.

In rapid succession I flipped the landing-gear control handle up to retract the wheels, then incrementally retracted the wing flaps. I was smiling beneath my oxygen mask. Every cat shot was an exhilarating experience, my favorite part of naval aviation. Getting tossed into the free air in an 11+-ton, bomb-loaded Skyhawk, accelerating from 0 to 130 knots over the short distance of 220 feet in less that 2 seconds, was one of the dramatic things that set me and every other tailhook aviator apart from all others who flew airplanes. Plus, it was fun! The world's most expensive thrill ride, and I was paid to take it.

I stayed low, 100 feet over the water, until clear of the pattern that recovering aircraft flew around the ship, then began a climbing turn. Three minutes later I settled into a left-hand rendezvous circle at 20,000 feet above the carrier. Tom Spitzer was flying a closing arc across the rendezvous circle, having launched from the starboard catapult a few seconds after me. As he neared my aircraft, he stopped his relative movement and paused momentarily on my left side before sliding smartly under my tail into a precise "parade" position off my right wing. I smiled again, remembering my own days as a wingman and my striving for precision. To a junior pilot it was important to make the right impression on the leader, especially if the leader was the squadron's skipper. In the combat zone, we flew parade formation only near the ship. In a few minutes the other two planes of our ministrike group would join us, and we would head for the beach in a spread-out formation called combat cruise or "loose goose."

In the meantime, Tom was trying to impress me with his "Blue Angel" exactitude. He didn't have to. I had reviewed his record shortly after he had reported on board *Oriskany*. He had high marks both in the regular flight-training program and in his follow-on specialized training in the Skyhawk. Indeed, the record had been a factor in my selecting Tom as my new wingman—the pilot who would function as my second set of eyes, ears, and senses—my alter ego during combat missions.

In succession, LCDR Marv Reynolds and his wingman completed the rendezvous. Marv was an experienced Skyhawk pilot who had joined the squadron several months earlier. I rolled out of the circle and steadied on a westerly heading toward the North Vietnamese coast. A few minutes later I waved bye-bye to Marv Reynolds, a prearranged signal telling him to proceed independently with his wingman to a point south of the target. At the designated TOT (time over target), Tom and I would attack the petroleum-storage area on a north-to-south heading, and one minute later Marv would lead his section in a south-to-north run. The attacks from the opposite directions were a tactical ploy to confuse the North Vietnamese gunners. The split attack wouldn't provide a significant advantage, but in war survival often boiled down to fractions of percentages.

With my gloved thumb I pointed toward the tail of my plane. It was the loose goose signal for Tom, telling him to move into a combat-cruise position about forty yards away from me. Another fraction of a percentage. The separation would give us both maneuvering room and reduce the chance that a single flak burst would hit both of us. The selected "coast-in," the point where we would cross the coastline and go "feet dry," was the southern end of Brandon Bay, an easily recognizable point at the westernmost indentation of the coast. There I would report our position to Red Crown, the southern SAR (search-and-rescue) ship stationed off the coast. The attack was planned for minimum exposure to AAA fire. We'd cross the coast going "downhill," descending and jinking at high speed to reach the roll-in point near the target. Each of us carried six 500-pound bombs on our wings. Tom would be a few seconds behind me, following me "down the chute."

After dropping our bombs, Tom and I would break left and rapidly retire to "feet wet" and the relative safety of the Tonkin Gulf. We'd be over the beach for as short a time as possible, less than three minutes. That was the "easy" first mission I'd planned for Tom's introduction to combat. The planned brief exposure to enemy AAA fire had nothing to do with bravado or courage or the lack thereof. It was merely pragmatic wisdom born in the Korean War and nurtured in the previous year of flying combat missions from Yankee Station. There would be nothing extra in my paycheck for intentionally dallying over enemy territory after completing a mission, no heroism Brownie points for needlessly exposing my fanny to antiaircraft fire. The philosophy of "one pass and haul ass" had long since become part of my combat thinking.

As if cued by a master script, flak bursts greeted us as we crossed the coastline. My jaw muscles tensed, and I instinctively tightened my loins, fighting the urge to urinate that always accompanied the fearsome sight of those ominous puffs of black smoke. The bursts, apparently barrage fire, were north of our track and all at a single altitude. They didn't appear to be an immediate threat because we were descending, increasing speed, and jinking. I glanced at the clock. We were on time, less than a minute from the roll-in point. I keyed the mike button on the throttle.

"Salt Two, heads up. Flak at two o'clock. Stay loose and keep jinking."[1]

I rolled my wings abruptly, first left then right, trying to spot the flak site. But no luck. I looked back into the cockpit, at the target-area chart clipped to my kneeboard, then at the altimeter. We passed 12,000 feet, descending, as we crossed the coast-in point. Eyes outside

---

1. VA-163's tactical call sign was Old Salt, abbreviated to Salt for communications between planes. As the flight leader, I used the call sign Salt One. My wingman was Salt Two.

For reference, the horizontal plane around the aircraft was divided into clock codes, twelve o'clock being on the nose.

the cockpit again, toward the target area, trying to pinpoint the petroleum-storage facility. Thirty seconds to roll-in.

I sighted the target and mentally ran through the three-dimensional air-to-ground attack problem: roll in at 8,000 feet, less than a mile from the target; establish a 45-degree dive; track the pipper to the target; check the crosswind drift; pickle the bombs off at 4,500 feet; pull out at 4 G; go no lower than 2,000 feet; turn hard left; keep jinking; head back to the Gulf. Twenty seconds to roll-in.

BA-LAM! Suddenly, the foggy mist of an explosive decompression swirled around me. The 400+-knot slipstream blasted through the cockpit. My helmeted head bounced against the headrest. I looked up. The Plexiglas canopy over my head and part of the windscreen in front of me were gone! I was flying an open-cockpit Skyhawk. My oxygen mask, tightly cinched, was still in place. My helmet visor was down. I felt no immediate discomfort, but the deafening roar of high-speed air enveloped me. My jet had been hit, no doubt about that, but how badly? There was a mild stinging sensation in my right elbow, but my attention was still outside the cockpit. The plane appeared to be flying OK, except the left wing was dropping slowly. I moved my hand to the right to level the wings. Nothing happened. *What the hell...?*

I glanced at the instrument panel and did a double take. An electriclike hot flash jolted through me, and for what seemed an eternity I stared in disbelief. The wall of instruments before me was a bloody mess. I glanced down. My right arm was missing! My gloved right hand lay like a macabre display atop the radio-control console on the right side of the cockpit. Stunned, I looked outside the cockpit, as if that would dismiss the awful spectacle from my mind. When I looked again I realized that I was not hallucinating. But I still did not believe my eyes. I could feel the stick gripped securely in my right hand. But there was no right hand on the stick! Again, I moved my right arm to move the stick, but nothing happened. Reality banged at my brain. I had no right arm!

My God! I thought. *This can't be happening to ME!*

Having mentally assisted the Liftmaster pilot through a successful takeoff, and having nothing to do as I lay strapped to my bunk, I let my mind drift. Several times I relived my final flight and the loss of my arm, which surely would end my Navy career. It seemed then such a short time ago that it had all started.

In 1944 I was a naive seventeen-year-old fresh out of high school. I joined the Navy's flight-training program to fight in World War II. A teenage romantic, I had learned my idealism and my concept of military aviation from war movies and noble "heroes" like John Wayne, Errol Flynn, and Robert Taylor. I wanted to do battle with Japanese Zeros in flak-filled skies over the Pacific, as they had done in the films.

In 1966, at the age of thirty-nine, droning over the Pacific, strapped in a bunk on a medevac aircraft, I no longer viewed war as a romantic or noble pursuit. I was emotionally confused. My part in the fight was over, and I was going home—alive—to see my wife and kids. That was good. I was missing one limb, a "traumatic amputation" in medical terms, but I'd already accepted that as part of the price of war. It didn't bother me. My choice of naval aviation as a career, and my specialty as a carrier pilot, had been voluntary and deliberate. There was an ethic involved. I didn't like fighting in a war, but I was a career military man. War was my job should it come along, and the possibility of becoming one of its casualties was something that I had long since accepted as part of the career.

Back home, misguided, confused idealists were already protesting the Vietnam War as "immoral," whatever that meant. There was no doubt in my mind that it was a lousy affair. But that had nothing to do with the rhetoric being spouted by antiwar protesters who were comfortably secure on the American continent thousands of miles away. The only immoral thing about the war from my viewpoint was the unwillingness of our civilian leadership to allow U.S. military air power, once committed, to be used effectively. The Vietnam War was lousy because it had given me a front-line view from the cockpit while irresolute politicians back home invoked a no-win policy. That was hard to take, even for volunteers like me.

The immediate focus of my irritation was an anonymous North Vietnamese gunner who had done me harm. And not just to my body. That gunner's almost accidental accuracy meant that I had to be removed from my command, from my tailhook squadron, from the best job in the Navy. It had taken sixteen years to reach that pinnacle. Yet, in a split second, in a hostile summer sky far, far from home, everything had changed suddenly.

Alone and injured, still over the beach, I was confused as I looked around the blood-spattered cockpit. Seconds seemed like minutes. I was in the midst of a weird kaleidoscope, conducting a mental wrestling match with myself. *Concentrate on basic emergency procedures,* I ordered. But strange thoughts kept getting in the way, and reality and reverie blended discordantly.

I remembered shipmates who had run into trouble on their own combat missions over North Vietnam. Paul Merchant, a close friend and fellow *Oriskany* pilot, was a "Spad" driver, flying the A-1 "Skyraider" during the carrier's 1965 deployment to Southeast Asia. Paul was shot down on a night mission and dramatically rescued. Other friends hadn't come back: Ed Davis, also a Spad pilot, also shot down at night; Jim Stockdale, *Oriskany's* air-wing commander in 1965, shot down as I watched; and Harry Jenkins, my predecessor as skipper of the Saints, lost on a daylight armed recco (reconnaissance) mission. All were POWs (prisoners of war).

Am I the next for a jail term in Hanoi? If I last that long. Who will stop the bleeding and patch up what's left of me if I parachute into a rice paddy?

I was living a nightmare in real time, half asleep, half awake. But there was a minor bright spot in the scenario: the war was over for one CDR Wynn Foster.

From somewhere within a voice screamed at me over the roar of the wind: *"Do something, stupid! Get your ass in gear! Take action!"*

I grabbed the stick with my left hand, rolling the wings level, and steadied it with my knees. Blood and bits of flesh covered the face of the airspeed indicator. I reached forward and wiped the gauge with my gloved left hand. The needle pointed to 200 knots, and I was surprised. Only seconds before that I'd been traveling at 450 knots. Two hundred knots was much too slow for a Skyhawk loaded with bombs, particularly in the flak-filled skies of North Vietnam. *How did I slow down so fast? Maybe the engine is damaged, and I'm without power.* I pushed the stick forward to lower the nose and pick up airspeed. *The best glide speed is....* I couldn't remember.

My frustrated thoughts jumped to Tom Spitzer. Was he OK? Again holding the stick with my knees, I pressed the mike button: "This is Salt One...." The oxygen mask was still clipped to my helmet and pressed snugly to my face, the integral microphone only a quarter of an inch from my lips. But with the roar of the wind, I couldn't hear myself talk. "This is Salt One," I shouted into the mask. "I'm hit. Salt Two, keep jinking and get clear of the area."

My left hand returned to the stick, and I banked the A-4 into a right turn toward the Gulf. Prior to reaching the coast-in point I had set my TACAN (Tactical Air Control and Navigation) to the frequency of Red Crown, USS *Reeves*, the SAR ship steaming several miles off-shore. The TACAN provided a direct readout of bearing and distance. As its needle swung toward the nose of my Skyhawk, I made a decision. *I don't want to be a POW!* I would fly to the SAR ship. For a moment I thought of trying to make it back to *Oriskany. Wouldn't that be dramatic?* A long-time friend, CDR Mike Chewning, another A-4 squadron skipper, had done just that a couple of months ago. He flew his Skyhawk back to *Ranger* and successfully landed on board after being injured by flak during an attack mission.

Just as quickly as the thought came, I dismissed it. I'd never make it that far in my condition. And even if I did, I'd endanger the crew and probably kill myself trying to make a one-arm, left-handed carrier landing. Besides, I needed medical attention as soon as possible.

Knees against the stick again, I pulled the emergency jettison "T" handle on the lower left side of the instrument panel. The aircraft shuddered slightly as explosive cartridges punched the external fuel tank, bombs, and bomb racks off the wings. The Skyhawk was immediately lightened, but my frustration returned. *What should I do next?* I couldn't remember.

The wind was noisy and irritating. I wished it would quiet down. The helmet's earphones were snug against my ears, but I heard nothing except the roar of the wind. *Did Tom hear my call?* I pressed the mike button. "Salt Two, do you read?" I couldn't tell if there was a response.

I forced myself to concentrate on flying. Again, I tried to remember the best glide speed. After several seconds it came. *Oh yes, 220 knots.* I wiped away more blood from the instrument panel and eye-balled the altimeter. Four thousand feet. *Be careful, don't give up your altitude too fast.* It occurred to me that I wouldn't make it to the SAR ship. I'd have to leave the plane soon and tried to remember the mini-mum altitude for ejection. But the answer wasn't there. Altitude, or lack of it, was a problem. If I ejected immediately I'd most certainly be captured. *Stay with the aircraft,* I told myself. *We've got to make it to the Gulf!* But I was without power and descending. *How far can I stretch the glide?* If I ejected too low to the ground or water, I'd be out of the "envelope." The chute might not open in time. *What's the minimum altitude for ejection?* I should have known that automatically, but I couldn't remember. Arbitrarily, I picked 1,000 feet. That was as good a number as any. An irrational thought flitted through my mind: *Ejection will be a new experience.* In all my flying career I'd never had to bail out of an aircraft.

The coastline inched toward my nose as I flew eastward, gradually losing altitude. I kept mentally chasing the mathematical problem of my glide. *Will I make it to the sea? Will I have enough altitude for a safe ejection when I get there?* But my mind wouldn't cooperate. I simply could not compute the figures.

The rearview mirror diverted my attention. A Skyhawk was flying off my right wing at the four-o'clock position. I felt a sudden sense of security. *Good old John, right there where he's supposed to be.* We'd flown dozens of missions together. If anything could be done to help me, John would think of it. *No, that was '65.* It wasn't John Shore flying my wing, it was Tom Spitzer. *How long had he been there?* I had no sense of time.

I studied my bloody flight suit with detachment. I guessed I was in bad shape, tired and light-headed, but strangely there was no pain. *Got to do something about the bleeding stump.* Putting the stick between my knees, I squeezed the stump with my left hand. *Will that stop the bleeding?* I still felt the mild stinging sensation in my right elbow, but I no longer had a right elbow. The tattered, bloody remnant of a flight-suit sleeve was empty. My lifeless, gloved right hand lay on the starboard console, a bizarre and gruesome still life.

The altimeter cranked down through 2,500 feet. *Pay attention, Foster. Concentrate. Fly the plane.* Staring at the instrument panel, I wiped blood from the face of the engine RPM indicator and was surprised to see the needle pointing to 70 percent power. *The Skyhawk engine idles at 52 percent, stupid!* Seventy percent wasn't enough power to maintain level flight, even without the drag of the bombs, racks, and fuel tank that I had jettisoned. Disgusted with myself for not recognizing the situation earlier, I pushed the throttle forward. The engine RPM wound up to 100 percent. The Skyhawk had new life. With the trim tabs set for a 220-knot glide, the added power pitched the nose into a climb, and I was ascending through 4,000 feet by the time I reacted. Easing back on the throttle, I retrimmed the plane for level flight.

Realizing that I had engine power was like receiving a shot of adrenalin. Suddenly, I was in a new ball game. I wouldn't have to eject over land after all! Not even close to land. I'd make it back to friendly hands. I had "escaped." I wouldn't become a POW that day.

But what should I do next? The clock on the instrument panel had escaped the bloodbath and was unobscured. It couldn't do me much good, but it made me wonder. *How long has it been since my cat shot?* I couldn't remember.

A faint, garbled radio transmission filtered through the noise, and I heard the word "position." Was the radio working again? Position? *You idiots! I've got enough trouble already. You should know where I am!* I keyed the mike button: "This is Old Salt Three Zero One. I am two four zero, one five miles from Red Crown." *Why doesn't Tom tell them that? Is his radio working? Has he been hit by flak, too? Who is that flying on my wing?*

The bleeding. I must stop the bleeding. A tourniquet. How? My .38 revolver, holstered in my survival vest, was attached to my torso harness by a nylon lanyard. The lanyard would make a good tourniquet. *How will I tie the knot? With my good hand and teeth while flying with my knees?* That was too complex.

Panic struck. *If they don't know where I am, do they know I'm injured?* I transmitted again.

"This is Old Salt Three Zero One." I spoke into the mike, loudly and slowly as if to a child. "I'm two four zero, one two miles from Red Crown. I've been hit. I'm hurt and bleeding badly. I'm going to punch out over Red Crown. I'll need immediate medical attention."

Was the call for medical attention superfluous? I wondered. Was there a doctor on board the SAR ship? Had the preflight intelligence brief covered that subject? I couldn't remember. I squeezed the stump of my right arm and thought about my favorite doctor, LT Dan Lestage, the flight surgeon assigned to my squadron. Doctor Dan, the Band-Aid man, in *Oriskany*. A hundred miles away.

With more than 1,200 hours piloting the Skyhawk, I was intimately familiar with the machine. Repeatedly, I'd drilled myself to respond to any and all emergencies, from catapult shot to arrested landing. But in the middle of the biggest emergency of my flying career my mind simply would not cooperate. I could not think of what to do next. Strangely, with the increase in power, it seemed the engine and wind noises had quieted down. I began to feel euphoric, just sitting there, as if I were just along for the ride.

A thin layer of wispy clouds drifted toward me, obstructing my view of the water below. I wanted to have the SAR ship in sight when I ejected, so I nosed down to fly through the shelf of thin clouds.

My peripheral vision sensed a dark void filled with swirling technicolor stars on either side of me. I was experiencing tunnel vision, able to focus only on what was directly ahead of me. For the first time I realized that I was in deep trouble. A safety slogan flitted through my mind: "An aircraft accident can ruin your whole day." Mentally, I paraphrased the slogan: *If I pass out in the cockpit and crash with the plane, it certainly will ruin my whole day.* My severed right hand was still resting on the starboard console, and I had a macabre notion. *Tidy up the cockpit. Shouldn't leave that behind.* I picked up the hand and tucked it between my life vest and parachute harness.

The SAR ship below was a beautiful sight, headed directly toward me with a "bone in her teeth," churning white water with her bow. Moments later she disappeared beneath my plane. The TACAN needle swung back and forth erratically, showing station passage. The slant range to the ship was less than a mile.

With my good hand I reached up, grabbed the face-curtain handle, and pulled. The rocket-propelled seat exploded out of the aircraft, taking me with it. The thrust of the ejection drained the remnants of blood from my brain, and I blacked out.

2 Off to War

 When the war in Europe ended in May 1945, I'd been an apprentice seaman student for nine months in the Navy's "V-12" college training program. The State Teacher's College in Dickinson, North Dakota, was about as far away from salt water as a Navy man could get. Three months later, while cooling my heels at the naval air station at Norman, Oklahoma, awaiting a vacancy at pre-flight school, the Japanese surrendered to end World War II. I took that as a personal affront. My secret dream of becoming a naval aviator war hero in the skies over the Pacific was in shambles, but eventually I made it through pre-flight school on the campus of the University of Iowa and was subsequently assigned to flight training at Cabaniss Field near Corpus Christi, Texas.

Frequent and often contradictory rumors confused the post–World War II active-duty picture. This or that bit of information or misinformation filtered down the pipeline, always from "reliable authority." At one point everyone was to be shipped home the following week because of a shortage of flight instructors. Except aviation cadets. We didn't have enough "points." Later, anyone who wanted to could stay in the flight program because everyone else was leaving the service. Peer pressure to "get out" was strong, but I resisted, hanging onto my dream.

I had a grand total of 12.3 hours in my flight logbook when all my options evaporated and the Navy made up my mind for me. I was "released from active duty" rather than discharged. The terminology protected me from being scooped up in the draft, and I went home to Minneapolis. Gentle prodding from my father led to enrollment at the University of Minnesota in the fall of 1946. The college credits I had gained from the V-12 program qualified me for entry as a sophomore, and for the next two and a half years I pursued a college degree. As graduation time approached, I was uncertain about what to do with my life. Flying was still my first love, and the exhilaration of my first solo remained fresh in my mind. Nothing else measured up to the smell, the feel, the sense of purpose of strapping into the open cockpit of a Stearman N2S "Yellow Peril" and going aloft on a bright afternoon over the south Texas plain.

By 1949 the post–World War II exodus of military pilots left hundreds of cockpits unfilled, and the Navy did an about-face. Six months prior to graduation I received an enticing "personal" recruiting letter. It offered a return to active duty. My college degree would net me a commission as an ensign, and I could reenter flight training with a fair prospect for a career in the regular Navy. In short, the Navy wanted me to fly its planes once again and was willing to pay me for that privilege. I considered the proposal for a full fifteen seconds before dashing to the recruiting office.

In short order in 1949 I received my degree, married my childhood sweetheart, Marilyn Hanson, pinned gold ensign bars on my collar, and headed for Pensacola, Florida. Marilyn and I bought a secondhand Chevrolet convertible and survived living in a series of tacky $65/month rental apartments in Pensacola and Corpus Christi while I worked my way over the multitude of flight-training hurdles.

The F8F Bearcat, a hot, single-seat, engine-with-a-cockpit-attached Navy fighter, was built toward the end of World War II to intercept and shoot down Japanese kamikaze aircraft. The Bearcat never made it into combat, but many of them went to the training command. On 14 December 1950, at the controls of a Bearcat, I made twelve arrested landings on board the carrier USS *Wright* in the Gulf of Mexico. The next day I received my naval aviator's certificate with a handshake from RADM Aaron "Putt" Storrs, the chief of Naval Air Basic Training. The admiral's dead-serious eyes almost pierced a hole right through me. That man's expression stayed with me over the years, as if to underline my achievement. Marilyn pinned on my "wings of gold," and a short time later we were on our way to California to join the Pacific Fleet.

The Korean War had erupted a few months earlier, and whatever combat thrills I had missed in World War II were again in the offing. Eventually, VF-721, a reserve fighter squadron recalled to active duty for the 1950s national emergency, became my official home. I logged seventy-five combat missions over North Korea, flying the F9F Panther from the carrier USS *Kearsarge*. The mission of VF-721 was air-to-air combat—protecting the task force and friendly aircraft from enemy fighters. The closest I got to that business was during the winter of 1952–53. The snug rubber collar of my cold-water immersion suit grated my neck raw on CAP (combat air patrol) missions while I kept a swivel head, searching for enemy aircraft in the cold sky over North Korea. But the Korean War did not produce many aerial dogfights for Navy fighter pilots. There was a lot more excitement in air-to-ground combat, strafing and dropping bombs, which comprised half of my missions. Being shot at by North Korean antiaircraft gunners wasn't as John-Wayne romantic as I had envisioned as a teenager, but I came through the war unscathed, a little wiser, and still enthusiastic about duty in naval aviation.

As a jet-qualified carrier pilot in the early 1950s, I was one of a unique group. Because of the Navy's transition to jet aircraft, the qualification was a career plus. On the home front, my family responsibilities had grown. Marilyn and I were the proud parents of a daughter, Corinne Susan. With no real inclination to pursue any other kind of livelihood, the bird-in-the-hand theory made sense to me. Drawing a regular paycheck for flying off and on carriers was much more appealing than having to work for a living.

Thus followed a variety of peacetime tours in which I tested air-to-air missiles, flew as a flight instructor, attended various schools, and spent lots of time on sea duty, driving ships. Toward the end of a minimum-flying, ship's-company tour in the carrier *Forrestal* in the late 1950s, getting tipsy at a party in the port of Cannes in the south of France brought a fortuitous boost to my aviation career. At his farewell party, departing *Forrestal* skipper CAPT Sam Brown asked what kind of assignment I hoped to get when my current tour was up. Having been a bomb-dropping "fighter" pilot in the Korean War, I said,

"Captain, I want to fly A-4s out of Oceana." At the time, the A-4 Skyhawk was the newest and hottest carrier-based attack (i.e. bomber) aircraft in the Navy's inventory.

Captain Brown, who had consumed about as many martinis as I, squinted and studied me briefly, but just long enough to make me wonder. Had I said something wrong? Perhaps it would have been smarter and more sophisticated to mention something more "career enhancing" such as the Naval War College or postgraduate school, rather than another flying tour. After a few seconds Captain Brown bluntly said, "You got it." Then he turned on his heel and walked away.

I wasn't sure how much influence Brown had, or whether he'd even remember our conversation come the morrow, considering the insobriety of the evening. But it was encouraging that he thought enough of me to ask. Needless to say, I was ecstatic about eight weeks later when I received orders—a two-year tour with the "Spirits" of VA-76, flying A-4 Skyhawks, based at Naval Air Station (NAS) Oceana, Virginia.

As operations officer of VA-76 I made two more Sixth Fleet deployments, on board USS *Intrepid* and the nuclear-powered *Enterprise,* logging plenty of time in the Skyhawk. The tour ended in January 1963, following forty tense days at sea in the Caribbean with *Enterprise* during the Cuban missile crisis. Our planes had been armed to the teeth, and we were in alert status daily, ready to pulverize Mr. Castro and the Russians if necessary. But Russian Premier Khrushchev "blinked," the world's superpowers stepped away from the brink of World War III, and I retreated to the routine of a peacetime Navy.

The summer of 1964 proved a heady one. I was assigned to the staff of the chief of Naval Air Technical Training in Memphis, Tennessee, when I was promoted to commander and positioned for a grab at the brass ring of a tailhook pilot's career. I screened for command and was placed on the list to lead a carrier squadron. A short time later I received orders to report to the VA-163 Saints as executive officer (second in command). If I avoided serious mistakes in that job, didn't bust any Navy aircraft, and refrained from ticking off my seniors, I would "fleet up" one year later to the top spot—squadron commander.

I looked forward to returning to the cockpit, but I was also sobered by the responsibility that accompanied such a job. The U.S. military involvement in the nagging war in Southeast Asia was expanding, and the Gulf of Tonkin incident in August pulled us in further. It was the third war in my lifetime, and my assignment to the West Coast–based Saints was assurance that I would be a participant in it. I left Memphis for California in September, knowing that the days ahead would be eventful but having little concept of the personal crisis that was in store for me.

The naval air station at Lemoore, California, was located in the "boondocks," thirty miles south of Fresno in the vast, agriculture-rich San Joaquin Valley. Its location in the middle of millions of fertile acres and occasional small towns prompted one bachelor officer to describe the place as "centrally located—two hundred miles from everything!" The base provided all the necessities for the married folks who lived in a large, on-base community of look-alike housing units. So we had it better than the bachelors. The local civilians, predominately farmers, were strongly promilitary, and they proved to be congenial and supportive neighbors.

VA-125, the West Coast Skyhawk training squadron, provided the back-in-the-saddle refresher that I needed before moving on to join the Saints. Except for the first two "fam" (familiarization) hops, my time there was uneventful. While descending to make practice landings at the outlying field at Crow's Landing in the northern part of the San Joaquin Valley one day, an unlucky bird darted in front of my Skyhawk. It was dispatched to avian heaven when it was sucked into the air intake. I sweated out an ominous rumble and engine vibration but made it back to Lemoore. The next day fog delayed the beginning of my second flight, a rather common occurrence at Lemoore. I got airborne during a temporary lifting, but the fog reassembled behind me and plunged the field into instrument minimums. Again I sweated while making my first actual instrument approach at the controls of an A-4 after nearly two years out of the cockpit. Safely back at the field, I paid a visit to my friend, CDR Ed McKellar, VA-125's training officer. Ed and I had served together in VA-76, and I joked with him about VA-125's "rough" fam syllabus.

I completed refresher training in the Skyhawk in mid-January 1965, collected my log book, and walked across the street to another hangar. There I checked in with VA-163's skipper, Harry Jenkins. A tall, lanky aviator with a droll sense of humor, Harry had only recently assumed command. His rawboned, laid-back, "country boy" demeanor disguised an acute mind and a professional competence as a pilot and a leader.

Prior to assuming command, Harry had served an unusual two-year stint—a "double cycle" in carrier-pilot talk—as the squadron's executive officer (XO), having been bumped aside when a more senior pilot was ordered in as skipper. In the process he had logged close to four hundred Skyhawk traps (carrier landings), an enviable peacetime accomplishment. Harry was very popular, as evidenced by his unofficial title "CinCSaint V," created for the squadron's fifth skipper by his fellow pilots.

Harry immediately took me into his confidence. He ensured that I understood the "short fuse" challenge the squadron faced in readying itself for combat. In April, three short months later, we'd be on board *Oriskany* en route to Vietnam.

The squadron had recently transitioned from the A-4B model Skyhawk to the newer A-4E with a more powerful engine, increased speed and maneuverability, and greater ordnance-carrying capability. In the pre–Vietnam War years Skyhawk pilots trained primarily for the possibility of global war. Readiness was based on the capability to deliver nuclear weapons against Russia and Soviet-bloc countries. Learning how to employ conventional weapons, although part of the training curriculum, had taken a back seat. The syllabus hadn't kept up with the times because budgetary limitations had diminished the availability of operating funds.

When I joined VA-163, I was the only Saint with combat experience. But having dropped 250-pound bombs from an F9F Panther over North Korea twelve years earlier didn't qualify me as an expert on bombing techniques for the escalating Vietnam War. During my time with VA-125 there had been routine training in the delivery of conventional weapons. But there was little evidence that the Commander Naval Air Force, Pacific (ComNavAirPac), who was in charge of fleet aviation training, was increasing his emphasis of conventional weapons because of the new war. The Saints selectively ignored training requirements that either could not be accomplished in the short time available or were superfluous to the forthcoming conventional war.

Harry Jenkins badgered the weapons-test people in Air Development Squadron Five at China Lake, California, into providing him with the details of the experiments in 60-degree dive-angle attacks that they had conducted with the Skyhawk. At the time 30-degree dives were the norm; a 45-degree dive was considered steep. The 60-degree run afforded both greater bombing accuracy and a tougher target for antiaircraft gunners.

Another inadequacy of our training for the war was the dearth of information about how it was being conducted. LTJG John Sloan, the squadron's cherubic, bespectacled air-intelligence officer, dug out what he could find. But it was a frustrating experience. The information that we needed the most—tactics and ROE (rules of engagement)—was classified and not readily available Stateside.

All-weather instrument flying, navigation flights, dive-bombing practice, and related tactics crowded our days. We pushed our aircraft's availability to the limit, routinely flying pilots twice a day, and completely expended our training allowance for conventional weapons. Twice during the three-month countdown the squadron deployed on board *Oriskany*, first to renew our carrier-landing qualifications and later for coordinated training with the ship and other airwing squadrons.

We enjoyed a break during the latter training when *Oriskany* put into San Diego for a weekend. At a Saturday-morning ceremony CDR James Bond Stockdale relieved CDR Thad Taylor as the CAG (rhymes with lag)—the commander of Air Wing 16.[1] The CAG was the coordinator of *Oriskany's* "main battery," the five squadrons and three smaller aviation detachments that comprised the wing. The two fighter squadrons, VF-162 and VMF-212, the latter a Marine Corps outfit, flew the F-8E "Crusader" and provided the air-to-air capability. The Saints and our sister A-4 squadron, the "Ghost Riders" of VA-164 ("Spooks" to the rest of the air wing), and the "Wild Aces" of VA-152 provided the air-to-ground punch. The Wild Aces flew the A-1 Skyraider, an obsolescent piston-engine aircraft of post–World War II vintage, affection-

---

1. An acronym for *C*ommander *A*ir *G*roup. Navy air groups were redesignated as air *wings* in December 1963, but the informal title for the wing commander persisted and, to the present, is firmly ingrained in the vocabulary of naval aviation.

ately dubbed the "Spad." Rounding out the wing were the three supporting aviation detachments—RF-8 Crusaders for photographic reconnaissance, E-1B Trackers for airborne early warning and electronic support, and A-3 Skywarriors for "heavy" attack and aerial-fueling support.

Jim Stockdale came to Air Wing 16 after commanding a fighter squadron. He had flown missions from USS *Ticonderoga* in connection with the Gulf of Tonkin incident.

After the change-of-command ceremony, the squadrons' skippers, execs (executive officers), and our wives got acquainted socially with Jim and his wife, Sybil, and the officers of Jim's staff during a delightful brunch at the Stockdales' home on Coronado Island. Later, Stockdale endeared himself to the Saints by spending considerable time in Lemoore, flying with us during the predeployment training cycle.

In March 1965 the air wing was back on board *Oriskany* for fleet exercise Silver Lance. A Navy press release described the exercise as "coordinated training and participation in interdependent land, sea, and air task force operations....the largest combined exercise of its kind since World War II." In plain talk, the exercise was a replay of the Navy's World War II Pacific experience—massive sea and air support of a major amphibious operation. Like the peacetime pilot-training syllabus, the exercise scenario was evidence that high-level thinking hadn't yet realized that we were involved in a different type of war. Silver Lance bore little resemblance to the fighting underway in Southeast Asia, unless someone was secretly planning a massive amphibious invasion of North Vietnam. An inordinate number of exercise flight hours was devoted to "boring holes in the sky" as we pretended to provide air-cover missions for marines assaulting the beach at Camp Pendleton, north of San Diego.

More productive were the bombing missions flown against targets in the Chocolate Mountains close to the California-Arizona border. Near the end of the exercise Don Martin, a meticulous pilot, proposed a scenario for an even bigger and better fleet exercise: "Operation Silver Pig." It would, Don said, combine the talents of the planners of Silver Lance with those of the planners of the abortive 1961 Bay of Pigs invasion. The end product would be the ultimate in futility.

In April 1965 we packed up to go to war. The only remaining hurdle was an ORI, an operational-readiness inspection. Conducted off

Hawaii, it would be a key measure of our readiness to go into battle. In peacetime a ship–air wing ORI was a major professional test. A failing grade could result in anything from a less-than-excellent fitness report to the ending of the career of a squadron's or ship's commanding officer. Higher authority, grade-sheet clipboards in hand, expected no less than peak performance, as well as the usual amount of "looking good." But for those of us in the cockpits, our involvement in a shooting war was already guaranteed, and we saw the ORI results as somewhat of a joke: pass or fail, we were going to the Tonkin Gulf.

Ready Room Five was the Saints' home and business hub while embarked. A converted armory, the ready room was a combination briefing area, training room, movie theater, office, coffee mess, lounge, and general gathering place for squadron personnel. "Ready Five" was furnished with rows of reclining seats—one per pilot plus a few extras, each having a pull-up, classroom-type desktop and a storage compartment for flight gear beneath the seat. There was a teletype machine that pecked out operational information, a desk for the duty officer, a telephone, an intraship-communications "squawk box," and other paraphernalia, not the least of which was the indispensable coffee mess. This last was essential because, second only to his flight helmet and flight jacket with colorful patches, a pilot's personally monogrammed coffee cup was his most prized possession, a symbol of squadron fellowship.

The Saints hadn't been on board *Oriskany* on a regular basis since their completion of the prior deployment in March 1964. In the meantime, the ship's company had used Ready Five, and for a variety of reasons it was in run-down condition and nearly uninhabitable. Because little flying would be scheduled at the outset of our Pacific crossing, rehabilitation of the ready room was a priority project. A thorough cleaning, a coat of paint, and new deck tiles were in order. We selected light blue as the color of the paint for the bulkheads, to match the color scheme on our squadron's aircraft identification marking. Also, blue was a "cool" hue, and anything that would make the ready room seem cooler would be a blessing when we reached the hot climate of Southeast Asia. CDR Alex Urquart, *Oriskany*'s gunnery officer, who was responsible for general housekeeping in our section of the ship, gave his OK to my rehab project before the squadron left the ship to return to Lemoore.

On Sunday afternoon, 4 April, I said sad good-byes to Marilyn and our three children, Cori, Scott, and Amy. Then I led a flight of eight Skyhawks from Lemoore to the naval air station at North Island, *Oriskany's* home port across the bay from San Diego. The tail end of a spring storm stopped pouring rain on the base just as we arrived. The air was fresh and clean, the sun was shining brightly around dramatic buildups of cumulus clouds, and the wet runway sparkled like champagne during my landing rollout. All eight of us taxied our A-4s across the main avenue of the air station and down the long, sloping ramp to the quay wall where *Oriskany* was moored.

We disembarked, and shortly, the ship's crane hoisted our planes to the flight deck. I set about inspecting the squadron's shipboard spaces. All were in good shape except for Ready Five. I was disappointed that the rehab project had not gotten off the ground.

Alex Urquart was on leave and Lieutenant Commander X, the assistant gunnery officer, was in charge. Upon learning of our rehab plan, Mr. X, a crusty, up-from-the-ranks black shoe (non-aviator) with no love for "flyboys," had halted the project. I learned that he had punctuated his decision with the exclamation, "Not only no, but HELL NO! *Nobody's* gonna paint *my* ship like a Goddamn rainbow!"

The squadron's personnel, equipment, and personal gear arrived at North Island in a combined air-surface lift. When everything had been stowed and berthing assignments had been squared away, I directed the leading chief petty officer to implement a generous "last night ashore" liberty policy for the men. I joined several pilots for Mexican food and margaritas at "MexPac," the Mexican Village Restaurant in Coronado, a favorite off-base watering place for Pacific Fleet aviators. Early the next morning Skipper Harry Jenkins flew in with the last of our planes and pilots. All hands were then on board. We were off to war, and when *Oriskany* got underway at 1015 on 5 April, not a single Saint had missed the ship.

LT Dan Lestage, a flight surgeon and one of the four ground officers assigned to VA-163, reported for duty shortly after I took over as XO, and we soon struck up a friendly relationship. Dan was a roundish, bespectacled, Tabasco sauce–loving Louisiana boy who had recently graduated from flight-surgeon school. Mild of temper, Dan fitted easily into the world of tailhook pilots—pilots who were an unusually healthy lot, seldom needing medical attention. Dan spent as much time in our ready room as his medical chores would allow, enjoying the repartee and enduring the sobriquets: "Attack Quack" and "Doctor Dan, the Band-Aid man."

But Dan was in a rare, foul mood one evening during the transit to Hawaii. He stormed into my stateroom and complained that there was no toilet paper in the head that served the area where his stateroom was located. Because my job as squadron exec included tending to housekeeping matters, Dan reasoned that I should "do something" about the situation. But I suggested that he call the ship's division officer responsible for his area. Surely, in this matter, a physician would carry more weight that a mere aviator commander.

Dan made the phone call and gave a sleepy division officer a polite tail-chewing, employing medical terminology that focused on a range of concerns, from sanitation and tropical humidity to pestilence and contagious infection. He wore an expression of smug satisfaction as he departed my stateroom. Fifteen minutes later Dan telephoned me to report that a sailor had just delivered a three-month supply of toilet paper to the head in question. I dozed off to sleep, believing that Doctor Dan just might have the makings of a fine naval officer.[2]

Oriskany arrived at Pearl Harbor on 11 April and departed a day later, after members of the Hawaii fleet air commander's staff had presented the ORI briefings. The period of relative inactivity that followed Silver Lance had dulled the fine edge of flight proficiency that the air wing had attained during that exercise. We hadn't flown much in late March or during the crossing. As a result, the ORI performances of both the ship and the air wing were less that spectacular. We were unsynchronized, slow in responding to the general quarters and other all-hands drills, and we missed too many flight hours because of aircraft-maintenance problems that shouldn't have occurred. Some good news offset the Saints' mediocre performance, however. CDR Art Heinze, the ship's executive officer, ruled in favor of our plan to rehabilitate Ready Five. Himself a pilot, Heinze had rejected the "Goddamn rainbow" philosophy of Mr. X.

With the ORI behind us, *Oriskany* returned to Pearl Harbor and

---

2. He did. As of 1991, he was still on active duty as a rear admiral in the Navy's Medical Corps.

moored at Ford Island near the submerged, rusty, forlorn-looking hulk of USS *Utah,* which remained where Japanese bombers had sunk her on 7 December 1941.

LTJG Charlie Stender, a young aviator assigned to the Saints, was nicknamed "Tuna" because of his resemblance to the sun glasses–wearing "Charlie the Tuna" character of Starkist Tuna's television commercials. "Tuna" was the squadron's material officer, and before going ashore in Hawaii, I counseled him on an important project. The standard Navy-issue linoleum was green, but my rehab plan called for blue-and-white tile on the deck, to match the design on our flight helmets. Tuna's instructions were to find suitable tile while we were in Hawaii, since it was unlikely that it would be available in the Gulf of Tonkin.

Then I hitched a ride ashore in the gig with CAPT Bart Connolly, *Oriskany's* commanding officer. As the coxswain guided the boat around Ford Island toward the Merry Point landing at the Pearl Harbor Naval Station, Captain Connolly and I discussed the air wing's relatively poor performance in the ORI. Connolly said that he wasn't too worried but had a plan to help the wing regain peak proficiency.

If possible, the wing would fly daily while the ship was en route to the Philippines. My spirits brightened at the prospect of having flight operations break up what would ordinarily be a tedious twelve-day crossing. However, I was amused because such flying ran contrary to NATOPS—*N*aval *A*ir *T*raining and *Op*erational *S*tandardization procedures, the "bible" of flight operations and aviation safety. NATOPS required that carrier operations be conducted within range of a suitable airfield ashore so that planes could be diverted there if an emergency precluded landing on the carrier.

In that era of Secretary of Defense Robert Strange McNamara's "cost effectiveness," there was pressure from the highest level to preserve all material assets. The requirement for a "bingo" (divert) airfield ashore was a hedge against the possible loss of expensive planes. The philosophy promoted cost effectiveness but not necessarily readiness. New generations of naval aviators were growing up half believing the myth that an in-range bingo field was a necessary element of carrier operations. Such airfields were virtually nonexistent in the mid-Pacific.

An alert, crusty old-timer, Bart Connolly led by instinct rather than by the book. An experienced carrier pilot himself, he'd won a Navy Cross, the second-highest combat award, in World War II.

"You guys are all good pilots," Connolly said, "and we're headed for combat. Next week, when we're one hundred miles west of Pearl, we should have a NATOPS-burning party on the fantail."

That was near heresy, but the words conveyed cheery news. Connolly wasn't going to let peacetime rules stand in the way of enhancing the readiness of *Oriskany's* aviators. Clearly, the ship's C.O. had confidence in us and was subtly employing me as a messenger, to the Saints at least: Despite our low scores on the ORI, we should not lose confidence in ourselves.

The Saints enjoyed three days and nights in Honolulu. One night I rendezvoused with Charlie Stender and LTJG John Shore, my usual wingman, at the officers club at Pearl Harbor. We sipped rum-laced Mai Tais and listened to Charlie's report on his somewhat harried but successful search for blue-and-white tile for the ready room. After dinner we taxied to Waikiki for the midnight show at the Barefoot Bar of the old Queen's Surf Hotel, where bare-chested Polynesian Apollos twirled flaming torches and wicked-looking machetes while lovely, brown-skinned wahines undulated sensuously in sparse bras and quivering grass skirts.

John Harrod Shore, my wingman, had a baritone voice. On the ground he was a pleasant conversationalist, but in the air he was a model of sound radio discipline. When John keyed his microphone, the transmission that followed was brief and businesslike. During the many hours that we had flown together as a team, John's most common transmission was the word "Rog," short for "Roger," meaning "OK" or "I understand." His "Rog" became a reassurance to me during the maturing of our airborne partnership. It reflected John's competence as an aviator and his skill as a wingman.

John was a slim, twenty-six-year-old bachelor and as good an officer as he was a pilot. When John wasn't flying, he supervised the squadron's "plane captains," the young, mostly nonrated men who serviced, cleaned, and "mothered" VA-163's aircraft on the flight and hangar decks. When it came to Navy paperwork, John was only average, and he was fairly typical of junior officers in resisting that irritating chore when provided the opportunity. But he loved to fly. John demonstrated a higher level of competence in that game than did many of his contemporaries. A fellow pilot remarked one day, admiringly, "When I get to be a skipper, I hope I have a whole squadron of John Shores."

After the intriguing floor show at the Queen's Surf, John, Charlie, and I, none of us exactly cold sober, removed our shoes and strolled barefoot along the beach toward Waikiki 's main "strip." While John and I wore aloha shirts and slacks, Charlie was attired more formally in a gray seersucker suit and sported a red knit tie. He looked out of place with shoes in hand and trousers rolled up to his knees.

At a palm-studded stretch of beach that easily could have been the place where Montgomery Clift was gunned down in the film *From Here to Eternity*, John Shore decided that he wanted to go swimming. Charlie Stender wandered on ahead while John stripped, unceremoniously handed me his clothes, and strolled naked into the surf. I imagined an unseemly headline in Honolulu's newspaper the next morning: SQUADRON EXECUTIVE OFFICER STANDS IDLY BY WHILE JUNIOR PILOT DISAPPEARS INTO OCEAN.

John returned to the beach a few minutes later, however, still alive but shivering uncontrollably as he struggled into his clothes.

"You feeling OK, John?"

"Rog."

We caught up with Charlie Stender as, still barefoot, he strolled along Kalakaua Avenue in his natty suit and tie, shoes still in hand, trousers rolled up to his knees, and returned to the ship.

3 First Line Period

 Captain Connolly was true to his word. Uncooperative easterly winds, opposite to the ship's required westward track, kept us from flying every day during the twelve-day transit to the Philippines. But fly we did. We had our "burning party" for NATOPS manuals, and for four days we severed the mythical peacetime tether to a "bingo" airfield ashore. The nearest *Oriskany* came to land was three hundred miles, and that was tiny Marcus Island, a mere flyspeck on the Pacific Ocean, 1,200 miles southeast of Japan. It didn't take a genius IQ to recognize that *Oriskany*'s flight deck was the only runway around and that all dry-flight endeavors terminated there. It was not surprising that our carrier-landing techniques became remarkably precise. For a time we were in a carrier pilot's Camelot. Operating as a "one and only" seaborne runway underscored the classic justification for the aircraft carrier—a self-contained, mobile, floating airfield capable of projecting air power nearly anywhere, independent of airfields ashore.

During one flying day I led a division of four Skyhawks high over the Pacific as we practiced the 60-degree dive-bombing tactic we'd borrowed from the folks at China Lake. The target was a small sled towed in the ship's wake. Our Mark (Mk) 76 practice bombs contained shotgun-shell charges and produced smoke puffs upon impact with the water. "Miss" distances became shorter with each run as we compensated for both wind drift and the movement of the ship. I liked the 60-degree dive. It was quicker than attacks at shallower angles and would expose pilots to antiaircraft fire for briefer periods. Equally important, the steeper dive angle accounted for decisively more accurate hits.

After the exercise we flew a "sightseeing" trek to Marcus Island, aside from *Oriskany* the only attraction on the ocean's surface for thousands of miles. We made two low passes in formation over the desolate speck of coral that had been a hotly contested prize during World War II. A few buildings dotted the island, and the short airstrip was apparently no longer usable. The structures appeared fragile, as if they would easily wash away in the first big wave of a storm. A dozen or so people rushed from the buildings to wave to us. They couldn't see me, but I waved back.

On another day I flew a late-afternoon tanker mission, acting as an airborne filling station. My Skyhawk carried a buddy store, a streamlined, 300-gallon fuel tank with a retractable hose and drogue. That fuel, added to what I was carrying in the internal tanks, meant that I had 900 gallons of emergency fuel and was the "friend indeed" should fellow pilots become thirsty for gas. But no one needed fuel that day, and the tanker mission was relatively boring. I flew circles over the carrier while other aviators engaged in more interesting pursuits.

The visibility was excellent, and the deep blue of the ocean created a knife-sharp horizon against the pale-blue sky. There were scattered cloud buildups, and the sun glowed golden behind a row of cumulus miles to the west of me. I was at 15,000 feet, listening to the terse radio conversations between pilots and the ship as the planes returned to *Oriskany.*

Then there was a call for me from the carrier.

"Old Salt Tanker, this is Childplay. Your signal is dump Charlie."

The last two planes were on their final approaches below me. My load of fuel was no longer needed. "Charlie" meant "come on down and land." I eased back on the throttle to begin my descent and flipped the toggle switch on the buddy store–control panel. As I banked my Skyhawk, I glanced in the rearview mirror. A misty stream of fuel trailed from my aircraft. The buddy store was dumping properly, and I would quickly be down to a safe landing weight. At 5,000 feet I glanced again to the west, at the dramatic sunset beyond the bank of cumulus, and for a few seconds an odd thought occupied my mind. Twenty-eight years earlier, around-the-world aviator Amelia Earhart and her navigator, Fred Noonan, had disappeared into the vast Pacific near Howland Island. I had been ten years old then, and the Earhart-Noonan disappearance had intrigued me. I had spent many hours trying to imagine what went through their minds as they motored, out of radio contact and alone in their plane, over the endless sea.

The needle of the altimeter wound down past 3,000 feet, and I was back in the real world, descending toward *Oriskany*. All other aircraft had landed, and I was alone in the mid-Pacific, the sole occupant of the only plane in the sky above thousands of miles of ocean. Well motivated, I summoned all my airmanship prowess and turned onto final approach. I flew "on speed" and "on glide slope" and caught the magic number three "target" wire for a perfect landing. Unlike Earhart and Noonan, I made it home safely.

Flight operations in the mid-Pacific had the pragmatic benefit of increasing the morale of both pilots and maintenance crews. For one thing, flying broke the monotony of the crossing. And our "birds" benefited. Aircraft fuel, hydraulic, and electrical systems became cantankerous when kept idle for long periods. Planes simply operated much better when flown regularly. Additionally, getting planes into the air unlocked *Oriskany*'s static traffic jam on the flight and hangar decks. The greater opportunity to move aircraft about was a boon to the maintenance effort.

To fill spare hours during the Pacific crossing, my friend and fellow *Oriskany* pilot LCDR Paul Merchant joined me to form a musical group. Paul was a short, mustachioed bundle of nervous energy assigned to VA-152, flying the aging A-1 "Spad." We'd met when assigned to the Naval Air Technical Training staff at Memphis, where we were allied by a common distaste for our less-than-challenging staff jobs. Paul had characterized our positions then as "retired on active duty." Frequent flights together while at Memphis had provided "escape" therapy and bonded our friendship.

Paul was a fair-to-middling mandolin player. He could close his eyes and strum sounds that conjured images of gondolas floating along Venetian canals. I played the baritone ukulele, and at Memphis Paul and I had occasionally entertained at staff parties. In *Oriskany* we drafted LCDR Eric Shade and LT Ed Davis from Paul's squadron and my wingman, John Shore, to create a playing-and-singing quintet.

Eric was an accomplished banjo player. Tall, personable Ed Davis claimed only "strumable" skills with his guitar, but he had a pleasant tenor voice. John Shore was just learning to play his ukulele but was a solid baritone. The five of us gathered frequently in the evenings for a hour or two of musical therapy.

Somewhere between Marcus Island in the mid-Pacific and Luzon Island in the Philippines the Saints' ready-room-rehab project came to a successful conclusion. The bulkheads and overhead of Ready Five were painted "cool," pale blue. The blue-and-off-white tile that Charlie Stender had bought in Hawaii was laid in a checkerboard pattern, and John Shore carved a "Saints" logo in the linoleum near the front of the room. A metalsmith from the ship assisted with his welding talents to reposition the metal furniture. The squadron's parachute riggers created blue-and-white Naugahyde headrest covers for the pilots' chairs. Our home away from home was elevated to what, after critical inspection, one of our macho young plane captains described as "a classy fuckin' ready room."

Pilots from other squadrons and several admiring men of the ship's company attended an informal open house, during which we showed off our handiwork. Notably absent, however, was Lieutenant Commander X, the ship's assistant gunnery officer, over whose objections we had painted the ready room "like a Goddamn rainbow." The first movie we featured in Ready Five after the rehab project was the James Bond epic *Goldfinger*. My supervisory role in the rehab efforts did not go unheralded. For several weeks thereafter the squadron's junior pilots referred to me, affectionately I hoped, as "Bluefinger."

On May Day I led three other pilots on a lengthy training mission. Two Skyhawk tankers accompanied us, and forty minutes after launch, while maintaining radio silence, we took on additional fuel. I patted my helmet and signaled to John Shore to take the lead, then jockeyed my Skyhawk into the plug in position, aligning my fuel probe with the skittery basket at the end of the tanker's drogue. Twelve minutes later all four strike aircraft were topped off, and I waved bye-bye to the tanker leader. He nodded acknowledgment, and the two tankers rolled away from the formation to return to the ship while we continued toward our "target."

Electronic aids to navigation were available, but the weather was clear, and we continued in radio silence. Testing my dead-reckoning skills, I had switched my radio-navigation gear to standby, and I was pleased when we made our planned landfall. After crossing hundreds of miles of open ocean, we hit the northern tip of the island of Luzon virtually on the mark.

We attacked the Tabones Rock off the west coast of Luzon with our Mk 76 practice bombs, then headed back to the ship. Three and a half hours and 800+ miles later, we were in *Oriskany*'s landing pattern. I was butt-weary. Also, I had a two-hour bladder, which dramatized the only significant shortcoming of the marvelous Skyhawk: the absence of a relief tube.

Oriskany put into Subic Bay, about fifty miles west of Manila, early in the afternoon of 3 May. The next morning Skipper Harry Jenkins, LT Art Avore, CAG Stockdale, and I went ashore to test fly some weapons. The squadron had been tasked with an operational evaluation of four new Bullpup II air-to-ground missiles. A larger, improved version of a weapon that had been in the inventory for several years, the "big Bullpup" was a radio-controlled, rocket-propelled drone—a standoff weapon that the pilot launched and "flew" by remote control to a distant target.

Harry led us to Tabones Rock, where we set up in a racetrack pattern. I was tail-end Charlie and watched the other three pilots fire their weapons. Finally, it was my turn. I began a shallow glide. When the target was only three miles away, I pressed the bomb-release pickle. The big Bullpup roared from beneath my wing. Using a thumb button on the control stick to send subtle up-down-left-right commands, I guided the big Bullpup as it streaked toward the target. The control of this weapon was smoother and easier than that of its smaller, older brother. Indeed, it was fun, almost like maneuvering a radio-controlled model plane.

But the toy I played with had a 500-pound, high-explosive warhead and produced an enormous fireball when it smashed into Tabones Rock. As I pulled off the target and joined the others, I tried to visualize using the big Bullpup in combat but couldn't see any great advantage. Theoretically, it provided a standoff capability, but its shortcoming was its need for visual guidance until it impacted the target. Maintaining a long, steady, descending glide path to control the missile would make me an easy target for antiaircraft gunners.

Harry led us on an impromptu "reconnaissance" flight after the Bullpup shoot so that we could explore central Luzon island. We circled over tiny Corregidor island, the "guardian" of Manila Bay. As I stared down at the abandoned fortifications grown over with vegetation, I tried to imagine what it was like in 1942 for more than eleven thousand ill-equipped Americans trapped there by the Japanese. They had endured a month-long siege with declining supplies of food, medicine, water, and ammunition. South of Corregidor was Lake Taal, familiar to me from my crossword-puzzle habit—a lake in the large crater of a dormant volcano. The lake held a smaller volcanic cone that, in turn, housed a smaller lake. The imagery made me grin beneath my oxygen mask: a lake on an island in a lake on an island in the ocean.

Oriskany was underway again later that day. I remained at Cubi Point with six other Saints to fly our planes to the ship. Late-afternoon thunderclouds boiled up, and a torrential rainstorm swept across Cubi Point as our departure time approached. The runway was glistening wet when I taxied my Skyhawk into position for a 1930 takeoff. The six other Saints were behind me. Ahead of us to the west was another mass of dark and threatening clouds. The South China Sea was infamous for generating huge and nasty thunderstorms and appeared to be living up to its reputation.

We took off and joined up, but it was soon apparent that we couldn't return to the ship as a group. *Oriskany* was fifty miles northwest of Cubi, and the granddaddy of thunderstorms was churning between us and the boat. The weather grew darker by the moment, and the turbulence was not conducive to flying in formation. After making radio contact with the ship, we split up for individual approaches under the guidance of the Childplay radar controllers. I rolled out on a westerly heading and was forced onto the gauges immediately.

The next forty minutes were a wild ride over a circuitous, two hundred–mile course. I was vectored around the worst of the thunderstorm cells, traveling one hundred miles west, then north for a bit, then back to the east. The turbulence was the most severe I had ever experienced. The lightning was spectacular to see but bad on the nerves. I gained new respect for the power of the weather.

During the final miles of my radar-guided CCA (carrier-controlled approach), the calm and reassuring voice of the controller was a godsend, a welcome contrast to the surrounding mayhem. My jet was tossed about wildly in a nightmarish black-and-white world. At one point a thunderstorm cell near the carrier buffeted my Skyhawk so violently that I gripped the throttle and stick with white-knuckle intensity. I felt as if I was literally hanging on for dear life. I kept my eyes glued to the red-lit instrument panel. Blindingly white, vertigo-inducing flashes of lightning punctuated the pitch black outside.

My muscles were tense. I turned the cockpit air conditioning control to maximum cold. Still I sweated profusely. My shoulders bounced against the canopy rails, and I felt like a Ping-Pong ball in a Chinese championship tournament. I was acutely aware of my diminutive size compared with the mammoth mass of angry winds, rain, and energy outside.

When I finally broke out of the worst of the weather, I spotted the lights that outlined the runway on the flight deck. Shortly thereafter I picked out the amber and green lights of the "meatball," the Fresnel optical landing system on the port quarter of the flight deck. I was overcome with relief. Normally, it was a struggle to maintain speed and proper glide path at night. But that time it was almost easy—an exaggerated sensation produced by the terror I had just experienced flying through the storm, and the subsequent welcome release from it.

I slammed down on deck and automatically jammed the throttle forward for full power. That was a habitual reaction in case the tailhook missed all four cables and convicted me of the embarrassing sin of carrier aviators, a bolter. But only my body surged forward, pressing against my shoulder straps, as the aircraft rapidly decelerated. I was "in the wires" on *Oriskany*'s rain-soaked deck. The other six pilots were soon home as well, safely on deck but a bit emotionally unsettled. When we reached Ready Five there was an abundance of genuinely sympathetic comments, and our perceptive Doctor Dan pressed two-ounce "combat rations" of medicinal brandy into our willing hands, "for duty above and beyond."

The flight deck of an operating aircraft carrier has always ranked high on the list of the world's most dangerous places to work. The Saints were reminded of that fact on 5 May as *Oriskany* steamed toward the war zone. During late-afternoon operations an F-8 Crusader was being maneuvered into position for launch. Following the signals of the yellow-shirt flight-deck director, the Crusader pilot added throttle to make a sharp turn. The jet blast from the fighter's exhaust caught five of the flight-deck crew unaware and swept them off their feet. They tumbled roughly toward the edge of the deck. One man grabbed an aircraft's landing-gear strut and hung on for dear life. Another clung to an aircraft's tie-down cable, even though it cut deeply into his hands. Two others took hold of the catwalk railing and slowed their roll enough to plummet into the safety net outboard of the flight deck. The fifth man, Airman Tom Prezorski, one of John Shore's young plane captains, wasn't so fortunate as the others. He was lifted completely off his feet and blown clear of the flight deck. He fell six stories into the ocean, and the impact with the water knocked him unconscious. The ship's helo hurried to the scene. Within minutes Prezorski was scooped from the water and returned to the flight deck. Dan Lestage was there to apply emergency resuscitation, but it was too late. At age nineteen, Tom Prezorski, a personable young man from Brooklyn, New York, had drowned, our first casualty of the Vietnam War.

In 1965 the war had escalated, and the Navy's supply system was unprepared to meet the demand for aviator flight suits suitable for missions over the jungles of Southeast Asia. The stock Navy flight suit was made of fire-retardant material and dyed international orange. In peacetime its high visibility was an advantage during search and rescue. But in combat it was a distinct disadvantage, crying, "Hey, here I am!" to a converging enemy force should a pilot have to bail out into a green jungle.

The supply system had an alternative, a flight suit coincidentally identified as "combat khaki." Still, its light-tan color had the same basic disadvantage. The situation called for naval-aviator ingenuity. A few farsighted individuals had purchased two-piece camouflage-pattern outfits at sporting-goods stores before leaving the States. Others had made "cumshaw" deals with Air Force and Marine Corps contemporaries in Hawaii and Subic Bay, swapping orange flight suits for blue-gray ones or for green fatigues. Plus, almost every pilot in Air Wing 16 tried his hand at dyeing an orange or khaki flight suit. The results were a bunch of dirty-looking, green-gray, one-piece outfits.

During *Oriskany's* brief stop at Cubi, I had instructed Charlie Stender to purchase a few packages of green dye at the Navy exchange so that the Saints could do some dyeing. After the Bullpup shoot I visited the exchange and noted that only four packages of green dye remained on the shelf. Not knowing if Charlie had been shopping yet, I purchased all four packages for insurance. I was unaware that John Sloan, the Saints' air-intelligence officer, had overheard my earlier conversation with Charlie. He had preceded me in visiting the exchange and, thinking he'd do Charlie a favor, bought three packages of the dye. Finally, Charlie had arrived at the exchange, only to discover an empty shelf. He rushed by taxi to the exchange at the Subic naval station a few miles away, where he purchased the last four packages of green dye in stock at that store. The next morning I was the custodian of eleven packages of green dye. After reading the instructions on one of the packages, I realized that I had enough coloring to dye the flight suits of every aviator in the Seventh Fleet for the next six months. When I learned that other pilots in the wing were grousing about the lack of green dye in the Subic Bay area, I cleared my conscience by informing the other ready rooms that the Saints had "a couple" of extra packages for sale at cost.

Later in the deployment, the supply system caught up with the demand. Pilots received flight suits made of dark green fire-retardant material suitable for combat missions. Initially, however, most of *Oriskany*'s pilots went to war in experimentally dyed, dirty-looking, greenish-gray coveralls.

"Dixie Station" was an operational "X" on the chart of the South China Sea, off the east coast of South Vietnam, 12 degrees north of the equator. It was created early in the summer of 1965 at the request of MACV, the Military Area Command, Vietnam. The purpose of having a carrier operate from Dixie Station was to augment the Air Force's tactical-air-support missions in South Vietnam. *Oriskany* was the first carrier to operate from Dixie Station, and we flew "in-country" missions during our first three weeks of combat. The term "in-country" was an Air Force euphemism used to distinguish their tactical missions flown *in* South Vietnam from those flown over Laos and North Vietnam. The latter missions were prosaically dubbed "out-country." Since we flew from a carrier at sea, "in-country" accurately described the Navy's air operations in the south, and the term was readily adopted.

But we could not bring ourselves to adopt the awkward "out-country" as descriptive of missions flown over North Vietnam from carriers on Yankee Station.

Missions flown from Dixie Station were considerably safer than those flown from Yankee Station, the carriers' operating area for the "northern war." Friendly troops operated in many areas of South Vietnam, but there were no friendly forces on the ground in North Vietnam. Enemy antiaircraft fire in the south was virtually nonexistent, while missions launched from Yankee Station routinely encountered moderate-to-heavy AAA. Experience had already proven that a pilot shot down over North Vietnam had a minimal chance of being rescued. In the south, the presence of friendly troops and the availability of U.S. helicopters significantly increased the prospects of rescuing a downed flyer.

Except for the live ordnance we carried and enemy small-arms fire—hazardous primarily to a pilot who pulled out too low from an attack run—our dawn-to-dusk operations from Dixie Station were not unlike Stateside training missions. In those three weeks my wingman John Shore suffered the embarrassment of being the only pilot in the air wing to return to *Oriskany* with a hole in his aircraft. During a routine post-flight inspection one of John's plane captains discovered a single .30-caliber bullet lodged in the fuselage of his Skyhawk.

A built-in bonus of flying from Dixie Station was working with FACs (forward airborne controllers) who guided our close-support efforts. They didn't fly at night, so our airborne chores were done for the day once the sun sank in the west. Dixie Station was a relatively calm environment compared with what was happening in the northern war, where disquieting intelligence reports showed a constant Communist buildup. The difference prompted one Saintly wag to post a Charles Schultz "Peanuts" cartoon with a personal observation on Ready Five's bulletin board. The cartoon's caption, "Happiness is a warm puppy," was rephrased to read, "Happiness is in-country!"

On Sunday morning, 16 May, a few hours before *Oriskany*'s planned departure for Yankee Station, there was an accident at Bien Hoa (Ben-wah) airfield, twelve miles northeast of Saigon. A chain reaction of exploding bombs and burning jet fuel created a holocaust on the flight line, killing more than thirty American and South Vietnamese personnel and injuring hundreds more. At first the cause was believed to be a Vietcong attack. But it was later learned that the culprit was a malfunctioning bomb fuze on a combat-loaded B-57 Canberra bomber, which exploded the bomb as the plane was starting up to fly an air-support mission. Along with the human cost, the accident at Bien Hoa was a blow to the inventory. Thirteen planes, including ten Canberras, were destroyed, and twenty-five others were damaged.

The accident directly touched *Oriskany*. One of those killed at Bien Hoa was Maj. Bob Bell, a popular Air Force exchange pilot who had been serving with *Oriskany*'s fighter squadron VF-162. Bob's F-8 Crusader had developed a fuel leak during an air-support mission near Saigon on that fateful Sunday morning. Rather than risking a flight back to the ship, Bob had elected to land at Bien Hoa to have a maintenance technician investigate the problem. He touched down at Bien Hoa a few minutes before the disastrous explosion and was killed on the flight line shortly after leaving his plane. Bob's death gave me a clammy "Grace of God" feeling when I next flew near Bien Hoa and looked down at the airfield. A couple of days before the disaster my Skyhawk had had hung ordnance—a bomb that wouldn't release and couldn't be returned to the ship. I had landed at Bien Hoa to have the bomb removed.

The loss of pilots and aircraft put a dent in the U.S. Air Force's tactical-bombing capability at a time when the Vietcong and North Vietnamese regulars had launched a "monsoon offensive." *Oriskany*, therefore, was retained on Dixie Station, and Air Wing 16 was pressed into service to fill the gap. From sunrise to sunset in the nine days beginning on 16 May the wing flew more than one thousand in-country air-support sorties. Morale was high as flight hours mounted, but the work was serious.

The unopposed missions we flew from Dixie Station were satisfying from the pilot's viewpoint. Frequently, each of us flew two sorties a day. We were the fortunate few who got away from the ship, if only briefly. That freedom gave me a new appreciation for the unsung heroes, the men of the air wing and ship's company who labored endless hours in our behalf. They got no break from the tedium—loading and unloading ordnance and servicing, repairing, maintaining, deck handling, launching, and recovering the aircraft. Their's was an 18–20-hour work schedule, day in and day out. While we were sleeping or eating breakfast, they were on the flight and hangar decks or in the multitude of compartments and spaces throughout the ship, doing their jobs. Their time clock was the regular one hour and forty-five minute cycle of aircraft launches and recoveries. And they were still hard at it hours after the last plane landed.

The heat and muggy humidity of the South China Sea made working conditions thoroughly uncomfortable for nearly everyone. Daytime temperatures hovered between 90° and 100° F. Jet blast from the aircraft and steam from the catapults exacerbated the conditions. At day's end the men might catch quick showers, if sufficient fresh water was available for such luxuries. The boilers and steam-powered catapults claimed priority for the output of the ship's aging and overworked fresh water–producing evaporators. As often as not, the men were victims of "water hours," when fresh water for bathing and laundering was turned off throughout the ship. Clean or dirty, the men tried to grab a few hours of fitful sleep. All night long the steel decks and bulkheads radiated the tropical heat absorbed during the day. Few berthing spaces in our twenty-year-old carrier were air conditioned. Often, they were hotter and more uncomfortable than the work centers that the men had just left. Some enterprising souls found sleep in the less stifling open-air catwalks and sponsons along the sides of the ship.

Somehow, in spite of the hard work and miserable conditions, there was a strong sense of purpose among the men. The troops of VA-163 seldom complained. Morale was high.

By tradition, the one thousandth arrested landing aboard an aircraft carrier, an easily identified benchmark, is an honored occasion. One afternoon in early May I broke my division of four Skyhawks overhead *Oriskany*, dropped the gear and flaps, swept astern the ship in a wide 180-degree turn, picked up the ball, and drove on in. After catching a wire, I was taxied to the forward aircraft elevator and immediately sent below to the hangar deck. A squadron mech passed by after I'd shut down and deplaned. "Congratulations, XO," he said. Confused, I could only smile. He was gone before I could ask the reason for the compliment. I made my way up to Ready Five, where I learned that mine had been the ninety thousandth arrested landing on *Oriskany*. A traditional cake-cutting ceremony after dinner in the wardroom the next day recognized my dubious accomplishment. I was presented with an engraved teak plaque made of flight-deck planking. In an age of all-steel ship construction, the small piece of lumber was a unique tribute to our World War II–vintage *Oriskany*, a part of whose flight deck was made of wood.

In late May *Oriskany* became involved in the part of the war in which antiaircraft artillery was a real threat. Operation Rolling Thunder was then three months old, focusing on supply and transportation routes that snaked their way from North Vietnam, through Laos, and into South Vietnam. Missions flown as part of Rolling Thunder had already proven both dangerous and discouraging. Twenty Navy planes had been shot down over North Vietnam in that three-month period, yet intelligence reports contained little evidence that the interdiction effort was having much effect.

Two days after departing Dixie Station, we were on Yankee Station in the Tonkin Gulf, and I was tasked to lead Air Wing 16's first strike mission over North Vietnam. The assignment was a minor distinction at best. Eight Skyhawks, loaded with 500-pound bombs, were to destroy a coastal railroad bridge over the Song Lua River at Ha Trung, sixty miles south of Hanoi. We were catapulted into terrible weather—thick, low-hanging clouds and torrential rain. It was 0930 on 28 May. I climbed through the "goo" on instruments and broke out into the blue at 20,000 feet. As the others joined me, I gazed at the weather below and had doubts about even finding our target, much less bombing it. Visibility on top was excellent, but all I could see below was a solid layer of clouds stretching to the horizon.

We proceeded toward the coast-in point, using TACAN bearing and distance from "Red Crown," the SAR ship stationed in the Gulf near the coast, as a guide. I kept examining my chart, as if it might contain a magic clue to help us get to our destination. I felt like a batter with two strikes. There were no visual references except for the horizon and the general east-west orientation provided by the sun and the compass. There I was, leading seven others to war, into unfamiliar territory none of us could even see.

The target was ten miles north of Than Hoa, a known hot spot. I hoped we didn't miss our mark and drift into that area. As we approached the coast—or, more precisely, where I *thought* the coast was—I felt that the chances of finding the target were zero. I considered aborting the mission, but then there was a surprise. Below me, at the ten-o'clock position, I saw a hole in the clouds. Incredibly, smack in the middle of the hole was the bridge, our target.

"This is Old Salt Lead," I broadcast. "Tallyho the target, in that hole at ten o'clock down. I'm going in steep, repeat steep, north to south. Check your switches."

"Steep" meant a 60-degree dive, the tactic we had practiced earlier. I hadn't briefed it that way back in the ready room, but I knew the other Saints would understand and wouldn't be bothered by the last-minute change of plan. However, two pilots from VA-164 were with the strike group, and I hoped that they could adjust. The "switches" call was an important reminder. Failure to select the correct ones might prevent the bombs from coming off and overstress the aircraft. A pullout with our bomb load could cause damage and possibly loss of control.

I tapped my helmet, pointed to John Shore on my wing, and started to blow him a kiss, the peel-off signal. John had moved into a close-parade formation on me and shook his head negatively in a silent, prearranged message. He didn't have the target in sight and would stay on my wing, diving with me in formation and pickling his bombs when I dropped mine.

I nodded an acknowledgment, then rocked my head to my left, signaling the beginning of the attack. Together, John and I did a wingover into a 60-degree dive. As we whistled down, flak whistled up from an unseen gun battery somewhere below the clouds. Bursts of AAA peppered the sky. For an instant I imagined that I was back in 1952, in the cockpit of an F9F Panther, diving on a railroad tunnel near Chongjin, North Korea. That had been my first unnerving exposure to antiaircraft fire. The flak from the North Vietnamese gunners below was no less unnerving.

The strike was over in less than a minute. We roared down, dropped our bombs through the hole in the clouds, and skedaddled clear of the antiaircraft fire. When number eight reported, "Off and clear," I relaxed a bit.

Immediately there was a surprise radio transmission. A Marine Corps "snooper" aircraft, probably an EF-10B flying out of Da Nang, was somewhere nearby and radioed BDA (bomb-damage assessment).

"You really clobbered the target," said the marine. "That's some of the best bombing I've seen, and I'm out here every day."

I was flattered, but where had he come from? He was on our tactical frequency and acted as if he knew what was going on and was supposed to be there. At the intelligence briefing there had been no mention of any snooper. As much as anything, I was concerned that we might have struck him as well as the target.

In the end, the Ha Trung–Song Lua bridge mission, Air Wing 16's first strike, seemed silly. Back on deck, we of the "first" had a hilarious time relating our experience to a ready room full of interested fellow pilots. The only other pilot to admit having seen the target was LCDR Don Martin. And he said that he was "hurting" for an aim point and spotted the bridge only seconds before bomb release. Like John Shore, the rest simply followed the leader, and the steep dive didn't bother our two brothers from VA-164.

My assignment as strike leader had been the luck of the draw. But with tongue in cheek, Harry Jenkins complained that he was "humiliated" by having the squadron's *second*-senior pilot "finagle" the lead of the wing's *first* strike from Yankee Station. His threat to banish me to the Philippines as "officer-in-charge of the squadron's Cubi Point detachment" (one non-flyable aircraft) amused the junior pilots.

The marine snooper plane remained a mystery. The squadron's air-intelligence officer, John Sloan, denied any knowledge of it. He dug into his files, found nothing, and chalked off the incident to "lack of high-level coordination." The final act of the drama was the viewing of the BDA photos taken by LT Hank McWhorter, the "photo beanie" pilot who tagged along behind the strike group in his RF-8 photo Crusader. Our "really clobbered...best bombing" caused only minor damage to the northern end of the bridge. We gave the thing a good scare, but it was still passable.

Typhoon Babe worked her way northwest across the South China Sea toward the Gulf of Tonkin. The deteriorating weather brought an unscheduled three-day stand down. On 31 May *Oriskany* was ordered out of the Gulf to avoid being trapped by Babe. Twenty-four hours later USS *Bon Homme Richard* arrived at Dixie Station as *Oriskany*'s relief, and we steamed toward Subic Bay and a brief respite.

Our first exposure to operations from Yankee Station was thus abbreviated, yet May had been a busy month. Filling in for the USAF from Dixie Station after the devastating accident at Bien Hoa airfield had propelled Air Wing 16 to a new high in combat sorties and hours flown.

Unfortunately, our efforts received little recognition because of self-serving military politics. The Navy and Air Force were competing for dollars because the Johnson administration was trying to finance the war on a peacetime military budget. The Air Force wasn't anxious to promote the case for carrier aviation by admitting that we had bailed them out of a tight spot. On the other side of the coin, operations from Dixie Station were a touchy subject from the viewpoint of the Navy's high command. There was the potential question: "Why not just base Navy planes ashore and eliminate the need for expensive aircraft carriers?" It was easier to justify operations from Yankee Station, and the Navy preferred that others focus on that aspect.

At the squadron level we weren't worried about high-level political concerns. But our high-time month did become part of naval aviation's traditional game of one-upmanship. When *Oriskany* arrived at Yankee Station on 26 May, Harry Jenkins sent LCDR Russ Weidman, one of our pilots, to visit the Skyhawk squadrons on board the carrier *Coral Sea*. "Coral Maru" had spent the entire month of May on Yankee Station, and Russ's mission was to collect firsthand information, pilot-to-pilot, on experiences in the north.

Among other things, Russ discovered that the "Silver Foxes" of VA-155 were feeling like peacocks, having logged a highly respectable 600+ hours of flight time thus far in May. Weather permitting, they said, the squadron might even set a "record" of 700+ hours of combat flying before *Coral Sea* left the line. Russ made small talk about other matters, politely avoiding the subject of flight hours and combat missions flown. *Coral Sea*'s pilots sensed a chance to one-up the "newboy" from *Oriskany* and wouldn't buy Russ's downplaying of the hours-missions issue. The question was posed directly: "How many flight hours have the Saints logged so far this month?" Russ answered honestly: "Nine hundred and seventy, with the prospect of breaking 1,100...weather permitting." The conversation was promptly terminated.

The twenty-three–day line period in May netted the Saints a "record" 1,132 flight hours and 402 combat missions, but the numbers do not reveal the truth of the effort. Each pilot spent about an hour and thirty minutes at flight-related activities—planning, briefing, and debriefing—for each hour of actual flight time. The result was that each pilot had a work day of 7–9 hours. Each hour a Skyhawk was airborne required that other squadron personnel spend about twenty-seven man-hours to service and maintain the airplanes, load and unload ordnance, and perform other related tasks. So our May record represented more than thirty thousand man-hours of effort, and VA-163 was but one of the five squadrons and three smaller aviation detachments that comprised Air Wing 16. In addition, there was the incalculable number of man-hours expended by the 2,500 ship's personnel.

Morale was high when we left the war zone for a few days of R and R. In Navy parlance, *Oriskany* was a "small deck" carrier, but we'd proven that our old "boat" was a strong contributor.

4 Second Line Period

 We usually ran a film in Ready Five after flying was over for the day. The movies provided a respite, an important opportunity to escape and unwind, albeit temporarily. The stag atmosphere of the ready-room "theater" usually generated an assortment of remarks from the audience. Charlie Stender, a master at such comments, bawdy or otherwise, was the hands-down winner of the "Couth Officer" title. On the other hand, LCDR Charlie Wack was the unchallenged leader in the trivia category. He could identify an amazing number of bit players by name and recite the details of their screen careers. LT Bob Hofford was "Mr. Perseverance." No film was too boring for Bob. Others might walk out on a particularly dull film, sometimes en masse, but not Bob Hofford. He reasoned that ready-room movies constituted free entertainment, and except for worrying about his next mission, there wasn't a helluva lot else to do anyway.

One evening we watched *Mutiny on the Bounty* with Marlon Brando as Fletcher Christian and Trevor Howard as the martinet, Captain Bligh. In one scene sadistic Captain Bligh was particularly cruel to a young officer. The lights came on to change a reel a few seconds later, and I took advantage of the break to busy myself with some routine paperwork. Charlie Stender boomed from the back of the ready room: "What's the XO doing, taking notes?" Later in the film, Captain Bligh flushed Fletcher Christian from the tropical undergrowth where the latter had been "studying botany" with a native lass. Bligh admon-

47

ished the young officer to "satisfy your lust at another time" and ordered Christian to return to the ship. Perhaps thinking of the ship's upcoming visit to the Philippines, Charlie Stender spoke again: "On second thought, XO, I hope you're *not* taking notes!"

Our brief respite in Subic Bay allowed maintenance crews to perform aircraft corrosion control on our A-4s. A month of intense flying and of exposure to salt air, jet-engine exhaust, gun-muzzle blasts, and smoke from the ship's stacks had left our planes "grungy" and in need of attention. Stop-gap corrosion control was a daily chore for the plane captains at sea, but there was no substitute for fresh water, cleaning compound, and scrub brushes to rid the Skyhawks of the long-term debilitating effects of corrosive elements. At sea, however, fresh water for washing airplanes was an unaffordable luxury. The steam catapults and ship's boilers claimed priority on the precious freshwater output of *Oriskany*'s aging evaporators, and the "Laundromat," Cubi Point's facility for steam cleaning aircraft, was popular.

The appearance of VA-163's planes prompted an unsettling remark from Lieutenant Commander X, the aviator-baiting assistant gunnery officer who had tried to sidetrack the rehab project for Ready Five. I met him on the flight deck the morning *Oriskany* departed Yankee Station, and Mr. X spoke bluntly.

"I don't get up here much while we're at sea 'cause you birdboys make all that noise. Your airplanes are looking pretty dirty and shoddy. You're not taking as good care as you used to."

Knowing that Mr. X had no sense of humor and was no stranger to ignorance of aviation matters, I skipped the opportunity for retort. He continued his monologue, changing the subject and announcing that he had received orders transferring him to another ship.

"I'll sure be glad to get away from this bird farm and back to the *real* Navy."

Again I held my tongue, knowing that our black-shoe friend was to be the target of aviator one-upmanship the following evening, after dinner in the wardroom.

In the presence of most of the ship's and air wing's officers, CDR Paul Engel, the air wing's operations officer, presided over a tongue-in-cheek ceremony recognizing the imminent departure of Mr. X. Paul presented him with a "bon voyage" gift—an aviator's leather flight jacket emblazoned with a personalized name tag, gold-embossed wings, and cloth insignia patches representing each squadron and detachment of the wing. Mr. X was at a loss for his usual caustic words about flyboys. He struggled to stay dry-eyed and was able to mutter only a soft, embarrassed "Thank you."

After that, the wardroom was partially converted to a stage for the debut of the musical group that Paul Merchant and I had formed. The ship's XO had "discovered" us, largely through our own self-promotion, and invited us to perform. We named ourselves "Four Wretched Amateurs and a Beginner" and put the finishing touches on a skimpy repertoire. Our "show" consisted of three numbers: "Ridin' down the Glide Slope" was a parody poking fun at the night carrier landings we made, to the tune of an old Roy Rogers cowboy ballad (see Appendix). "The Country's in the Very Best of Hands" was a commentary on ineptitude in Washington, D.C., borrowed from the musical *Li'l Abner*. And our finale was "The Biggest Parakeets in Town," a suggestive but nonexplicit poem borrowed from an early issue of *Playboy* magazine, set to a simple tune. The recital was well received by the wardroom audience, but we harbored no illusions. Our shipmates were starved for entertainment of any kind after an extended period at sea, and we appreciated performing for an audience that didn't shoot back.

While in Subic, the Saints enjoyed a wet but relaxing all-hands picnic, replete with beer and massive quantities of hamburgers, hot dogs, potato salad, and baked beans. Pilots told and retold "sea stories" of their recent flying experiences to the enlisted men, and there was the inevitable talk of home. Rain periodically interrupted a few innings of softball, a volleyball game, and some rounds of horseshoes, and a game of tackle football in the mud bore little resemblance to the civilized version played back home. On some fragile pretext the exuberant troops tossed Harry Jenkins and me into the bay. In the end, no one was hurt, no one got too drunk, and all enjoyed themselves as much as possible, insofar as there was a war going on and we were going back to it shortly.

After six days of R and R, we left the Philippines with a load of freshly scrubbed aircraft and returned to Dixie Station. There we were soon back into a routine of one hundred–sortie days.

The catapult flung me from *Oriskany*, and a few minutes later four of us were headed west over South Vietnam. Upon checking in with an Air Force control station, we were referred to a FAC, who would direct our mission. Flying from Dixie Station, we seldom had advance knowledge of our targets. Usually when we left the ship, we were equipped with only a set of geographic rendezvous coordinates and the FAC's call sign. Most of the lush, green South Vietnamese countryside appeared tranquil from our altitude. But the thick foliage that we saw from 20,000 feet was actually the top of a rain-forest jungle that concealed all sorts of activity.

I spotted the FAC as he skimmed the treetops thousands of feet below us in a vulnerable, low-powered, light aircraft and keyed my mike:

"Wagon Wheel, this is Old Salt Three Four Two. Four Alfa Fours, each with six 250s and 20 mike mike. I have you in sight."

"Roger, Old Salt, I have a Charlie storage area two clicks east of the junction of the two roads below me. Make runs west to east. Marking now." The FAC fired a smoke rocket to identify the target. "Charlie" was the unseen enemy, and a "click" was a kilometer. Not being metrically oriented, I never had a full appreciation of how much lineal territory was spanned by a click, especially from my lofty perch, so I waited for the next transmission.

"Storage area is about two hundred feet north of my smoke." Two hundred feet. That made more sense to me.

"Roger, Wagon Wheel. Salt One has smoke in sight. Ten seconds to roll in." The smoke was bright white against the deep green as it drifted upward, but the target itself was hidden by the dense trees. We took its existence on faith. I rolled into a 45-degree dive, and I checked the bombsight pipper. There was no wind drift. I gathered speed, glanced at the altimeter, and pickled a bomb.

Some referred to that type of in-country assault—attacking trees—as "making toothpicks." There was no ground fire to deter us, so we bombed and strafed in run after run from an overhead racetrack pattern. It was almost like our training flights back home. Occasionally, if we were deadeye accurate and clobbered the first target in a couple of bombing runs, the FAC would shift us to a second target. But that mattered little to us. One mass of trees and undergrowth looked pretty much like the next. Frequently, when we were through, another formation was standing by for the FAC's guidance, and we would depart with little knowledge of the effectiveness of our hits. Sometimes a FAC would be complimentary and give us a "score": "You clobbered a series of Vietcong bunkers" or "We really messed up a brown-rice storage area today." Less enlightening was the FAC who gave a numerically coded report. A cryptic "90 slash 60" meant that 90 percent of our bombs had dropped into the designated target area with a 60-percent coverage of that area.

For three days in June 1965 in-country missions were refreshingly different. We were called to support major U.S. ground activities near Dong Xoai (Dong Z-wah), fifty miles north of Saigon. For a change, we could see our targets and could discern clear-cut patterns of tank and troop movements on the ground. Gratuitous comments by the FACs spiced up the drama, and mindful of our "friendlies" on the ground, we dropped our bombs with maximum precision and accuracy. In that brief episode I had a feeling that, for once, I was actually contributing to the Allied effort in Vietnam.

But Dong Xoai was the exception. The rest of the time our in-country missions just produced toothpicks.

Some of our assigned targets were in the wide, wet delta of the Mekong River southwest of Saigon. They required 400–600-mile round-trips from Dixie Station. To accommodate the extra distance, we carried two 300-gallon external fuel tanks on each aircraft instead of the single centerline tank common on Yankee Station. And the ship's operating cycle between takeoffs and landings was extended to two hours. Still, the two-tank configuration meant a commensurate reduction in our bomb loads and available time over the target. Additionally, we frequently had to circumnavigate towering thunderstorms generated by the summer monsoon. That ate up fuel, leaving us with small reserves upon our return to *Oriskany.*

In contrast, we were occasionally assigned targets in the central highlands of South Vietnam, a relatively short distance from Dixie Station. There we would work with a FAC or a ground controller, drop our bombs, and have spare time on our hands before recovery. One time-consuming option was to volunteer as a "bogey" or adversary for the Crusader pilots assigned as CAP (combat air patrol). The southern location of Dixie Station made the probability of an actual enemy air attack on our carrier slim, and flying CAP was mostly boredom. We provided the fighter pilots with a chance to hone their air-to-air intercept skills against live targets. Flying as a bogey was not dramatically exciting, but I loved the brief dogfights with the Crusaders at the end of the intercepts. I never "won," but that was OK. Winning that sort of mission was a fighter pilot's business.

Once there was no bogey work to be had, so I led my division out over the South China Sea for some cloud hopping and formation acrobatics. Bob Hofford invented a time-consuming game—determining the maximum altitude that a Skyhawk configured with two 300-gallon fuel tanks and an empty, high-drag bomb rack could reach. I made it to 41,000 feet one day, but no Saint exceeded Bob's record of 42,000 feet.

Bob and I were involved in a "crunch" in mid-June. After trapping on *Oriskany*'s flight deck, I taxied forward under the arm-waving directions of the yellow shirts to a deck-edge parking space atop the starboard catapult. Bob landed after me and taxied clear of the landing area. My plane had just come to a stop when I felt a thump-bump that rocked the cockpit. I knew something, perhaps a ground-support vehicle, had collided with my plane. Glancing into the left rearview mirror, I was surprised to see Bob's Skyhawk tucked close against the left side of my plane, too close to qualify as normal parking distance. Bob's left wheel brake had failed as he was taxiing forward. His A-4 had rolled toward mine, presenting him with a dilemma. Bob could use his good right brake to avoid a collision, but that would swing his machine toward the edge of the flight deck and result in a sixty-foot plunge into the water. Wisely, he opted for the collision. A plane captain threw a chock under the wheel of the moving aircraft just as Bob's canopy bumped and slid beneath the left horizontal tail section of my Skyhawk.

The damage was relatively minor—a shattered canopy and a bent fueling probe on Hofford's plane (side number 340) and a dented, misaligned tail section on mine (number 341). Both Skyhawks were struck below to the hangar deck, where the maintenance crew replaced the tail section of 341 with that of 340. Instead of having two planes out of service, we were shy only one the next morning when a "new" aircraft appeared on the flight schedule: number 340 1/2.

As our warm-up assignment at Dixie Station wound down, I knew we would soon miss the relatively safe missions that we were flying there. Intelligence reports from Yankee Station reflected a growing AAA threat. In addition, Russian-built MiG-17 fighters had recently made their debut in the northern skies, shooting down two Air Force F-105s and a Navy F-4 Phantom.

Rolling Thunder and Steel Tiger, operations aimed at interdicting North Vietnam's supply lines and troop movements into South Vietnam, were in full swing. Two vulnerable mountain passes—choke points between Laos and the southern panhandle of North Vietnam—were prime targets of this campaign.

The politics of Rolling Thunder and Steel Tiger were darkly amusing. The whole world knew about the Ho Chi Minh Trail and how it was being used. Nevertheless, convoluted rules of engagement restrained and frustrated us. The ROE precluded our dealing with the Ho Chi Minh Trail as a single tactical problem. Instead, Rolling Thunder operations, which were public knowledge, allowed direct flights between Yankee Station and North Vietnamese targets. Included were those portions of the Ho Chi Minh Trail on the North Vietnamese side of the border. On the other hand, Steel Tiger operations, instituted in early April against those portions of the trail in "neutral" Laos, were classified secret. They were considered so politically sensitive that their very existence was publicly denied. Tortured diplomatic logic saddled Steel Tiger missions with a complex system of prior approval. In some cases, advance authorization from the U.S. embassy in the Laotian capital of Vientiane was necessary.

An Air Force unit in South Vietnam coordinated Steel Tiger missions. American pilots could attack Laotian targets only if under the "control" of a Laotian FAC in the area. The Laotian air force had precious few pilots, and in my tactical radio conversations during Steel Tiger I noted that the "Laotian" FACs had decidedly American accents. The diplomatic charades extended to pretending that missions from Yankee Station really weren't going to Laos. The direct route from Yankee Station to the key choke-point targets on the Laotian portion of the Ho Chi Minh Trail was obvious—a 110–20 mile track that crossed the North Vietnamese panhandle, where we regularly flew armed recco missions. However, to reach targets on the Laotian side of the border, we were required to fly south from Yankee Station and proceed across South Vietnam, below the 17th-parallel "demilitarized" zone. A reciprocal track was prescribed for the return flight.

In the ready room the "Alice in Wonderland" aspect of Steel Tiger made us wonder who was being fooled. The circuitous route to the Laotian targets accomplished little more than adding 150–60 miles of travel to each mission. More important, it decreased our useful time over the target considerably.

Fortunately, the complex ROE for Steel Tiger were a minor irritation because those missions were infrequent compared with the number of sorties flown against North Vietnamese targets. But the operations that were part of Rolling Thunder provided their own frustrations because of the limitations on what targets we could hit. Air action against North Vietnamese targets of any significance was tightly controlled from Washington, D.C. They were listed in the "Alfa" section of a master target list drawn up by the Joint Chiefs of Staff (JCS), and missions against those targets became known as "Alfa strikes."

Each Alfa strike required specific approval from Washington. There was no question in my mind that the limitations and the cumbersome long-distance control served only to prolong the war. Our resulting irritation prompted CAG Stockdale to mutter to me after an early Alfa strike, "We fly through flak thick enough to walk on, directly past the world's largest hydroelectric power plant, to bomb some blankety-blank JCS-approved outhouse in the middle of a rice paddy." Alas, even Jim's cogent account was inaccurate. Along with the power plants, the rice paddies were also sacrosanct. We were not permitted to attack dikes or irrigation facilities because disrupting North Vietnam's agricultural production would apparently be an unfair blow. The North Vietnamese weren't as naive as the politicians in Washington, of course. It wasn't long before we began seeing enemy antiaircraft batteries atop the protected dikes.

An Alfa strike was a major undertaking. Each involved large numbers of aircraft that would penetrate deep into enemy territory to strike heavily defended targets. Any combat mission in the north carried personal risks, but each Alfa took on a life of its own. The mere intonation of the words "Alfa strike" sent shivers up my spine.

Our Alfa strike of 20 June was on the Moc Chau army barracks, sixty miles west of Hanoi. The control stick flopped back into my waiting hand as I was fired off *Oriskany*'s bow. I slapped the gear handle to retract, nursed the flaps up, and climbed to rendezvous altitude. CAG Stockdale was the leader of the twenty-six–plane strike group—twenty bomb-loaded Skyhawks, with six Crusaders for protection against

MiGs. Moc Chau was a "far piece" from Yankee Station, a round-trip of more than five hundred miles. We cruised at 26,000 feet, each of us with one eye on his fuel gauge. A limited number of up aircraft that day meant that tankers were available only for the most dire emergencies.

The sky was dramatically clear and deep blue, with fluffy white clouds scattered below us. We were wary of MiGs because they had been active recently. Three days earlier, in the Navy's first decisive air-to-air combat over North Vietnam, F-4 Phantoms from the carrier *Midway* had shot down two MiG-17s.

The trip to and from Moc Chau took us a scant fifty miles from Phuc Yen, North Vietnam's main fighter base near Hanoi. My head was on a swivel, scanning the skies to the northeast for signs of enemy aircraft. The view brought to mind a sortie in another war, on an equally clear but bitter cold day in December 1952. I saw my first MiG in the sky above Unggi, North Korea, while flying TarCAP (target combat air patrol, to protect a strike from enemy fighters) for an attack on a Yalu River bridge. Russian MiGs had scrambled from Vladivostok, northeast of our position. They circled menacingly a few miles away over Peter the Great Bay, daring us to cross into Soviet territory, but nothing came of it.

Black puffs of antiaircraft fire blossomed below and to our right as we approached Moc Chau. The flak was lighter than we had expected, but I still had MiGs on my mind. The escorting Crusaders were reassuring, but a MiG attack could throw a monkey wrench into even the best-planned attack, scattering the bombers and reducing our effectiveness. And we were vulnerable. The Skyhawk was neither designed nor properly equipped for air-to-air combat.

There were no MiGs. I temporarily shifted my concentration to the large cluster of buildings that comprised the military complex west of the town. CAG led the first eight Skyhawks into their dives, attacking from the east. Flak bursts continued as I led the remaining jets in an arcing turn north of the target, where we fanned out for our individual attacks. The fan would complicate the task of the enemy gunners.

I "kissed off" John Shore and rolled in. Roaring down toward the ground, I corrected for a slight west–east wind drift and pickled my bombs. Pulling off to the left on a southeasterly heading, I immediately reverted to my rubberneck mode so that I could watch for MiGs as my division reassembled and headed for home. The MiGs didn't come out.

On the following day we flew a second strike in the same area, against the Qui Hou ammunition-storage facility forty miles southwest of Hanoi. The target was even closer to the Phuc Yen MiG base, but again the enemy elected not to take the bait. The MiGs didn't come out to play, and the antiaircraft fire was surprisingly light. The mission was nearly a milk run. But instead of leaving me relieved, the unusual lack of opposition left me a bit spooked, wondering what the enemy was up to.

A few days later I led a sixteen-plane strike to cut the runway of the Vinh Airfield, well south of Hanoi. Intelligence photos showed that no enemy aircraft were based at Vinh, but the runway appeared intact, and the field was MiG-capable. Only ninety miles from Yankee Station, it posed a threat to our carriers.

Four Crusaders accompanied my strike group, but the MiG threat was minimal for the mission. The MiGs hadn't ventured out on the closer probes, so the enemy probably wouldn't risk sending fighters to protect an unused airfield 150 miles away. Antiaircraft fire would not be minimal, however, because Vinh was consistently a hot spot.

Inbound at 20,000 feet, we crossed the coast and descended to pass south of Vinh. We then made a sweeping U-turn to the right and spread out, peeling off for individual attack runs. The enemy knew we were coming, and the U-turn tactic didn't provide any surprise. It was designed to keep the strike group over land for the shortest possible time. If a pilot was hit, the west-to-east heading would minimize the time needed to make it to the sea.

Even before we had completed the sweeping turn toward the east, black flak bursts filled the sky. As I reached the roll-in point I saw below and ahead three separate flak sites winking muzzle flashes at me. But the strike was successful. We cut the Vinh runway in two places, making it at least temporarily unusable. More important, everyone made it safely back to *Oriskany*.

Harry Jenkins led a forth Alfa strike, attacking a POL-storage facility at Nam Dinh, forty miles southeast of Hanoi. Fierce antiaircraft fire opposed the group but no MiGs. Again all planes returned safely, but the results were discouraging. The target was only partially damaged, and that meant that somebody would be sent back there to try again. Then, after the four days of heightened excitement, the Alfa-strike assignments unaccountably dropped to zero, and we returned our attention to interdiction of the Ho Chi Minh Trail.

The pace was slower on Yankee Station than it was on Dixie Station. Pilots averaged one mission every other day, compared with two or three per day down south. In spite of the 14–16-hour working days on Dixie Station, morale there had been sky high. The opposite seemed true on Yankee Station, where the days were just as long but events seemed to unfold in slow motion. Up north, there was less good-natured repartee in the ready room—a recognition by our pilots that combat flying over North Vietnam was more hazardous to one's health. Tempers seemed shorter, and there was more griping about trivial things.

Occasionally, there was uplifting news. On 20 June, the day of the Alfa strike on Moc Chau, an Air Force pilot was shot down during an unrelated action and parachuted uninjured into the mountainous, sparsely-populated terrain west of Thanh Hoa. The Air Force mounted a SAR effort but, before sending a "Jolly Green" helicopter to pick up the downed pilot, called for support in suppressing ground fire. Flying an armed recco mission nearby, four A-1 Skyraiders from the carrier *Midway* responded. The Air Force's tactical coordinator made an error by not ensuring that fighter cover was available, however. Shortly after the Navy's A-1s arrived on the scene, they were pounced on by two North Vietnamese MiG-17 fighters. The appearance of MiGs at the scene of the SAR was unusual because they had not bothered the major strike groups sent to attack Moc Chau and Qui Hou. Perhaps someone in the command structure at Hanoi sensed an easy kill against the relatively slow, unprotected Skyraiders, which were not designed for air-to-air combat.

In any case, the two MiGs ventured seventy-five miles from their home base. LT Charlie Hartman and LT Clint Johnson lucked out that day when the apparently inexperienced MiG pilots displayed poor tactical savvy. They surrendered their speed and altitude advantages, electing to attack the Skyraiders at low altitude and slow speed, and under those conditions the A-1s had superior maneuverability. A brief melee followed, characterized by much "flailing around" and the expenditure of a lot of 20-mm ammunition. The Hartman-Johnson team shot down one of the MiG-17s. The second enemy pilot fled northward. The Air Force's pilot was rescued, and the success of the SAR reflected favorably on the Navy. *Oriskany's* Spad pilots were not involved in the incident, but they were ecstatic that the tired Skyraider they flew had achieved unexpected fame in the skies over North Vietnam.

Another incident in June 1965 that brought smiles was the U.S. Air Force's first B-52 "Arclight" bombing raid over South Vietnam. Staged from Okinawa some 1,900 miles away, the B-52 missions over South Vietnam had no connection with our operations. But even on Yankee Station we couldn't avoid the public-relations campaign that followed the first "carpet bombing" raid that spread bombs over hundreds of acres of real estate. The Pacific edition of the worldwide military newspaper *Stars and Stripes* gave the B-52s a glowing account. Reading the article left the impression that the Strategic Air Command had all but won the war and that I'd be wise to book passage on the first plane home.

We would have quickly forgotten the B-52 raid in spite of the embellishment of the *Stars and Stripes* article, but because the newspaper did not give the results of the raid, I browsed through the classified intelligence reports and discovered that the results were "inconclusive," yielding a post-strike "body count" of one dead Vietcong. Paul Merchant speculated that the B-52s' bombing had merely disinterred a body that had been buried previously. Much later in the war, the B-52 raids would contribute significantly to the continued destruction of North Vietnam's war-making capability and would hurry the eventual peace efforts, but we got a chuckle from the first one.

Infrequent humorous episodes aside, operations on Yankee Station were a twenty-four–hour grind, with carriers operating alternately on twelve-hour schedules. The goal was to keep around-the-clock aerial-interdiction pressure on North Vietnamese efforts to resupply the south. In late June *Oriskany* was assigned the midnight-to-noon flying schedule. Our working "day" began an hour before midnight with the spotting or positioning of aircraft for a midnight launch. While the pilots were awakened for late-evening breakfast and mission briefings, the deck crews loaded bombs and flares and readied the aircraft for the upcoming missions. The first catapult launch came at the stroke of midnight, beginning the day's hour-and-a-half launch–recovery pattern. The last plane trapped aboard shortly after noon. By 1400 the pilots were in bed for their "night's" sleep. On deck, unused ordnance was unloaded, aircraft were serviced and spotted for the next launch, and everything was readied to repeat the evolution when midnight rolled around again.

The war was still young in June 1965, and interservice politics often confused the routine on Yankee Station. Missions flown by the Air Force over both North and South Vietnam came under the overall direction of MACV. That headquarters in Saigon detailed the specifics of the missions in daily "frag" orders. Navy missions flown over South Vietnam and Laos were likewise subject to the Air Force's coordination. But the Navy wasn't willing to relinquish the operational control of its aircraft carriers to MACV.

Thus, while both services were engaged in Operation Rolling Thunder over North Vietnam, the Yankee Station commander who worked for the Commander-in-Chief, Pacific Fleet (CinCPacFlt) tactically directed the Navy's missions. We all were involved in the same war, however, and an interservice Rolling Thunder Coordination Committee (RTCC) was established. Coordination became the operative buzzword. Under the initial efforts of the RTCC in 1965, policies and procedures for assigning missions in North Vietnam were tested and refined almost daily. The coordination efforts added yet another level of frustration to the daily existence of the pilots in the cockpits. Unexpected, last-minute mission substitutions, modifications, and cancellations frequently beset *Oriskany*'s daily air plans during the month of June.

Sometimes the amendments were explained, but just as often their purpose was mysterious. More than once I spent the better part of two hours planning and briefing a mission, only to have it scrubbed without explanation and replaced by an entirely different mission. The cyclic nature of the carrier's launch schedule always made planning substitute missions a hurry-up affair that precipitated abbreviated preflight briefings and a rush to man the aircraft on the flight deck.

Several times I sat drenched with sweat in a hot cockpit while the scheduled launch was delayed for a half hour or more and finally canceled altogether. Then, it was back to the ready room to repeat the cycle. By the end of the working day my frustration factor was in a dead-heat tie with my physical exhaustion. When I did fly a mission,

SECOND LINE PERIOD **59**

enemy flak and all, it was almost a relief compared to the flak we were getting from our own people in the "coordination" war.

In one three-day period the Saints were treated to three bonus strike missions. The missions were tacked onto the regular schedule, at just about the time we otherwise would quit for the day. None of the bonus missions had any greater tactical significance than our other daily missions. And they were particularly discouraging because they didn't come out of any high-level coordination with the Air Force's operations. The bonuses were the product of an overly fertile mind on the Yankee Station commander's staff. I suspected that someone at that level, with nothing better to do and no great compassion for the working guys, conjured up the bonus missions to look good when his next fitness report was due. In each of the three instances our pilots planned and briefed their bonus missions, and planes and ordnance were readied and loaded. But the missions were scrubbed before they were launched. Instead of normal 14–16-hour working days, our "bonus" was a trio of exhausting 18–20-hour days.

Truck hunting was a principal thrust of our daytime armed recco missions during Rolling Thunder. We were failing to produce the expected results, however. Intelligence reports indicated that our inter-diction efforts were not significantly decreasing North Vietnam's resupply of its Army units and of the Vietcong in South Vietnam. In fact, the opposite had occurred. Supplies were being moved at night, and the apparent lack of success of our daytime efforts gave added importance to the nighttime armed recco missions. Those missions in the A-4 Skyhawk were primitive and experimental. Time and tense time again I was launched into the black for one of those missions, musing that neither my Skyhawk's weapons systems nor its navigation equipment was suited to the task.

Nighttime target-hunting and attack techniques in the A-4 in 1965 were identical to those used in broad daylight, but without the benefit of daylight visibility. Success in a given night armed recco mission depended on a pilot's wits and eyeballs. Our A-4s were equipped with simple terrain-clearance radar systems designed for navigation while delivering nuclear weapons. But the radar was useless in filling our biggest need during nighttime missions over North Vietnam—detecting moving targets on the ground.

We were equipped with state-of-the-art MCBRs (multiple-carriage bomb racks) that significantly increased the Skyhawk's bomb load; but those racks had a cartridge-piston device designed to physically kick bombs away from the plane, so the MCBRs could not carry the thin-skinned Mk 24 parachute flares that we needed for nighttime target illumination. By sheer chance we had a fall-back option—the PMBRs (practice multiple-carriage bomb racks). Logically, because storage space on board ship was at a premium, most of the practice racks should have been left in dead storage at Lemoore. However, at the last minute before moving on board *Oriskany,* someone had decided to take the PMBRs with us. Older and simpler in design, they operated on a basic retracting-latch principal well suited for use with the fragile parachute-flare canisters.

Using PMBRs to carry flares was not officially sanctioned, but necessity overcame regulations. The squadron's ordnance technicians jury-rigged the PMBRs so that they could carry multiple flares on the A-4's outboard wing stations.

Our Skyhawks were equipped with semiautomatic computers for the "loft" delivery of nuclear weapons, but that bit of automation was useless for delivering conventional weapons. Day or night the pilot of a 1965 Skyhawk making an air-to-ground attack depended on an optical bombsight and his own mental computations of the best dive angle, the wind velocity, the target lead angle, and the weapons-release altitude. In the end, the bombing techniques I used in the Vietnam War differed little from those I had used twelve years earlier as a "fighter" pilot in the old F9F-2 Panther, dropping 250-pound bombs in Korea.

John Shore and I launched on a late-June nighttime armed recco mission. I climbed for the designated rendezvous area, and John joined me in a few minutes, using my exterior lights as a visual reference. I tuned my TACAN to the SAR ship's frequency and took up an intercept course toward the coast-in point.

The night was hazy, and we flew over a layer of broken clouds. Ahead, through the breaks in the clouds, I watched the enemy's unsophisticated but effective night-air-raid warning system go into action. The enemy listened and communicated. Alerted by the sound of our approach, he halted traffic and turned off lights, and his trucks became lost in the darkness.

I eased the throttle back, and we descended to the coast-in point. John flew close to me to keep me in sight while we were over water. Some wingmen preferred to have a single taillight illuminated on the leader's aircraft as a visual reference. But John and I had discussed the tactic and preferred to fly "dark," with all exterior lights off. Our theory was that the possibility of providing an illuminated target for an enemy gunner wasn't a fair exchange for what little flight intelligence the taillight would provide for the wingman.

"Red Crown, this is Old Salt Three Four Two. Feet dry with two at your three four five, fifteen miles."

The controller in the SAR ship acknowledged my transmission. The lights on the landscape below, seen earlier from a distance, had long since been extinguished. We crossed the coast, descending through 5,000 feet, and switched to our tactical radio frequency. Relying on the SAR ship's TACAN information, I headed into the assigned recco sector where, for safety reasons, John and I would be the only two aircraft operating for the next forty-five minutes.

"I've got 4,000 feet, John," I radioed.

"Rog, going five," John replied. For safety again, we flew at different altitudes, with John stepped a thousand feet above and about a half mile behind me. My recco altitude was a compromise: high enough to avoid running into mountains but low enough to see the features of the terrain and any clues of ground activity. As we proceeded inland the terrain became progressively higher. Periodically, I told John my altitude, and he adjusted accordingly.

Preplanned and lettered tick marks along the intended flight path dotted my kneeboard chart. While searching the ground, I frequently glanced at the elapsed-time clock in the dimly red-lit cockpit and cross-checked the time with the tick marks. I maintained a steady stream of radio chatter, keeping John informed of where I was and of my direction of movement, my altitude, and my intentions.

"At Alfa, coming right. Forty-five hundred."

"Rog."

John and I had an arrangement regarding radio contact. If we lost contact for sixty seconds or so, we would automatically abort the mission and return to the Gulf, flying to a prearranged rendezvous point and turning on our lights. If one of us didn't arrive at the rendezvous within fifteen minutes, the other pilot would return to the ship and file a missing report. Luckily, we never had to use the back-up system.

A white light blinked up ahead. A truck driver had taken a chance, or made a mistake. He had turned on his lights for a few seconds and thus became a target.

"Passing Delta. I've got a light on the ground about a mile ahead."

Twelve seconds later I was over the best-guess location of the truck.

"Pickling one flare. I'm at four grand. Left orbit."

"Rog."

I made a south–north run, dropping a flare at 3,500 feet and pulling into a left circular pattern at 4,000 feet of altitude. John positioned himself between 5,000 and 6,000 feet, as close as he could guesstimate to the opposite side of an imaginary circle that I would be flying around the target. Seconds later the flare sparked to life, and an area of countryside a mile in diameter was flooded with the eerie, silver-white glow of a one-million-candle-power flare. Luckily, I was right on. Two trucks were nestled under the trees at the side of a road.

"Rolling in hot, east to west."

Attacking under the light of a flare was an uncomfortable experience. The basic techniques were the same as those used in daylight, but the brilliance of the flare destroyed night vision and hampered depth perception. A different set of cockpit disciplines was required. The milky sphere of the flare's light and the stark shadows it cast on the ground below warped everything into two dimensions and made me nervous. To avoid vertigo and the possibility of a low pullout, I flew half visual and half on instruments and made shallower bombing runs than I would have used in daylight. Night recco missions never made me feel very tigerlike.

The descending flare burned for about ninety seconds, its circle of illumination shrinking steadily. We made two runs each, planting our bombs as close to the trucks as possible. A secondary fire flared up. A hit! But I couldn't tell what was burning. Gasoline perhaps.

The flare sputtered and went dark, returning me to the black void. The only remaining light was the orange flame of the burning truck. I afforded it no more than a quick glance and devoted my full attention to the flight instruments while my eyes slowly readapted to the darkness. I went back to the recco track diagrammed on my kneeboard chart. I marked the location of the truck and turned the plane north toward point Echo, the fifth tick mark. I saw the shadowy silhouette of a mountain and a momentary, dim, silver-gray reflection of starlight from a bend in a river. I drew a quick circle on the chart—the spot where I thought I was.

A single white tracer streaked off to my right. That woke up the butterflies in my stomach. I marked the antiaircraft-fire site on the chart with an "X."

"Alfa Alfa north of Echo," I radioed to John.

"Rog. Got it."

We followed the mission plan, reversing course at Point Foxtrot, retracing the route toward the Gulf. With no radar to assist us in discovering ground targets, night recco for the most part was an exercise in dead-reckoning navigation, visual clue hunting, and educated guesswork as to where trucks would most likely be hiding. From habit, I glanced periodically at the lazily swinging TACAN needle, but it provided little helpful information. TACAN was line-of-sight equipment, and numerous ridge lines lay between us and the SAR ship. Even a momentary lock on was only marginally helpful because the SAR ship was permitted to steam anywhere within a five-mile circle in the Gulf. Twice more we illuminated possible choke points, places where there might be ground activity, but there was none. I continued to check off the tick marks. There were no more ground clues, and after forty-five minutes over the beach our hunter-killer mission had amounted to a lot of hunting but precious little killing. Time was running out, so I illuminated a final choke point with my last flare, a small bridge across a river. We made two runs each, dropping the bridge into the water. Maybe that would slow them down a bit when they came to that spot on their supply route.

"Salt Four Two is steady on one two zero, climbing. Let's go home, John."

"Rog."

Again over the Gulf, I flipped the switch on the outboard side of the throttle, turning on my exterior lights as a visual reference. John slid into formation off my right wing a minute or so later, and we cruised on home.

"Red Crown, Old Salt Three Four Two is feet wet with two, switching to Childplay."

The results of our mission were insignificant. If nothing else, we were told, the nighttime interdiction campaign served as "tactical nuisance value," an expression that begged the question: "A nuisance to whom?"

Nighttime armed recco was sobering work. The regular radio chatter with John, with me doing most of the chattering, was helpful psychologically to both of us. But in the dark over hostile territory, in a single-pilot plane, each of us was constantly aware of one fact. If shot down or otherwise required to part company with the plane, we had only two hopes—that the other pilot had kept a reasonably accurate dead-reckoning track to pinpoint the location, and that the downed pilot would be able to avoid capture. Friendly rescue forces were a long way off, and any rescue attempt was at least as far away as the dawn's early light. The enemy was a lot nearer.

5 A Secret Airmen Share

 By July we were two months down and five to go. Early that month Harry Jenkins led a second Alfa strike against the POL-storage facility at Nam Dinh, forty miles southeast of Hanoi. The earlier effort there had produced ragged results, and Harry was determined to make the second attempt successful. I stayed behind. Except on rare occasions, Harry would not allow the two of us to be scheduled for the same strike mission. The odds were against it, but he refused to run the risk that we would both be shot down simultaneously, depriving the squadron of its top leadership.

Harry's thirty-plane group placed all of its bombs squarely in the target area and destroyed about half of the petroleum facility. There was heavy AAA, but all aircraft returned safely. LTJG Dick Pennington received the only significant damage. His Skyhawk took a hit from a flak burst that almost surgically removed the top six inches of the vertical tail fin. Morale was high in Ready Five when poststrike photos of Harry's mission confirmed the heavy damage. One photo showed a large and fiercely burning petroleum fire spewing a column of dense black smoke 20,000 feet into the air over Nam Dinh.

A short time later *Oriskany* went south for a few days of duty on Dixie Station. CAG Stockdale nominated Harry Jenkins for a Silver Star medal and sent him to Saigon for a press interview about the Nam Dinh mission. Harry's trip revealed some interservice "image" rivalry.

Air Force tactical bombers had struck Dien Bien Phu, 160 miles west of Hanoi, at the same time that *Oriskany*'s planes had attacked Nam Dinh. The English-language *Saigon Daily News* gave extensive front-page coverage to the Navy's strike, featuring Harry's interview and the photo of the towering smoke cloud. Later, many Stateside newspapers would also put the Nam Dinh strike and the dramatic photo on the front page. But the Pacific edition of *Stars and Stripes* gave three columns on the front page to the Dien Bien Phu strike, reporting the Navy's effort in a three-line "elsewhere in the war" vein on the back page.

The enemy gave the Nam Dinh strike much greater attention. In an English-language broadcast, Hanoi radio accused the "criminal, imperialist, war-mongering LBJ-lackey pilots" from *Oriskany* of killing and maiming countless women and children and of destroying Nam Dinh's hospitals, schools, and orphanages. We learned that two of our planes had been "shot down burning by the heroic People's Army of the Democratic Republic of North Vietnam," but there was nary a mention of what had caused all that black smoke.

The reaction to the Nam Dinh strike from some people on our own side was disappointing. After several weeks the paperwork nominating Harry Jenkins for a Silver Star finally worked its way through the red tape of the Navy's Pacific Fleet awards board and was returned to *Oriskany*. The proposed Silver Star award had been downgraded to an Air Medal, an outright insult to Harry and all the other pilots who daily risked their fannies flying missions over North Vietnam. CAG Jim Stockdale was furious.

Under the existing rules, an Air Medal was automatically awarded to a pilot or aircrewman for each ten combat missions flown, and most of us had already earned several of those awards. It appeared that some of our Navy brethren, safely ensconced in Hawaii, were pathetically unaware of, or at least insensitive to, what was happening in the combat zone. To the credit of ADM Roy Johnson, the new commander of the Pacific Fleet, the anachronistic practices of the PacFleet awards board were corrected a short time later. But that initial reaction to the successful completion of a major strike mission made it clear that some folks on our side were still asleep to the fact that we were at war. The squadron's morale had been high immediately after the mission, but the awards board's rejection was as psychologically damaging as anything the North Vietnamese threw at us. At least we could dodge the enemy's flak.

We were also frustrated by an inconsistent high-level attitude about napalm, the gelatinous gasoline mixture that became a fire bomb. In 1965 napalm was just another tactical weapon. It had been used in World War II and the Korean War and had not yet been elevated to the status of a cause célèbre by indignant "burn baby" war protesters back home. Napalm was being used routinely in South Vietnam, but we were not allowed to use it against targets in North Vietnam. The rationale offered was that napalm required low-altitude delivery, placing the pilot and aircraft at too great a risk of being hit by antiaircraft or small-arms fire. That was partially true. But we also used "Snakeyes," bombs equipped with fins that popped open into four miniature barn doors upon release. The high drag of these fins rapidly retarded the bomb, dropping it almost vertically on the target. The retard feature permitted highly accurate low-level bomb delivery while providing sufficient time for the delivering plane to fly clear of the bomb's fragmentation pattern. Low-level Snakeye bombing was certainly no less dangerous than delivering napalm. The AAA and small arms couldn't discriminate between the two. But the authorities weren't concerned about the inconsistency.

Another bit of specious high-level reasoning that irritated combat pilots was an official admonishment from Mr. Robert Strange McNamara's Defense Department. In the summer of 1965 combat commands were directed to cease using the phrase "shot down" in reference to aircraft shot down in the northern war. Apparently, the phrase was too warlike for Washingtonian sensitivities. The acceptable Pentagonese, we were told, was "lost in combat."

The height of high-command unreality in the midst of war, however, came one day just before I launched on an Alfa strike. A priority official message from the Commander, Naval Air Force Pacific exhorted squadron commanding officers to redouble their efforts to meet their quotas for United Fund charity contributions.

An ominous signal came our way shortly before *Oriskany* left Yankee Station on 2 July. LT Hank McWhorter, a pilot in the air wing's photo-reconnaissance detachment, took some excellent pictures of several oblong crates stacked on the docks at the North Vietnamese port of Haiphong. The crates looked hauntingly familiar. I'd seen their duplicates in other intelligence photos while deployed on board *Enterprise* during the 1962 Cuban Missile crisis. The crates on the Haiphong dock contained SAMs—Soviet-built SA-2 "Guideline" surface-to-air missiles—and their associated equipment. High tech had joined the war in Southeast Asia.

Earlier, in April, intelligence sources had pinpointed activity in the Hanoi area that signaled the construction of probable SAM sites. However, the photos of Haiphong showed that actual weapons were being delivered. Seeing the photos frustrated me. The SAM crates on the docks were a clear invitation for a meaningful Alfa strike. But an inane U.S. government policy kept us away from that port city, protecting those docks. I wasn't so naive as to believe that an Alfa strike against Haiphong would stop the eventual use of SAMs against us. But the destruction of the enemy's largest and most important port facility certainly would have delivered a clear message to North Vietnam that we wouldn't passively accept the development.

With the arrival of SAMs came increased vulnerability. The Russian-built antiaircraft weapons had been around for several years. A SAM had shot down Gary Powers's U-2 reconnaissance plane over Russia in 1960, and the Cubans had the SAMs in their antiaircraft arsenal in 1962. Sophisticated electronic equipment existed to detect and warn a pilot of active SAM-controlling "Fan Song" radars. But in 1965 peacetime budget constraints had precluded our A-4s from being equipped with such countermeasures gear. Having SAMs in North Vietnam tilted the tactical odds in favor of the enemy.

Oriskany's arrival on Dixie Station, which pilots viewed as the beginning of a minivacation, brought a rude Fourth of July surprise to the Saints. The air-conditioning unit in Ready Five broke down and created a special kind of hell. A replacement part to repair the machine was neither in *Oriskany*'s supply bins nor available anywhere else in Southeast Asia. The temperature in the ready room soared from a cool 75° F to a sweltering 100 + ° F. A twenty-six-inch floor fan did little but turn the ready room into a miniature, overheated wind tunnel.

Discomfort was one thing. But the constant heat would physically debilitate the pilots and increase the possibility of accidents in the air and on deck. The replacement part to fix the air conditioner would not be available until our visit to Japan some three weeks hence. In the meantime, Harry and I kept a close eye on our pilots' performance.

From Dixie Station we again worked with FACs on a daily basis. LCDR Bill Smith came up with an idea: invite some FACs to visit *Oriskany* for a few days to see our side of in-country missions. Within days of the invitation six Air Force pilots came on board. They toured the ship from primary flight control to the engine rooms, sat in on mission briefings, and rode as "back seat" observers in A-3 Skywarriors. The exchange was a huge success.

When the FACs returned to South Vietnam, they reciprocated by inviting several of Air Wing 16's pilots ashore to see their operations. Spad driver Paul Merchant of VA-152 was among those who went to visit the Mekong delta southwest of Saigon. In Kien Phong province Paul flew a spotter mission in the back seat of a tiny L-19 and watched *Oriskany's* planes attack Vietcong targets. Paul and his FAC landed at the Cao Lahn airstrip after the mission, where they met a contingent of Army Rangers en route to conduct a body count in the area just bombed. The Rangers invited Paul and the FAC to join them, and they accepted, Paul later insisting that he didn't have enough sense to say no.

The Rangers provided their new recruits with .30-caliber carbines and gave them some unnerving instructions: "Don't get lost, and if you see anyone other than Rangers, shoot!" Then they traveled pell-mell by jeep to the target area. Temporarily abandoning the vehicles, the Rangers entered the jungle at dog-trot pace. Paul and his FAC companion soon wearied of the follow-the-leader game, falling twenty or so yards behind the Rangers. Well into the "boondocks" they entered a jungle clearing just as the Rangers disappeared into the greenery on the far side. Suddenly, a man popped up from an underground bunker in the middle of the clearing, facing in the direction of the Rangers. Confronting "a real enemy person" was something a pilot seldom experienced. Paul froze in his tracks for a moment that seemed to last forever. Then he followed instructions. He aimed his carbine at the bunker and fired a burst. The figure disappeared, and the Rangers came storming back into the clearing. They emptied a few clips of ammunition and lobbed hand grenades into the bunker.

The dead man, a North Vietnamese soldier, was the sole occupant of the bunker, and there was no clue as to why he had remained behind. The Rangers found a North Vietnamese battle flag, documents indicating that the site was a command post of the 502nd NVn Regiment, and a hand-carved wooden eagle. The eagle was a symbol of strength to the Vietnamese, a Ranger interpreter said, giving the carving to Paul as a souvenir.

After the jungle outing, Paul visited the headquarters of a district chief in a "safe" Vietnamese village. The chief, also the commander of the local militia, proudly showed Paul a strange but vaguely familiar object pickled in a bottle of murky fluid. A grisly but matter-of-fact explanation was offered. The chief said that his militiamen were given monetary rewards for killing Vietcong. Most of the men were illiterate and marginally trustworthy, so the chief had devised a scheme to confirm body counts, requiring a militiaman to cut off the left ear of a dead VC and deliver the trophy to headquarters in exchange for payment. However, the chief lamented, that method had proved unreliable. Militiamen sometimes cut off both ears and turned them in for double payment. Therefore, the chief had changed his method of proof, requiring his militiamen to go below the belt to cut off a unique part of the male anatomy. The bottle contained the first such claim presented for payment under the new system, the chief said proudly as he offered it to Paul as a souvenir. Paul declined as gracefully as possible, stating that the wooden eagle was more than enough trophy to take back to *Oriskany*. But he later admitted that he would have liked to have seen Doctor Dan's reaction to the chief's trophy.

The brisk pace of dawn-to-dusk operations on Dixie Station continued unabated in the first half of July. It looked as if we were on our way to another record month. On 10 July a "newboy" arrived on board to join the Saints. LTJG George Lundy was a quiet, innocent-looking young man in his mid-twenties, about five feet eight inches tall, tipping the scale at no more than 130 pounds. Lundy's slight build prompted LTJG Dave Small to remark, "Jeez, what a moose," and the timing of the comment was such that the nickname stuck. From his first day with the Saints, George Lundy was "Moose" to the other pilots.

Lundy's arrival presented a challenge. *Oriskany* was scheduled for a three-week absence from the war zone to visit Yokosuka (Yo-KOOS-ka), Japan, departing one week after the young pilot reported aboard. After the visit, we would go directly from Yokosuka to Yankee Station. If we didn't get Moose into the air promptly, he would be quite rusty, after eight weeks out of the cockpit, when he was plunged into combat. Russ Weidman, who was temporarily grounded because of eye problems, took Moose under his wing. For two days Russ pumped the newboy's head full of the rules of engagement and *Oriskany*'s operating procedures while the rest of us flew the in-country mission schedule. Moose was back in the air on the morning of his third day on board. He made several hook-up touch-and-go landings before his first trap (arrested landing) on *Oriskany* and that afternoon flew his first combat flight as my wingman. The next day Moose flew as Harry Jenkins's wingman. When Harry and I compared notes, we were pleased with Moose's performance. Our newboy was an excellent pilot who would be no cause for worry, even with our upcoming vacation from combat.

Lundy's piloting skills even brought a favorable comment from Captain Connolly. The ship's skipper made a call from the bridge to Ready Five on the squawk box after observing Moose's first few carrier landings: "Lundy's landings are better than those of either Jenkins or Foster. Perhaps he hasn't been aboard long enough to pick up either of your bad habits."

Harry Jenkins landed aboard one day when *Oriskany*'s flight deck had a slight starboard list. It was an occasional condition resulting from a temporary imbalance in the loading of the ship's fuel tanks and in the location of aircraft on the flight and hangar decks. The list was irksome but not dangerous and required only a little extra attention to carrier-landing technique on the part of the pilots. Walking aft on the flight deck after landing, Jenkins glanced up at the bridge and saw Captain Connolly looking down at him. Harry held his arms out, spread-eagle fashion, and rocked to one side, indicating with body language his opinion that the deck could be a bit more level. When Harry reached the ready room, another squawk-box message arrived from the bridge: "To Commander Jenkins from the Captain. Remember our agreement: You fly the airplane, I drive the ship."

Late one afternoon I was leading a four-plane strike group home from the Mekong delta. The long day's sun was sinking toward the horizon behind me as we cruised eastbound at 25,000 feet. The TACAN gauge on the instrument panel indicated 105 miles from *Oriskany*, and I keyed the mike.

"Childplay approach, Old Salt Three Four Two is inbound with four at one hundred miles."

"Roger, Old Salt, your signal is Charlie on arrival."

That meant that we were the last jets airborne for the day and would be cleared to land immediately. On the heels of my call, I heard Eric Shade, my banjo-playing friend, report in with a flight of Spads at forty miles. The ship's response to Eric's report was out of the ordinary: "Old Salt and Ace, you're the last two flights airborne. Captain says last one home is a rotten egg."

A quick drinking-from-my-thumb signal to the other three pilots brought return hand signals indicating that we all had enough fuel to play a hare-versus-tortoise game. I eased the stick forward, lowering the nose, and let the airspeed pick up to 410 knots. Up ahead somewhere Eric was also accelerating his flight of A-1s, to a maximum airspeed about half ours. Sixteen minutes later I spotted Eric's Spads already in the landing pattern as my flight of jets raced toward the ship.

Anxious to show off, the pilots of my division had tucked into a tight "Blue Angel" formation. The standard airspeed for entry into the traffic pattern around the ship was 250 knots. If I slowed my flight in compliance with that edict, however, all of the Spads in Eric's flight would probably land aboard first. I maintained 360 knots as my flight whistled past the ship at 300 feet, and we broke into the downwind leg of the landing pattern. I brought the throttle to the idle stop and opened my speed brakes to slow down. Then I dropped the gear and waited until I passed abeam of the ship before easing the flaps down.

Three Spads had already landed when I closed upon the fourth, which was ahead of me on final approach. NATOPS rules gave jets landing priority because of our higher rate of fuel consumption, so the LSO (landing signal officer) gave a wave-off signal to the last Spad. All four Saints trapped on board before the solo Spad pilot lumbered around the pattern for a second landing try. Obviously, glorious victory was ours to claim. Eric Shade met me on the flight deck to argue a lot of nonsense about my cutting his boy out of the landing approach, and to suggest that the LSO (Bill Smith of the Saints) "naturally favored the jets." We parted after a brief discussion of landing-pattern ethics, still friends, but resolved to settle the important "rotten egg" matter over drinks at the officers club when we reached Japan.

Sunday, 18 July, our last operating day before *Oriskany*'s departure for Japan, began in eager anticipation. The aircraft of the first morning launch were turning up on the flight deck when I arrived in Ready

Five to brief a second mission with John Shore, Bob Hofford, and Duke Tyler. The first launch began with a familiar dull thump as a catapult sent a shudder through the ship. Then someone muttered, "Oh, Jesus," and I tensed involuntarily. Spinning around, I looked at the closed-circuit television monitor on the welded bracket above the duty officer's desk. Through the camera's eye I saw the last few seconds of a Skyhawk's settling toward the water from the bow, seeming to hang precariously a few feet above the sea before it disappeared in a mountainous geyser. Airman Jerry Worchal, the young enlisted man who manned the ready room's sound-powered-phone circuit during flight operations, spoke a number out loud: "Three-four-four." My eyes darted to the board at the front of the ready room where the flight schedule was posted. Next to the number 344 was the name Avore.

Our eager anticipation of the upcoming trip to Japan dissolved when that plane flew into the water about four hundred yards ahead of the ship, breaking up and sinking immediately. LT Malcolm A. "Art" Avore, one of the sharpest aviators I'd ever known, was killed instantly. Nothing was recovered to help establish the cause of Art's accident, and as is the case with many such incidents at sea, we were left to rely on visual and written records, eyewitness testimony, and speculation. Personnel on the flight deck said that it sounded as if Art's plane had momentarily lost engine power during the catapult shot. Harry Jenkins and I reviewed the plane's maintenance records but found no prior malfunctions to suggest a possible cause for the accident. We watched the TV tape of the launch over and over, searching for clues.

The catapult officer reported that the cat shot had been normal in all respects, and the videotape showed that Art had held the proper flight attitude right up to impact, wings level, with no unusual movements of the flight-control surfaces and no erratic motions on the part of the aircraft. It appeared that Art was in control, flying his plane right to the end. The ejection seat didn't fire, indicating that Art may not have considered himself in extremis. He was a cool, competent pilot not given to panic under stress. Perhaps he had experienced an unexplained, momentary loss of engine power and, having regained it, was trying to fly out of his predicament. We could only guess.

In a carrier squadron, particularly one in combat, the lives of the pilots are closely entwined on a daily, hourly basis. A fellow pilot is a brother in a family bonded by shared yet highly personal experiences, by camaraderie, and by challenges, successes, disappointments, beauty, hazards—by the magic of being part of a highly specialized team in a risky, demanding business. The loss of a squadron pilot is a crushing blow. The grief is cutting but not maudlin, and seldom does it live beyond the next mission. To continue successfully in his chosen calling, a tailhook aviator cannot long allow himself to wallow in pity or dwell on thoughts of death. When death takes a fellow aviator, those remaining erect invisible shields against the harsh realities of the chosen profession. The shields shut out the pain and permit only fond recollections to filter through.

In the 1950s a professor at the University of Kansas lost a son who was a naval aviator in an aircraft accident. Recording his thoughts in an attempt to find meaning and comfort in his loss, Professor F. C. Bates wrote:

> There is a secret airmen share. Men who have experienced the quiet communion with God in the vast reaches of the night sky can never die. Death is but one more solo, beyond which an air-man can shed the chains of wings and fuel, and dwell free in that cathedral he has learned to love, forever and in peace.

Art Avore was dead, and in July 1965 in Ready Room Five aboard USS *Oriskany*, the Saints of VA-163 shared that secret.

Yokosuka had changed little in the twelve years since I had first visited that Japanese coastal city during the Korean War. Inflation had driven up the price of a martini at the officers' club from fifteen to twenty-five cents, and in the dining room chateaubriand was a staggering $2.15, up from its former buck and a quarter. Traffic signals had been installed at the street intersection outside the main gate of the naval station. That innovation significantly reduced the hazards presented to pedestrians by the steady stream of Japanese taxicabs, each driven by a surviving Kamikaze pilot.

Close by the naval station gate was Thieves Row, a succession of bars and retail stalls. The streets had been paved since my last visit, and covers had been placed over the "binjo" ditches. Strolling in Thieves Row was less hazardous than before, but the prevailing aroma confirmed that the gutter method of sewage disposal was unchanged.

There were more bars than I remembered, and the advertising, intended to lure sailors inside, had improved in both imagination and color. Large, gaudy signs proclaimed:

BLACK ROSE, a grand Cabaret. Look at our record, years of outstanding service be entertained by our fine characters taste. a vote for BLACK ROSE is a vote for honest pleasure always entertaining. fifty beautiful sexy girls are always waiting for you. Floor show every hour no cover charge.

Shangri- La Bar.
Ugly broads. Lousy service.
Take a look.

Heaven and Hell Bar. U.S. hero of Com 7th Fleet So sorry to have troubled you at Vietnam. Please stay at loveliness of an earthly paradise as long as you like this evening. We give service for you in anything what ever you please. All sexy girls skin show every hour.

Dear sirs: It's enchanting! Clean, Grand, and full of beauties. Try it with a coal draft beer.

My favorite was:

BRASSRAIL. This is a good bar but—not a great bar. Be feel like home with SHITKICKING MUSIC.

Jimmy Lee, an enterprising Japanese tailor of wide reputation among WestPac (Western Pacific) sailors, had been an important attraction to Yokosuka's visitors since shortly after World War II. At any given moment in modern history, so it seemed, Jimmy the Tailor was responsible for outfitting at least half of the U.S. Seventh Fleet in tailor-made civvies. Jimmy's store backed up to the fence of the Navy's property two blocks from the main gate and sported a discrete advertising message on its back wall, visible to all who trod the streets of the naval station. During the Korean War the message was simple: "James S. Lee, Tailor". But times had changed. Jimmy's sartorial success had spawned a me-too competitor, "James Lee, Tailor," who had opportunistically set up shop immediately outside the main gate. Meeting the competition head-on in 1965, Jimmy had enlarged and reworded the sign on the back of his building. Below the freshly repainted identification "James S. Lee, Tailor" were added some pragmatic words: "This is the *real* James S. Lee, Tailor, not the one outside the main gate!"

An impromptu getaway trip with Paul Merchant and Dan Lestage was relaxing. We braved the Japanese rail system, pointy-talking our way from Yokosuka to Kamakura to Odawara by regular trains, and switchbacking our way up the mountain into Hakone National Park via a two-car "Toonerville Trolley." Near the park, dramatically secluded on the side of a mountain, was the delightful village of Miyanoshita (ME-ya-no-SHE-tah) and the elegant Fuji Hotel. It was a visit to Miyanoshita and the hotel that fired a love affair with Japan when I was a young pilot during the Korean War. In 1953 the Fuji Hotel was a military R and R facility operated by the U.S. Army, but it had since reverted to civilian control. It's specialty in 1965 was catering to well-to-do, upperclass Japanese.

We had not booked rooms in advance, so when we arrived unexpectedly at the hotel's registration desk, we were coolly received by a clerk formally attired in a cutaway. He apparently spoke little English. I mustered my maximum reserve of diplomacy and, in English, apologized for our thoughtlessness. I was uncertain if the clerk understood me as I told him of my earlier love affair with the hotel and surrounding village when I was a young naval officer. Explaining that my friends also were naval officers who would be visitors in his beautiful country for only a few days, I expressed my hope that they, too, might enjoy the pleasure of staying at the famous Fuji Hotel.

The clerk listened politely, but stiffly and without expression. Then he excused himself and stepped to the far end of the polished-wood reception counter. After a minute or so of subdued conversation with another formally attired gentleman, the clerk returned, bowed slightly and graciously, and announced in perfect English: "Yes, we can accommodate you, sir."

Paul, Dan, and I ate a leisurely lunch at the grill, then wandered about the hotel's carefully sculptured gardens. After our walk we bathed in the hotel's "Dream Pool," an elegant version of that wonderful Japanese creation, the "hotsi" bath. Drinks at the bar and afternoon naps rounded out a delightful day. I dozed off, totally relaxed, listening to the birds outside my window as they intoned a half-strident, half-melodious "gaw-reep, gaw-reep." The sound of a brook gurgling over the rocks beneath my window accompanied the birds. But the most enjoyable part was the knowledge that there was no salt water nor a gray-painted bulkhead as far as the eye could see.

The visit to Yokosuka didn't lack for party invitations. Harry Jenkins and I attended two soirees as guests of the squadron's enlisted personnel. An evening with John Shore's plane captains, the modern day squires who served the pilot-knights and cared for our Skyhawks, was an eye-opener. A $300 slush fund that they had saved since leaving Pearl Harbor paid for a gala evening, with food, drinks, a band, girls, dancing, and a floor show.

The food and drinks were plentiful, the music loud, and the dancing—the twist, the frug, the swim, and other popular moves—frantic. No one became obnoxiously drunk, nothing of consequence was broken, there were no fights, and everyone had a good time. The floor show consisted of "sexy dancing girls," a so-so male singer, and a Japanese band that played American hillbilly music. I was amused because the plane captains, whose average age was twenty, clapped, hooted, and hollered louder and more appreciatively for the hillbilly band than for the "sexy" dancers.

The visit to Japan introduced me to the mysteries of the fast but bewildering Japanese train system and involved more than one traumatic experience with Japanese taxis. On our last night in port several Saints pilots dined at an *ichi ban* (number one) restaurant and were entertained by a geisha. Our main sinful involvement with the geisha was a coaster-tapping, Japanese version of American "chug-a-lug," which did little more than get us all tipsy. At the tag end of our party, two pilots from our sister squadron, the Ghostriders of VA-164, joined us with their wives, who were visiting from the States. The wives instigated the visit, I suspected, to discover what debauchery occurred in the presence of a geisha. I also suspected that they were a bit disappointed at finding us engaged in an innocent game of manual coordination. Our visitors joined the game, and the wives turned out to be the least coordinated, consuming a considerable amount of warm sake.

On 5 August, with a pleasant period of R and R behind us, *Oriskany* slipped slowly from beneath the monstrous overhead crane at Yokosuka's Piedmont Pier, cleared the breakwater into Tokyo Bay, and headed back toward the war. The weather was clear and crisp with a fresh breeze, but the sea was rough as we headed south from Japan, plowing through the outskirts of Typhoon Jean. *Oriskany*'s deck heaved, sending shudders through the ship, slopping coffee out of cups, and causing cancellation of a bilateral war-game exercise with the Japanese Maritime Self-Defense Force.

Forty-eight hours later we were near Taiwan in a calm sea with only a gentle swell. I launched for a mission that was part of a second bilateral exercise, with the Nationalist Chinese defense forces providing opposition. Instead of climbing to a higher rendezvous altitude, I stayed at 500 feet, flying a sweeping arc around the carrier until John Shore joined me. We headed south, hugging the deck to stay below the "enemy's" radar coverage. Legally flathatting, we zipped along at 340 knots, 100 feet above the wave tops. Fun, but not relaxing. A second of inattention or misjudgment at that altitude spelled doom. At our speed, an impact with the sea would be no different from hitting a concrete wall.

We flew a 170-mile dogleg track, south then west, to a landfall at the southern end of Taiwan. Thirty minutes after leaving the ship, I saw through the windscreen the rugged southern tip of the island as it took shape on the horizon, right where it was supposed to be. Pleased with my dead-reckoning skills, I turned north and paralleled the eastern coast of the island.

It was my first view of Taiwan. From my 100-foot vantage, the island's range of "broken glass" mountains loomed dramatically above us, rising and falling in steep cliffs from 13,000 feet to a narrow coastal strip. Occasionally, a village or a small cluster of houses flashed past my wing tip, and I spotted railroad tracks snaking along the coast. But except for the here-and-there signs of civilization, southeastern Taiwan appeared remote and inaccessible. I made a mental note not to bail out over that part of the world.

Two-thirds of the way up the island, I spotted the town of Hualien. Easing back on the stick, I popped up and altered my heading to the northwest, climbing to clear the spine of the mountains. Minutes later we made a successful surprise "attack" on our target, the capital city of Taipei. Then we headed for home, our part in the exercise over. Neither of us had seen hide nor hair of the Nationalist Chinese air force.

Oriskany bypassed a Dixie Station warm-up and went directly to Yankee Station, an apparent indication that those in command felt that we had attained big-boy status. It was 10 August. We not only returned directly to combat flying, but even after almost a month's absence, we were scheduled to fly Alfa strikes on our first two days on the line. As Harry Jenkins, Jim Stockdale, and I planned the strikes, a potent new element—SAMs—strongly influencing our thinking. The crates spotted earlier on the docks at Haiphong and the construction of suspected SAM sites announced by intelligence reports had meshed into operational reality. Fan Song radars that guided the SAMs had been detected in the field in late July. On the day *Oriskany* put into Yokosuka an Air Force F-4 Phantom flying northwest of Hanoi had been shot down. It was the first SAM victim of the Vietnam War.

Our Skyhawks' inability to deal with the Fan Song radar made our mission planning a sobering experience. We were totally dependent for airborne early warning and electronic support on the capabilities and limitations of the air wing's "Willie Fudds" (E-1B "Tracker" aircraft), of the Marine Corps's EF-10B "Willie Whale" jammers flying from Da Nang, South Vietnam, and of the Navy's EC-121s staged out of Cubi Point. The support they provided was helpful but still gave only general threat warnings. The A-4 pilot's principal butt-saving insurance, when *he* was the target of a specific SAM, consisted of his own eyeballs and tactical maneuvering abilities.

The first two Alfa strikes were against a military barracks–ammunition storage complex at Son La, 110 miles west of Hanoi and 40 miles farther from Yankee Station than the Moc Chau strike that we had flown in June. Some weeks later North Vietnam would be carved into geographical route packages with specific areas of responsibility divided between the Air Force and the Navy. Most of the North Vietnamese terrain west and northwest of Hanoi would become Air Force territory, while the Navy had predominant control in the areas east and south of the capital city. When we returned to the line in August 1965, however, vested rights to the enemy's geography had not been positively established at the working level. The Son La mission was a long haul—a 600 + -mile round-trip from Yankee Station—and required flying at a high altitude to consume less fuel.

Harry Jenkins led the strike scheduled for 10 August, and I was assigned the next day's effort. My plan for the twenty-six-plane mission took us west from Yankee Station over northern Laos (diplomacy be damned) to approach Son La from the south. I knew that enemy radars would easily track us at altitude. The dogleg route would keep us about one hundred miles from the MiG base at Phuc Yen. Also, the route avoided known SAM sites. I was nervous about the mission because a follow-on attack against any target, particularly a distant one with limited approaches, allowed for little surprise. We'd be at high risk from a ready-and-waiting enemy, and our necessary high-altitude flight profile would make us nearly ideal targets for both SAMs and MiGs.

A confident intelligence officer assured us that no SAM units were known to be operating outside the Hanoi area. I didn't carry the intelligence officer's confidence with me into the cockpit. When we approached the target on schedule, I kept my eyes moving, scanning the skies and ground.

We throttled back and descended into the Son La area, where, to our pleasant surprise, antiaircraft fire was minimal. We were in and out in short order, getting good hits with our bombs. But our pleasure with the successful strike gave way to concern on the return trip. The assurances of the intelligence officer were small comfort as we flew southwest of Vinh at 25,000 feet on our return leg.

I glanced down, and my heart leapt to my throat. Something ignited fiercely on the ground, and the billowing cloud of pale yellow and white smoke was the unmistakable characteristic of a SAM booster.

"This is Salt Lead," I transmitted. "Missile away, ten o'clock down! Spread out and prepare for individual evasion."

The latter remark was unnecessary. Upon hearing the word "missile," each pilot instinctively began thinking of evasive tactics. The group was in an awkward position. At 25,000 feet we were precisely the sort of target for which the Soviet SA-2 missile was designed. I waited tensely for the missile's lift-off. Once we saw that, the formation would become twenty-six planes scattering all over the place.

But luck was with us. The expected "telephone pole" did not emerge from the billowing smoke. The SAM had apparently malfunctioned and was burning on its launch pad.

We were still tense during the mission debrief. We came close to having been numbered among the Navy's first SAM losses. CAG Stockdale had flown a Saints Skyhawk as an ordinary wingman for the Son La strike. He had seen the SAM misfire and agreed with my recommendation: no more long-range, high-altitude missions over North Vietnam.

The reality of the SAM threat was underscored that night. A few hours after my mission had landed, a Skyhawk flying from USS *Midway* was shot down during an armed recco mission. The pilot was flying sixty miles south of Hanoi, not far from the route we had taken to come home from Son La. LTJG Donald H. Brown, Jr., of VA-23 was KIA (killed in action), the Navy's first loss to a SAM.

Our response to the introduction of the SAM in the war was a matter of mental conditioning, convincing ourselves that the situation wasn't hopeless. We knew the missile's capabilities, limitations, and operating characteristics. But no one had firsthand experience with the Soviet-built weapon. The SAM booster unit, the smoke we had seen on the ground near Vinh, was an excellent visual clue. It burned for about five seconds as it lifted the missile itself into the air. After the booster burned out, the SAM was more difficult to see. However, it was sluggish in responding to the commands of the guiding Fan Song radar during the first few seconds of acceleration. Since our Skyhawks were not equipped with electronic countermeasures or missile-decoy gear, our SAM defenses depended on the pilot's alertness and the aircraft's maneuverability. Also, at low altitude, we could use terrain masking as an additional defense against the Fan Song.

SAM hunt-and-destroy missions, code-named Iron Hand, began on 13 August, the day after the loss of the *Midway's* plane. Because of the operating characteristics of the SAM and its Fan Song radar, it was decreed that the best defense was to fly low, beneath the SAM's envelope. Prophetically, 13 August fell on a Friday. The SAM hunters came up empty that day, but the Navy lost four low-flying aircraft to conventional antiaircraft fire. One of the losses particularly saddened me because it was CDR Harry Thomas, a long-time friend from flight-training days who was serving as skipper of VA-53 on board USS *Coral Sea*.

The fly-low order didn't hold up for long. From the cockpit we quickly recognized that such a tactic, ostensibly protecting us from SAMs, merely placed us at increased risk from conventional antiaircraft and small-arms fire. The Skyhawk's operating altitude was changed to a minimum of 3,000–4,000 feet above the ground, where visibility was better and the pilot could take advantage of the aircraft's excellent maneuverability against the initially slow-moving SAM. We couldn't shrug away the SAM threat, but we learned not to trade exposure to one antiaircraft hazard for another.

After the back-to-back strikes at Son La, Air Wing 16 was assigned only three other major strikes in the next two weeks. We were unsuccessful in trying to destroy the Ham Rong railroad-highway bridge across the Song Ma River. Commonly called the Thanh Hoa bridge because of its proximity to that town, the target was destined to take on increased, almost mystical significance. The other two strikes focused on the demilitarized area between North and South Vietnam and were relatively easy and only lightly opposed.

Iron Hand missions became a regular part of our daily flying, but the main focus continued to be truck-hunting armed recco missions. In practice there was little difference between the recco and the Iron Hand missions; but for reasons obscure to those doing the flying, Iron Hands were restricted to the area south of the twentieth parallel. And they all came up empty. If the North Vietnamese had deployed SAMs south of the Thanh Hoa, they kept them well hidden and were careful not to fire them when we were around.

6 Hornet's Nest

 Air-intelligence photos taken in late August revealed a SAM site under construction near the North Vietnamese MiG base at Kep, thirty miles northeast of Hanoi. The construction, per se, was nothing new, but for unclear reasons that particular site was branded as a priority target. A three-wave strike was laid on for 23 August.

A partial bombing pause, ordered by the president, heightened our pre-mission tension. The pause had been in effect for two weeks, and the Kep mission would be our first venture north of the twentieth parallel in that time. A lengthy absence from any area of North Vietnam always increased our concern for what changes the enemy might have made in its antiaircraft defenses in the meantime, and where. Additionally, Kep was virgin territory and our closest approach yet to North Vietnam's capital city, where the majority of the enemy's antiaircraft defenses were concentrated.

The mission was characterized as "an exploratory strike," a confusing euphemism. Essentially, that meant that we were cleared for deep penetration into the North Vietnamese heartland for a look-see, with limited license to attack whatever we found that most closely resembled a SAM site under construction. My guess was that someone up the line, concerned that the newly inaugurated SAM-hunting Iron Hand program had so far been unproductive, was getting desperate for positive results. Intelligence material for the Kep target was minimal. It consisted of two oblique-angle aerial photos of earth-moving equipment and nonspecific construction activity atop one of dozens of hillocks in the surrounding countryside.

To avoid flying directly through the known heavy AAA concentrations in the Haiphong-Hanoi heartland, and to take advantage of what little surprise we might muster, we selected a dogleg route to and from the target. North from Yankee Station our track would take us to a coast-in point northeast of Haiphong. From there, we'd fly northwest at low level, using the mountains to mask us from radar, and attack the target from the northeast. However, the available aerial-navigation charts covering the overland portion of that route were based on French survey data of 1950. The blank portions of terrain along the intended flight path, labeled "uncharted," were not exactly reassuring.

Three strike groups were scheduled to hit the Kep target, each composed of eight A-4 Skyhawks with maximum loads of 500-pound bombs. Four Crusaders would accompany each group as protection against MiGs. Aerial tankers would be available, E-1B Trackers would provide electronic intelligence and countermeasures support, and a photo Crusader would snapshot the results. Harry Jenkins was tasked with leading the first wave, with CDR Jack Shaw, the skipper of VA-164, spearheading the second, hot on Harry's heels. I had the third wave.

During mission planning Harry, Jack, CAG Stockdale, and I discussed at length the rather massive effort—twenty-four Skyhawks carrying thirty-six tons of bombs—that was being mounted against a target for which there was so little meaningful intelligence. We agreed that my third wave would be held in reserve, to be launched only if either of the first two groups found something significant to attack in the target area.

I'd been sitting in the hot cockpit with the canopy open, strapped in and fidgeting for thirty minutes, when the air boss ordered, "Standby to start engines." The ship was steaming downwind, and precious little air was stirring across the flight deck. The sun was bright and hot, the humidity high. Sweat trickled down inside my flight suit. Starting the engine meant that I could close the canopy and find relief in the cockpit's air-conditioning.

For the umpteenth time I reviewed the photos of the target. Our impending launch meant that Harry or Jack had found something near Kep for us to hit, something that warranted a follow-on strike. I put on my helmet as the starter units around the deck whined to life. When it was my turn, the plane captain gave the turn-up signal. Power from the starting unit spun the engine compressor. I moved the throttle outboard to click the solenoid switch and fire the igniters. A hollow "whump" announced the completion of the ignition sequence, and the low-pitched moan of the turbine grew into a high, steady shriek.

I put on my oxygen mask to keep from inhaling the acrid jet exhaust that swirled around the deck. People in colored shirts scurried beneath my cockpit, completing the post-start chores before disappearing. Soon the noisy deck became a ballet of pantomime motion as aircraft moved toward the catapults under the arm-waving commands of the yellow shirts.

I taxied to the starboard catapult and was quickly tensioned between the shuttle and the holdback rig. A red-shirted ordnanceman emerged from beneath my Skyhawk and held up two handfuls of red streamers, indicating that he had removed the bomb's safety pins. With the plane at full throttle, 100-percent power, I scanned the instruments, then saluted the catapult officer. The catapult fired, and I was airborne under the clear, blue sky.

Twelve aircraft joined me at the rendezvous circle—seven other bomb-loaded Skyhawks, then the four Crusader escorts with 20-mm cannons and air-to-air missiles, and, finally, Hank McWhorter, the "photo beanie" in his unarmed, camera-equipped Crusader. Hank's mission was to capture photographic evidence of whatever mayhem we, and the two flights before us, rained on the "suspected SAM site."

I headed for the coast-in point 180 miles to the north and switched to the strike group's tactical frequency. Twice I called Harry Jenkins. No answer. His group had apparently switched to the approach frequency in preparation for landing. But Jack Shaw responded to my second call.

"We hit what I *think* was the target," Jack said, adding, "It's confusing real estate up there." His comments were not helpful, but his report of very light flak took an edge off the tension I felt.

The coast-in point was a small bay north of Hon Gay, twenty miles east of Haiphong. As the alluvial delta surrounding the Haiphong roadstead came into view at my ten-o'clock position, I cross-checked with the navigation chart clipped to my kneeboard. We were about forty miles from coast-in. Unconsciously, I tugged against the shoulder straps of my seat harness to ensure that they were locked, then I keyed my mike.

"Salt Lead, 80 percent." I eased back on the throttle and began a descent. From habit, I nodded my head backward against the headrest, the visual signal for power reduction. But the group was spread out in combat-cruise formation, and only John Shore was flying close enough to see the signal. A few minutes later we were twenty miles south of Hon Gay, eight Skyhawks spread out in a loose formation, cruising along at 340 knots a few feet above the wave tops. A glance in the mirror confirmed that the five Crusaders were behind us, a few feet higher. Flying close to the surface at high speed was thrilling, but the excitement was secondary to its purpose of keeping us below the enemy's radar horizon for as long as possible.

Da Cat Ba Island slipped by on the left, then we whisked over a profusion of jagged limestone formations that jutted from the placid water like shards of broken glass. On the chart the rocks had a colorful French name—"Archipel Des Fat Tsi Long." We had long since Americanized the name to "Fatso Rocks."

Here and there between the rocks were innocent-looking sampans, probably just poor fisherman, but I wouldn't have been surprised to learn that amidst that apparent innocence someone was radioing a report of our passage. We knifed over a narrow inlet a half-mile west of Hon Gay, and I noted that the port facility was empty. Thirty seconds later we roared across a triangular bay and over the mainland, a hundred feet off the ground. I reported, "Feet dry" to Red Crown behind us in the Gulf and eased the stick to the left, turning the strike group to a northwest heading.

Without signaling, I nudged the throttle forward to achieve the prebriefed airspeed of 360 knots. There was nothing magic about the number except that it is six miles per minute, a mile every ten seconds, an easy rule of thumb for dead-reckoning navigation. We skimmed the tops of rugged mountains and sped over the thinly populated countryside northeast of Haiphong. To our left was a 3,000-foot ridge line shielding us from the Red River delta and the enemy radars. To our right, northeast, were more mountains and the Chinese border.

Our 100-foot altitude behind the ridge line protected us from probing enemy radars, but I knew we weren't fooling anyone. The Soviet "trawler" that shadowed the carriers on Yankee Station was loaded with electronic equipment and had probably already informed Hanoi that we were coming. Besides, the enemy couldn't be sleeping too soundly after a twenty-four-plane "reveille," courtesy of the Harry Jenkins and Jack Shaw groups. The earlier strikes had probably also given the enemy a good clue as to our objective.

The visibility was excellent under the clear sky, and navigation was a cinch as we raced along the terrain contours, across the tops of the mountains and down through the pastoral valleys of farmland. The people below may have been farmers who for years had tended their rice paddies, but they were also the enemy. I felt no real compassion for them. The roar of jets engines for a third time in the last forty-five minutes had assuredly sent them scurrying for cover. Briefly, I thought of what they might do if I fell into their hands. I was one who regularly rained bombs on their homeland, and to them I was the devil incarnate. Surely they would think nothing of beating me to a pulp or killing me.

Beyond one valley was a ridge, then another valley and another ridge. Four and a half minutes after coast-in we emerged over a flat area twenty-three miles east of the target. The initial point for our run-in was two minutes away—a lake, about a mile in diameter, depicted on the chart. At the lake I'd turn southwest and increase speed for the run to the target, ten miles farther down the line.

Once again I glanced at the photo of the target. Jack Shaw's less-than-reassuring remarks nagged at me. Butterflies banged around inside my stomach as if to underscore my lack of confidence in finding anything worth attacking.

Seconds ticked by, then more seconds. Concern became anxiety. There was no lake, only farmland and another karst ridge dead ahead. So much for French survey data.

"Salt Lead, popping up for a look-see." I climbed to 500 feet. Beyond the karst ridge were the tracks of a railroad that snaked northward from Hanoi to the Chinese border. Damn! I began a left turn. Bill Smith, leading the two-plane section immediately behind me, saw the error too.

"We've overshot, Ex-Oh," he radioed.

"Roger. Salt Lead is coming left," I replied, mentally recomputing the problem. There was still time to make a corrective "S" turn, toward the southeast then southwest. That would put us back on the run-in heading.

Bill Smith had anticipated my maneuver and, with his wingman, Charlie Stender, turned more sharply. As my Skyhawk swung eastward, Bill's two-plane section was off to my left, about a quarter mile ahead and crossing left to right. The difference in our turn radii placed my section behind Bill's. I glanced to my right, toward the target area. The intelligence photos showed the suspected SAM site atop a hillock. Great! The entire countryside around Kep was dotted with hillocks, each one revoltingly similar to its neighbor. Jack Shaw had been right, the real estate was confusing.

At 360 knots we were fast running out of time. Deep in enemy territory was no place to mill around at low altitude to reorganize.

"Do you have the target in sight, Smitty?" I radioed.

"I think so," he answered. That was good enough for me. I decided that the solution was to follow Bill rather than trying to regain the lead.

"Roger. I'm at your four o'clock. You have the lead."

The sky erupted. Black puffs of flak and tracers streaking orange and white appeared everywhere. The North Vietnamese were wide awake and waiting for us with guns manned and ready.

Ahead and off to the right I saw what I thought was the target—several vehicles and pieces of construction equipment clustered atop a hillock. "Two o'clock, Smitty," I radioed.

Bill acknowledged, and at the same moment I saw Hank McWhorter's photo Crusader making a steep turn over the same hillock. "I'm directly over the target...now," Hank radioed, his Crusader seemingly engulfed by tracers from the ground.

I muttered to myself, "Thank you, Hank, but you've more guts than sense."

Bill Smith put his section into a steep right turn toward the hillock. I counted aloud to myself—one thousand one, one thousand two—as I continued on my southwest heading, distancing myself from the target. Our bombs were equipped with Snakeye fins for retarded low-level delivery. A delay in my run-in was necessary so that John and I wouldn't fly through shrapnel from the exploding bombs dropped by Bill and Charlie.

At one thousand five I wrapped my Skyhawk into a hard right turn and jammed the throttle to 100-percent power. Just as quickly, I eased it back to 99 percent to preclude outrunning John. Tracers and antiaircraft shells crisscrossed in the sky ahead, creating a wall of frightening flak. My airspeed indicator showed 400 knots. I watched Bill's and Charlie's bombs explode and create great clouds of dirt and debris.

My throat was dry, and my heart was pounding, my stomach churning. I breathed heavily through the oxygen mask. A half mile ahead there were several trucks and a bulldozer parked in a neat row. Whether they were constructing a SAM site was academic at the moment. Over the ambient engine and air-conditioning noises of the cockpit, I heard the cracks of enemy guns and shells bursting along my flight path. It was like sitting astride a popcorn popper. I peered through the bombsight, a pale yellow reticle projected onto the windscreen. The pipper crept toward my aim point, the nearest truck. That would allow me to "walk" my bombs along the whole row of rolling stock. The sky was hazy gray from loitering flak smoke, and for a second or two I had a perverse admiration for the defensive effort, the fireworks display of 37-mm tracers and bursting 57-mm shells lofted by the North Vietnamese gunners.

As I moved my thumb over the bomb-release pickle on the control stick, I heard Charlie Stender's unemotional voice transmit, "Salt Four. I'm hit."

The pipper moved over the first truck, and I pickled the bombs. My Skyhawk shuddered slightly as small explosive charges kicked the weapons from the racks. I pulled sharply up and to the right and jammed the throttle full forward, as if to shove it through the instrument panel. Wishing that the Skyhawk had an afterburner, I was amazed that I'd gotten through all that flak without being hit.

Twisting in the cockpit to look back toward the target, I tried to assess the damage and to find John Shore. Dust and smoke were boiling from the hillock, obscuring the target, but our hits appeared to be right on.

Good, but where was John? I turned steeply in the opposite direction. Two Skyhawks were fast approaching the target from the west. Charlie Wack and his wingman, I assumed. But where was John?

Tracers flew past me. I yanked my bird around to the right, again twisting in the cockpit, anxiously holding my breath. There was no telltale black smoke near the target, no burning jet fuel to signify an airplane crash. Partially relieved, I exhaled, took in another gulp of oxygen, and pressed the mike button.

"Salt Two, do you have me in sight?" An agonizing silence followed. Long seconds, then I heard that single reassuring word: "Rog." John was OK.

But we weren't out of the woods yet. LTJG Ken Kreutzman of VA-164, flying as "Tail End Charlie," the fourth aircraft in Wack's division, radioed that he too had been hit. Then his section leader reported that Ken's plane was streaming fuel. But at least everyone was off the target. No one had been shot down.

Each pilot checked in with his fuel state. Charlie Stender added that he was "running a little rough." Bill Smith reported bullet holes in his own wing. Ken Kreutzman said that he was losing fuel rapidly but was otherwise OK. "Leaking like a sieve" was his wingman's comment. Superheat One, the leader of the four Crusaders, checked in, and finally Hank McWhorter reported, "Off and clear," having finished his post-strike photo-taking.

It was decision time. Two planes were badly damaged, and we were fifty miles from the Gulf. The safest retirement course was to backtrack at low level on the reciprocal of our inbound route, over sparsely populated territory. That would hide us from radar, behind the shield of the mountains. But it would cost more fuel and would keep us over enemy territory for the longest time. Besides, low altitude provided the least maneuvering room.

At the rate Ken Kreutzman was losing petrol, it was doubtful that he could make it to safety on the backtrack route. The severity of the damage to Charlie Stender's aircraft was a matter of conjecture. Both Ken and Charlie needed time to maneuver should the conditions of their aircraft deteriorate. They needed to climb to higher altitude.

The shortest route to the sea was southeast, but a beeline track in that direction meant flying close to Haiphong and possibly encountering a volley of SAMs. MiGs were a possibility, too, from Kep airfield behind us. Of the two threats, MiGs would be the more acceptable. The enemy wouldn't fire SAMs if its own fighters were in the air, and we'd brought along four Crusaders for cover. And the electronic watchdogs over the Gulf had broadcast neither SAM nor MiG warnings.

"Salt Lead is climbing on one three zero," I radioed to the strike group, "direct to feet wet." It was a calculated risk. For good measure I added, "You fighter guys keep your eyes open in case you have to earn your pay today." The Superheat leader clicked his mike button twice in businesslike acknowledgment. It wasn't necessary to mention SAMs. Everyone knew they were a serious threat.

Charlie Stender calmly reported that his engine was running progressively rougher. He was experiencing heavy airframe vibration and abnormally high engine-exhaust temperature. Those symptoms meant that his power plant might soon begin spitting out compressor blades. One or more of those blades could tear through fuel lines or the fuselage fuel cell, create a fire, and dictate an immediate ejection. Every second got Charlie a little more altitude, a little closer to the water.

Ken Kreutzman's plane was still flying well, but he needed a tanker—right away.

The cockpit of the Skyhawk was a small place. It became even smaller and hauntingly lonely when trouble was brewing. There were no words of encouragement I could give to Charlie and Ken, and neither pilot expected any.

Ten minutes later we were "feet wet," and I heaved a sigh of relief. No SAMs had been fired, and no MiGs had come out to pick us off from behind. If Charlie or Ken had to punch out, at least it would be over water, where the prospect of rescue was significantly increased. The pilot of the strike tanker stationed over the Gulf was Johnny-on-the-spot. He homed in on our radio transmissions and met Ken Kreutzman over Haiphong even before we were feet wet. Ken plugged in and returned to *Oriskany* without further difficulty.

Charlie Stender was having a more difficult time. With his plane vibrating uncontrollably at lower power settings, he flew with his throttle jammed all the way forward at 100 percent. His engine EGT (exhaust-gas temperature) hovered close to the redline danger zone. Using his speed brakes, landing gear, and wing flaps as his only means of controlling the airplane's speed, Charlie nursed his Skyhawk down from altitude and into *Oriskany's* landing pattern. Like a concerned mother hen escorting an injured chick, Bill Smith flew a close wing on Charlie all the way.

Charlie rolled his wings level astern of the ship. As usual, he radioed his fuel state and the word "ball," indicating that he had the glide-slope indicator of the Fresnel lens in sight. But the rest of his radio call was anything but routine. "My EGT is in the red, and the engine is making funny noises," he said.

From overhead, I watched the approach with a helpless feeling, knowing that Charlie would have but one chance at the deck, one chance for a landing. If he missed the arresting wires and boltered, his engine probably wouldn't hold together, and he'd have to "punch out." Ejection at low altitude always carried an increased risk of injury or death, more so if the aircraft was marginally controllable.

When Charlie's plane was in the groove, a couple of hundred yards astern of the ship, Bill Smith radioed even more somber words to the LSO: "Take him, paddles. He's on fire."

Charlie's landing was perfect. Within seconds he caught the number three wire, came to a stop, shut down his engine, opened the canopy, disconnected himself from his seat, and made a fast exit from the burning plane. It was an absolutely marvelous performance under extreme pressure. The flight-deck crew extinguished the fire rapidly and pulled the aircraft clear of the landing area.

Ken Kreutzman landed next, unplugging from the tanker a half mile astern, and the rest of us followed in order. The afternoon's ordeal was over.

The Kep mission was a baptism of fire, the heaviest and most concentrated antiaircraft fire any of us had witnessed so far in the war. A small favor was that the enemy had not launched any SAMs. In the ready room I found myself shaking nervously as I drew a cup of coffee. We had poked our heads into a hornet's nest and had all come out alive.

If nothing else, the mission proved that the Skyhawk could absorb punishment. Inspections revealed that five of the eight planes had taken flak damage. Charlie Stender's plane was so badly torn up and damaged by fire that it would require an overhaul. It would be off-loaded in port. Ken Kreutzman's plane was a sieve, as his section leader had reported, but was deemed locally repairable. Bill Smith and Charlie Wack had taken shrapnel and small-arms hits that tore jagged holes in their planes and caused minor internal damage. And John Shore was just plain lucky. A 57-mm projectile had torn a hole through the lip of his right engine's air intake, inches behind the cockpit. Our low-level Snakeye delivery had spared John a fiery death over Kep because the 57-mm projectile didn't have time to arm before it tore through his plane.

The Kep mission had been a frustrating mess, and its apparent overall stupidity irritated me. In the debrief, none of the pilots reported seeing SAMs or any associated launching equipment. If the construction activity we attacked was intended to produce a SAM site, it hadn't progressed far enough to be recognizable.

After the debrief I unloaded my frustrations to CAG Stockdale. The mission had involved a "nothing" target, had unnecessarily risked the lives of pilots and the loss of aircraft. The two waves led by Harry Jenkins and Jack Shaw had found nothing. The third wave should not have been launched. We had harassed the enemy, but that was about all. The flight might have been justified if we had hit a significant target—the MiGs at Kep, the northeast railroad between Hanoi and China, or the docks at Haiphong. Jim had no control over the selection of targets but was a patient and understanding audience.

Hank McWhorter, whose gutsy flying had helped to pinpoint our target, returned with his photo coverage. After viewing the pictures, the intelligence officer said that we'd struck the wrong target.

"We weren't given any credible intelligence to establish the *right* target!" I snapped at the intelligence officer.

CAG Stockdale interceded, agreed that launching the third wave probably hadn't been justified, and expressed his thanks that we all returned safely. He then asked what I thought we had attacked. Other than some construction equipment, I wasn't sure, but with all that flak I figured that they must have had something up there that made them mighty proud.

Later I learned from Stockdale that the operations officer attached to the staff of RADM Ralph Cousins who was embarked in *Oriskany* had upset the mission plan. The staff ops officer had appeared in *Oriskany*'s strike-operations center, interposed himself into the tactical direction of the mission, and, ignoring both the mission plan and the advice of the ship's strike-ops officer, given the order to launch my wave. Jim Stockdale was airborne at the time as leader of the fighters escorting Jack Shaw's wave and learned of the change of plan after he had landed on board. As soon as Kreutzman and Stender nursed their crippled birds safely onto *Oriskany*'s flight deck, CAG stormed up to the flag bridge for a private audience with Admiral Cousins—a face off about who was running Air Wing 16. Cousins agreed with Stockdale's position, and thereafter the staff operations officer was seldom seen in the ship's strike-ops center.

That evening I wrote two recommendations for the Distinguished Flying Cross (DFC). One was for Charlie Stender, who had kept his cool in a hazardous and demanding situation. His plane was a valuable asset and, even though damaged, could be repaired and used again. And if being shot up during a combat mission, nursing his plane back to the ship, and making a perfect carrier landing while on fire didn't qualify as distinguished flying, nothing did.

The second recommendation was for Hank McWhorter. In the midst of a heavy barrage of antiaircraft fire he had completely disregarded his own safety to help the strike group locate the hillock among hillocks that most closely resembled a "missile site under construction." No one would have thought less of "noncombatant" Hank if he and his unarmed photo Crusader had avoided the hot area. His sole responsibility had been to make a post-strike pass over the target to gain photographic evidence. But Hank was a tiger. He'd helped when help was needed.

I was deeply pleased when CinCPacFlt later approved both DFC recommendations. Sadly, one award was made posthumously. Six days after the Kep mission my friend LT Henry S. "Hank" McWhorter was killed in action while flying another mission over North Vietnam is his unarmed RF-8 photo Crusader.

7 A Grim Day

 Southeast Asia's summer monsoon machine was at full efficiency in late August and early September of 1965. Almost every day the Gulf of Tonkin was a cauldron of thick clouds, low ceilings, rainstorms, and uncertain flying conditions. Twice *Oriskany* temporarily moved south to Dixie Station when prolonged poor weather completely clobbered all targets in North Vietnam. When we did get over the beach from Yankee Station, the low, ragged overcast made the time spent flying armed recco missions both abbreviated and tense. It was a challenging grab bag of trying to maintain visual flight conditions while searching for targets and maneuvering to avoid enemy AAA fire, mountains, and midair collisions.

When trucks or other ground targets were found, we were often faced with a "Catch-22" situation—the overcast was too low to permit us to drop bombs safely. For the better part of those two months the weather provided as many challenges as the enemy. We flew to the beach and back through solid overcasts extending from 400–500 feet to over 30,000 feet. Strong, gusting winds kicked up the sea, and frequently, after an instrument approach through heavy rain and turbulence, I couldn't see *Oriskany*'s pitching flight deck until I was 500–600 yards astern of the ship. In less than ten seconds at the Skyhawk's closing speed I had to acquire the ball, orient myself on the proper approach angle, and make any corrections before slamming down onto the wires.

On the flight deck, working conditions for the crews varied from moist to soaking wet, but there was a minor plus to the miserable weather. The almost constant overcast and the rain allowed the ship to cool down to about 80° F, providing the crews with more tolerable, if not entirely comfortable, sleeping conditions when their work was done.

Another kind of crew—from CBS television—was on board *Oriskany* on 24 August to film a segment of a news special entitled "Vietnam Perspective." While I was briefing several pilots for one of our periodic strikes to recut the runway at the Vinh airfield, CBS correspondent Murray Fromson and his crew entered Ready Room Five, ostensibly to conduct an interview but in effect putting on a demonstration of efficiency. In the space of a few minutes the crew set up camera, lights, and sound equipment while Mr. Fromson asked a few preliminary questions about my background. I was on camera for about thirty seconds while I continued the strike briefing. Then, just as rapidly as they had arrived, Fromson, TV equipment, and film crew disappeared. The episode left me wondering how much of a perspective could result from what appeared to be superficial coverage of what we were doing.[1] Alas, unknown to Mr. Fromson and the vast American viewing audience, bad weather canceled our Vinh mission before we got off the deck.

On the day following my thirty-second television career, the "Four Wretched Amateurs and a Beginner" gathered in Paul Merchant's stateroom to practice new song parodies for a planned comeback as wardroom entertainers. New additions to our repertoire were "Wingman, Ho Chi Minh, and Me" and "The Fighter Boys" (see the Appendix). The first was a broad bit of in-house fun about the bombing business we conducted; the second, a good-natured needle pointed at fighter pilots because of their absence from the scene during the shoot down in June of the North Vietnamese MiG-17 by the *Midway's* A-1s. Being Spad drivers, Paul Merchant, Eric Shade, and Ed Davis took a

---

1. I didn't see the TV program, but Mr. Fromson was kind enough to send me a copy of the program's companion paperback book. In retrospect, it was encouraging to see how my mission briefing fit nicely into the *Oriskany's* segment of the story, which, in turn, was an abbreviated but honest portrayal of the carriers' role in the war.

particular fancy to the latter song. The five of us looked forward to entertaining in the wardroom for a second time, but twenty-four hours later our plans changed dramatically.

During the night of 26–27 August guitar-playing tenor Ed Davis was shot down. Flying on an armed recco mission in the southern panhandle of North Vietnam, Ed's A-1 Skyraider was hit at low altitude and crashed within seconds. It was a pitch-black night, and Ed's wingman reported seeing no chute or post-crash signal from the ground. It seemed highly improbable that Ed could have survived the crash, and CAG Stockdale officially reported Davis as KIA.[2] Ed's loss sent our amateur musical organization into abrupt retirement. The camaraderie that we had built was strong, but stark reality had intruded upon us. Without Ed, "show biz" wasn't fun anymore.

It would have been nice if the ROE were simple, something like, "In war, if someone shoots at you, you get to shoot back." However, early in America's experience in Vietnam, over-cautious, senior armchair tacticians meddled with the local tactical situation. The number and complexity of ROE increased rapidly, even as operations on Yankee Station took on a predictable, stereotyped sameness. The ROE reflected the ambivalent philosophy of the Johnson Administration. We were at war with North Vietnam, but we really didn't want to hurt the North Vietnamese. We would love to quit punishing Mr. Ho Chi Minh if only he would quit trying to dominate South Vietnam. The concept of conducting a "humane" war was self-contradictory, frustrating, and difficult to reconcile in the cockpit.

We were ordered to fly out and bomb the enemy, to interdict the flow of supplies and material from North to South Vietnam. But we were prohibited from attacking North Vietnamese villages. The enemy's response was predictable. More than once after a fruitless daylight armed recco mission spent hunting for the trucks that transported supplies and equipment, I was irked to fly past a village and see rows of poorly camouflaged supplies and equipment stored right in the streets.

2. Davis survived the crash and was later confirmed as a POW, remaining in that status until repatriated in 1973.

The ROE prohibited us from attacking targets within two miles of any known hospital. Predictably, previously nonexistent "hospital" buildings, clearly marked with large red crosses, soon appeared near the approaches to strategic bridges.

The ultimate stupidity in the formulation of the ROE, however, was that Washington provided sanctuaries for the enemy. The JCS Alfa list placed arbitrary restrictions on the ability of on-scene tactical commanders to order opportunity strikes against major targets. Equally arbitrary restrictions were placed on strategically important chunks of the enemy's geography. Imaginary circles were drawn around the capital city of Hanoi and around Haiphong, North Vietnam's only major seaport. Inside of those circles, offensive air operations were either restricted—made only with Washington's prior permission—or altogether prohibited.[3]

The ROE were generally published in a two-part "situation" and "rule" format, and hardly a week went by that didn't bring an urgent message adding, changing, or amplifying some ROE. It wasn't long before the pilots' frustrations led them to savage the ROE, at least in Ready Room Five. Anonymous "notices" mysteriously appeared on the bulletin board:

SITUATION: Night road recco. RULE: Don't go below 10,000 feet. Better yet, don't go!

SITUATION: Day road recco, Route Kilo or Juliet. RULE: If you launch on this mission, you haven't yet learned to conduct a thorough preflight inspection of your aircraft! [Juliet and Kilo were the two most flak-infested recco routes.]

SITUATION: Strike mission at Vinh. RULE: Lower seat to floor of cockpit; close eyes; enter dive at 25,000 feet; recover from dive at 20,000 feet!

SITUATION: Strike mission at Thanh Hoa. RULE: Buy your way into the Squadron Duty Officer watch and stay aboard ship. Money is no object!

---

3. For a more detailed critique of the rules of engagement, see *On Yankee Station: The Naval Air War Over Vietnam* by John Nichols and Barrett Tillman (Naval Institute Press, 1987).

SITUATION: Strike mission at Kep. RULE: Disregard. Kep does not exist. It's just a practical joke perpetrated by staff planners!

A variation of the theme came in the form of a NOTAM (Notice to Airmen) familiar to Stateside flyers:

NOTAM. HOT AREA—North Vietnam. Aircraft cautioned to avoid flying over North Vietnam where possible. Widespread, unannounced surface-to-air gunnery and missile practice conducted day-night at undisclosed locations, particularly Hanoi-Haiphong areas. Exercise caution all quadrants Vinh area due in-flight hazards of various sizes from 37-mm to 85-mm.

After an eternity of the topsy-turvy midnight-to-noon operating schedule, *Oriskany* shifted to a more normal noon-to-midnight assignment in late August. Shortly thereafter, newboy Moose Lundy flew his first night armed recco mission. He'd flown several daylight missions over North Vietnam and had been scheduled to fly a couple of "easy" night recco missions with experienced pilots. However, poor weather and an aircraft malfunction had intervened, and he had not been able to complete either night mission. Moose added some night flying time in his log book, but he'd not yet been over the beach at night by the time he was assigned to fly with Harry Jenkins. In the unrelenting sameness of our daily grind, Harry did not realize that this flight would be Moose's first night recco mission. The skipper assumed that the young pilot had already experienced the pucker factor that accompanied nocturnal combat and didn't cover that in the preflight briefing.

Moose's subsequent night experience over the beach was wild. The weather at the target was poor, the night was as dark as the ace of spades, and the parachute flares turned the sky into a shimmering milk bowl without a horizon. Bouts of vertigo were frequent, and it seemed to Moose that every North Vietnamese gunner was mounting a special effort to shoot him down. He found that dodging flak while trying to keep track of Harry Jenkins as they sought out targets was sweaty, hard work.

When the combat portion of flight was over, Moose spent a tense forty-five minutes struggling to stay on Harry's wing as they made their way through turbulent weather and a solid overcast that extended almost from the surface to 30,000 feet. Moose made an instrument approach and needed seven tries to land on *Oriskany*'s wildly heaving deck. One by one the other planes landed, while Moose repeatedly flew his lonely way around the night landing pattern.

Ready Five was tense as the Saints eyeballed the remote TV monitor and listened to the controller talk Moose around for a seventh landing attempt. The ceiling over the ship was a ragged 300 feet, rain was heavy, the ship's recovery course was taking it perilously close to the coast of North Vietnam, and Moose was getting low on fuel.

I knew the pressure that Moose was experiencing. Under normal conditions, *one* night approach and carrier landing were a challenge. Seven, made under instrument flying conditions while having to contend with a badly pitching, rain-swept flight deck, would make even the most experienced pilot go bonkers. I felt knotted up as I sat in the ready room. Mentally, I was in that cockpit with Moose. Harry Jenkins sat beside me, feeling worse by the second. The predicament was not of Harry's making, but he felt responsible and deeply concerned for his young wingman.

On his seventh pass, Moose touched down safely, and we in the crammed ready room heaved a collective sigh of relief.

A few minutes later Moose came through the door. All eyes were focused on our newboy. He looked physically exhausted, yet he was emotionally keyed up. Moose stared at us for a moment, then flung his helmet violently at a nearby chair and issued a totally uncharacteristic expletive: "I'm fuckin' glad to be alive!"

The room full of combat-experienced pilots erupted in a chorus of cheers. Moose Lundy had joined the club. He was no longer a newboy.

A steep valley in rugged karst mountains about fifty-five miles southwest of Hanoi was the stage for an impromptu strike mission that yielded our best armed recco results to date. In early September Bill Smith and Charlie Stender were truck hunting along a road that snaked up the narrow Song Ma River valley northwest of Thanh Hoa. There was an overcast with intermittent rain, and the clouds were lowering. Further recco was useless, so Bill turned his section back toward the Tonkin Gulf, intending to go home. Skimming above a ridge and over an adjacent valley, he spotted "a bee-utiful sight." Along a precarious stretch of narrow road carved into a mountainside was an eighteen-truck convoy. The North Vietnamese had taken a calculated risk in putting the convoy on the road in daylight. Either they desperately needed to move the supplies, or they had relied on bad weather to keep air opposition out of the area. The stretch of road had no exit, so Bill and Charlie quickly attacked and destroyed the first and last trucks in the line, trapping the remaining vehicles on the narrow road. Then Bill radioed for help.

Fifteen miles north, John Shore and I were grubbing through the weather on a luckless, truckless recco mission. I heard Bill's call and turned south, flipping on the ADF (automatic direction finder) homer to get a bearing on his position.

"We've got a real turkey shoot here" was Bill's message. The call for help also brought in Jim Stockdale and Harry Jenkins from their southern recco route.

In a racetrack pattern along the axis of the narrow valley, the six of us swarmed back and forth, bombing the trucks and riddling them with 20-mm cannon fire. At low altitude under the overcast, there was the possibility of being hit by small-arms fire. But a greater risk was the possibility of damage from the blasts of our own bombs, and of midair collisions in the narrow sky suddenly cluttered with aircraft.

On one pass at the target I scared myself by pulling up too steeply into a wingover after dropping a bomb. I entered the dark overcast, leveled my wings, and rapidly transitioned to instrument flying. Easing the nose down a bit, I hoped to regain visual flight conditions immediately. I figured that I had about five seconds of leeway before having to break up and out of the pattern, lest I tangle with a mountaintop or run into a fellow pilot. Four seconds later I was visual again. The tension eased, and I chastised myself for getting carried away in all the excitement.

Thirty miles downstream from the "turkey shoot," just outside the coastal city of Thanh Hoa, was the Ham Rong railroad-highway bridge, which spanned the Song Ma River. It was the notorious "Thanh Hoa Bridge," a seemingly invulnerable link in the North Vietnamese north-south, road-rail coastal supply route. Designed and built by the Vietnamese, the bridge was completed in 1963, the first major non-French engineering project in their country. It connected two steep banks at a narrow bend of the Song Ma River called "Dragon's Jaws." The bridge was a prime target. Destroying it would force the enemy to detour traffic many miles to the west.

The degree of antiaircraft protection given the Thanh Hoa Bridge reflected both its strategic value and North Vietnam's pride of accomplishment. Air Wing 16 flew Alfa strikes against the bridge in July and August, but neither was successful. Other air wings failed as well. The Thanh Hoa Bridge thus became a challenge to us as periodic reports of its destruction proved false. Its alleged indestructibility gave birth to tongue-in-cheek theories. The bridge was the hinge holding the world together, and God simply would not allow its destruction. Or, less theistically, the bridge was merely an illusion, done with mirrors.

Oriskany was again tasked to hit the bridge on 9 September. At CAG Stockdale's urging, we scheduled a maximum effort featuring thirty-two bomb-loaded Skyhawks and Crusaders. Another eight Crusaders would fly fighter cover. Four tankers, an electronics early-warning aircraft, and two photo beanies would play key support roles. Harry Jenkins was assigned to lead the first wave of twelve Skyhawks, followed by Jack Shaw of VA-164 with another twelve. Each Skyhawk would carry eight 500-pound bombs. A third wave of eight Crusaders from our marine fighter squadron, VMF-212, would perform a very unfighterlike mission. Led by LtCol Ed Rutty, a former Blue Angel, each marine would carry two 2,000-pound bombs. The load was so heavy that the Crusaders would launch with partial fuel loads and top off from airborne tankers. Stockdale assigned himself as strike coordinator, and I was his backup, flying on his wing.

The weather had been marginal for the twenty-four hours preceding the strike. The 1030 launch time was delayed while we awaited a final weather report from an aircraft launched from another carrier. In my cockpit I sat, holding the canopy partially closed against the periodic rain showers that swept across the flight deck. Running through the prelaunch-launch checklist for the fourth or fifth time, I wondered if the mission would go. I thought about the flak that surely would greet us at Thanh Hoa.

The weather was reported as OK, and the Yankee Station commander gave us the go. All the strike group had been launched by shortly after 1100. While we were rendezvousing, the pilot of the weather recco plane called CAG Stockdale with an amended report. The weather at Thanh Hoa had deteriorated to "zero-zero." When the strike group had joined, Stockdale reluctantly directed it to split up, sending the division leaders on their secondary missions.

For twenty minutes Jim and I orbited off the coast near Vinh, sixty miles south of Thanh Hoa. The four-plane division led by Harry Jenkins scoured the countryside near Vinh, looking for a roving SAM unit believed to be in the area. If Harry's group found the target, Jim and I would assist in its destruction. However, Harry reported no success, and at ten minutes to noon my fuel supply had dropped to decision state, a prebriefed level that meant that it was time for us to proceed on an alternate mission.

I notified Jim, and he rolled out of the orbit and headed north in a slow descent, parallel to the coast. Our secondary mission was to destroy some camouflaged equipment discovered earlier, stored beside the coastal railroad track fifteen miles south of Thanh Hoa. We flew north at 300 knots, parallel to the coast and just above the wave tops. Four minutes after passing Hon Me Island, Jim gave me a prearranged "bye-bye" signal and broke away in a left turn toward the coast. I punched the button on the elapsed-time clock and made a modified S-turn to the right, then back toward the coast.

The maneuver placed me about a mile behind Jim and would ensure that I didn't fly through the blast pattern of his finned Snakeye bombs. Our coast-in point was a few miles south of Thanh Hoa. As I steadied on a westerly course, I saw our primary target area to the right. It was hazy over the Thanh Hoa Bridge, but the weather was considerably better than what the recco pilot had reported. The ceiling had lifted to 4,000–5,000 feet, and the overland visibility was improving rapidly. From my low-level perspective it appeared that the bridge strike could have gone after all. I was disappointed because of all the wasted planning and preparation.

Stockdale's Skyhawk was a dark slice against the gray-green tideland as he went feet dry five miles south of Thanh Hoa. A few seconds later he banked sharply to the left and headed south along the railroad. Another twelve seconds elapsed, and I rapped my plane into a left bank, rolling out to parallel the railroad tracks. I checked my armament switches and scanned ahead through the bombsight reticle, watching Jim as he passed over the target. His aircraft scooped up into a climbing left turn toward the Gulf. His bombs exploded.

My aim point was the near end of a long row of something covered by tarpaulins. I glanced at the clock. It was four minutes after noon as I closed on the tarp-covered row. At the far end, equipment lay in disarray from the damage caused by Jim's bombs. My pipper slid smoothly to the near end of the row, and I pressed the pickle four times in quick succession, "walking" my bombs two at a time along the length of the target.

The target disappeared beneath my nose, and I climbed to the left, toward the Gulf. I saw Jim ahead at about 3,000 feet, silhouetted against the noonday sky. I also saw something else. There were black flak bursts just behind Jim's plane. Before I could press the mike button for a radio warning, I heard Jim transmit: "Uh, Three Five Three, Mayday."

Jim's Skyhawk lurched over into a steep dive.

I keyed my mike button. "Pull up, CAG. Pull up," I said. But the jet continued to plummet toward the ground.

"Eject, CAG. Eject," I shouted.

Stockdale's canopy flew off the plane, followed by the dark form of the ejection seat as Jim rocketed out of his crippled plane. I pawed clumsily at my radio controls, rotating the selector to guard, the emergency distress frequency.

"Mayday, Mayday, Mayday. This is Old Salt Three Four Two. Salt Three Five Three is hit and has ejected one two miles south of Thanh Hoa. Repeat, one two miles south of Thanh Hoa."

Fifteen seconds later I was over the scene. Jim's unmanned Skyhawk crashed into a tidal flat about one hundred feet from the water's edge, and my heart sank as I watched Jim's parachute float slowly downward toward a small coastal village. The situation was grim, but there was still a chance that Jim's parachute might drift clear of the village. If CAG made it to an uninhabited area or to the water, I could provide support with strafing runs. Other aircraft nearby would drop what they were doing and head our way in rapid response to the Mayday call. I broadcast again on guard, saying that I had a good chute and correcting the position to fourteen miles from Thanh Hoa. The code words "good chute" alerted the pilot of the rescue helicopter stationed on board the SAR ship in the Gulf. His service might be needed.

If Jim could evade capture, even for a few minutes, there was a chance that he could be snatched to safety. I charged my 20-mm cannons and turned tightly over the village. Jim was hanging beneath the parachute risers, but I couldn't determine his condition, whether he was injured.

The situation quickly turned to hopeless. Jim had ejected at about 1,000 feet and simply didn't have enough time to drift. The chute collapsed alongside a street in the center of the village. Within thirty seconds, before I could complete another 360-degree turn overhead, the chute disappeared from sight, gathered in as someone might dispose of dirty laundry before company came.

An empty, nauseous feeling came over me. There would be no rescue. For the first time I felt a deep hatred for the enemy that I had never seen, who heretofore had been but an impersonal target on the ground.

I flipped the master armament switch to on and dove to make a pass over the village. ROE be damned! I had every intention of strafing the hell out of that village with my cannons. I wanted to punish whoever was down there. But my reason returned soon enough. I turned the master armament switch off and erased revenge from my mind. I didn't care crap about the ROE or about inflicting civilian casualties, but Jim's exact location was unknown. Strafing would be just as dangerous to him as to anyone else. At 400 knots I roared low over the thatched-roof huts and pulled up at the far side of the village. Above me, I saw that my interest in the ground was attracting reciprocal interest in the air. Twenty or thirty flak bursts peppered the sky. The low pass was a dumb idea. Nothing but my own stupidity would be proven if I, too, got shot down. I climbed to a safe altitude, flying clear of the village and broadcasting a heavy-hearted "no chance." That terminated any SAR operation.

I was low on fuel and had to head back to the ship. Bill Smith, who had just launched from *Oriskany,* arrived on the scene to relieve me, but there was no rescue operation to coordinate. I relayed to Bill what I had observed, then turned for home.

In his brief six months as commander of Air Wing 16, James Bond Stockdale had proved himself a capable and popular leader and, to me, a good friend. A scholarly thinker, sometimes almost esoteric, Jim nonetheless had an engaging sense of humor and a colorful flair. In one mood, he could expound philosophically on man's natural penchant for war. In another, he used his name to capitalize on the current popularity of Ian Fleming's "James Bond" novels and movies.

The Navy's official call sign for the commander of Air Wing 16 was "Smoke Tree," but Jim never used it. He preferred "Zero Zero Seven." Once he delighted in posing for a tongue-in-cheek publicity photo, wearing a long black cape over his flight suit. It was just before he was to fly a "cloak and dagger" mission in an E-1A Tracer, an airborne early warning–electronics countermeasures aircraft. Although he was generally quiet and low key, there never was any doubt about who was in charge of the air wing. Jim never was heavy handed or meddlesome in the affairs of the several squadrons, but he always knew what was going on. He allowed skippers free rein in running their outfits while masterfully molding their efforts into the highly effective main battery of USS *Oriskany*.

I felt close to Jim because he was a patient listener. More than once, like an older brother, he had absorbed my frustrations with the war, my comments on the stupidity of this or that ROE, and my concerns over some inane procedural matter dictated by the brass. He always responded thoughtfully, calmly.

And I enjoyed listening to him. The flow of his ideas when he launched into one of his occasional minilectures on philosophy was always enlightening.

Jim's background as a naval aviator was in fighter aircraft, but he had earned the respect of everybody by flying with every squadron, in every plane that operated from *Oriskany*. His drive and personal commitment obliged him to fly frequently, often two missions per day, and it was his rigorous, self-imposed schedule that had become a cause for concern. Along with the other senior officers in the air wing, sometimes I wondered aloud if Jim was pushing himself too hard, spreading himself too thin. Flying back to *Oriskany* that September day, I tried unsuccessfully to visualize the air wing without CAG.

By the time I arrived at *Oriskany*, all of the other aircraft had landed. My approach to the ship was something less than that of a picture-perfect, precise naval aviator. I was given an "immediate charlie," meaning that I was to land on board without delay. I was also instructed to make a nonstandard right turn to the final approach. It was a simple maneuver but a departure from the habitual left-hand carrier-landing pattern ingrained in the thinking of every tailhook pilot. The different procedure, coupled with my mood, resulted in a minor error. As I rolled into the "groove" astern of *Oriskany,* thinking that I was all set for landing, I heard Bob Hofford, the LSO, transmit a single word, "Hook."

I felt foolish. I'd forgotten to lower my arresting hook and angrily slapped the control lever to the down position. The hook was the exclamation point in my naval aviation career. It set me and every other carrier pilot apart from other pilots the world over. The oversight was harmless but, even under the circumstances, embarrassing. By tradition I owed Bob a bottle of his favorite booze.

After landing, I made the long climb from the flight deck up the island ladders to the bridge. There was a look of anguish on the face of Captain Connolly as I related the details of Jim's shoot down. Then I returned to a melancholy Ready Five. John Sloan's intelligence debrief was short and unenthusiastic. Bob Hofford's remarks concerning my landing were just as perfunctory. He didn't mention the tailhook.

I talked quietly with Harry Jenkins while other pilots and several enlisted men gathered around to listen. There were a few halting, half-hopeful questions, but I could provide no encouraging answers. VA-164's skipper Jack Shaw stopped by for a few minutes, as did Paul Merchant. Conversation was difficult. Dan Lestage pressed a two-ounce combat ration of brandy into my hand.

We all lost a lot on the ninth of September, a grim day for Air Wing 16 and a traumatic one for me.

The author as a seventeen-year-old apprentice seaman, 1944. (*Author*)

The author as a Navy Aviation Cadet at pre-flight school, University of Iowa, 1945. (*Author*)

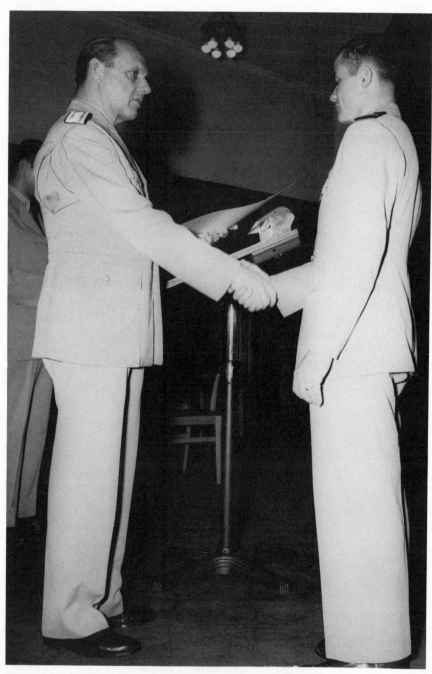

The author (right), receiving his naval-aviator designation certificate from RADM Aaron "Putt" Storrs, Pensacola, December 1950. (*U.S. Navy*)

A Grumman F9F-2 "Panther" over North Korea. During the Korean War the author flew seventy-five combat missions from the carrier USS Kearsarge while assigned to the VF-721 "Starbusters." (*U.S. Navy*)

Pilots and ground officers of VA-163 on the flight deck of USS *Oriskany* (CVA 34) in April 1965 just prior to the squadron's first combat cruise. Standing (left to right): LTJG Jim Taylor, LT Fred Mitchell, LTJG Dave Small, LTJG Larry DeSha, LT Art Avore, LTJG Charlie Stender, LT Dick Tulley, LTJG Floyd Oakes, LT Larry Spear, LTJG Dick Pennington, LTJG Jim Tyler, LT Bob Hofford, LTJG John Shore, and LTJG John Sloan. Kneeling (left to right): LCDR Russ Weidman, LCDR Don Martin, LCDR Roy Bowling, CDR Harry Jenkins (CO), Foster (XO), LCDR Charlie Wack, and LT Bill Smith. (*U.S. Navy*)

The attack pilot's singing group, "Four Wretched Amateurs and a Beginner," entertaining in USS *Oriskany*'s wardroom, April 1965, while the ship was en route from Yankee Station to a port visit in Yokosuka, Japan. The author is center. Others are (left to right) LCDR Paul Merchant of VA-152, LTJG John Shore of VA-163, LCDR Eric Shade of VA-152, and LTJG Ed Davis of VA-152. The singing group was disbanded in August 1965 when Davis was shot down over North Vietnam and became a prisoner of war. (*U.S. Navy*)

An A-4E Skyhawk of the VA-163 "Saints," approaching the flight deck of USS *Oriskany* for a trap (arrested landing), summer 1966. The ship in the background is a plane-guard destroyer, assigned to shadow the carrier in a rescue-alert status and to render assistance to a pilot in the event of an accident. (*U.S. Navy*)

A combat-loaded Douglas A-4E "Skyhawk" of VA-163 about to be launched from the port catapult on the flight deck of USS *Oriskany*, summer 1966. The author matched the squadron's number, flying 163 combat missions in Vietnam before being shot down. (*U.S. Navy*)

CDR Harry Jenkins (right), briefing VA-163's pilots in Ready Five on board USS *Oriskany*, May 1965. Left to right: Foster (face, lower left), LT Bill Smith, LT Art Avore, LTJG John Sloan (air-intelligence officer), LT Dick Tulley, LCDR Charlie Wack, LTJG John Shore (author's wingman), LTJG Dick Pennington, LTJG Charlie Stender. LCDR "Hap" Bowling, the squadron's operations officer, who was killed in action in November 1965, is hidden behind Jenkins's hands. (*U.S. Navy*)

The cake prepared for the author to commemorate his making the 90,000th arrested landing on board USS *Oriskany* on 8 May 1965. (*Author*)

The author, center, during a cake-cutting ceremony in USS *Oriskany*'s wardroom, commemorating the carrier's 90,000th arrested landing, which Foster made on 8 May 1965. Seated at left, holding a cigarette, is CDR (later VADM) James Stockdale, commander of *Oriskany*'s Air Wing 16. Stockdale, shot down over North Vietnam in September 1965, spent 7 1/2 years as a prisoner of war and was subsequently awarded the Medal of Honor for his leadership in that capacity. (*U.S. Navy*)

The author (right), briefing for a night armed recco mission with LTJG Dave Small in 1965. (*Author*)

The author at Cubi Point's BOQ mess, May 1965. (*Author*)

LTJG John Sloan, the air-intelligence officer during the 1965 cruise, napping in the ready room in the middle of the night while waiting for pilots to return from armed recco missions. (*Author*)

A "crunch" on *Oriskany*'s flight deck occurred in mid-June 1965 when LT Bob Hofford in aircraft number 350 partially lost hydraulic braking while taxiing. Rather than rolling over the side of the ship forward of the island, Hofford elected to turn his aircraft toward and collide with 351, piloted by the author. (*U.S. Navy*)

LT (later RADM) Dan Lestage, the flight surgeon assigned to VA-163. (*Author*)

LT John Shore by an A-4E Skyhawk before acombat mission in 1966. Shore was the author's wingman during VA-163's 1965 combat cruise. (*J. H. Shore*)

LTJG John Shore, the author's wingman, at breakfast in USS *Oriskany*'s wardroom, prior to a combat mission in 1965. (*Author*)

LTJG John Shore, the author's wingman, at NAS Lemoore, 1965. (*J. H. Shore*)

The author (left) and LCDR "Hap" Bowling (center) greet LCDR Charlie Wack (right) upon the latter's return to *Oriskany* after his 7 November 1965 shoot down and rescue (chapter 9). LTJG John Sloan (glasses), VA-163's air-intelligence officer, is between the author and Bowling. Nine days after this photo was taken, Bowling was killed in action during an Alfa strike against the Hai Dong bridge. (*U.S. Navy*)

Official portrait of the author as commanding officer of the VA-163 Saints, Naval Air Station Lemoore, California, January 1966. (*U.S. Navy*)

The author (left) with CAPT Bart Connolly, commanding officer of USS
Oriskany, during VA-163's awards ceremony at NAS Lemoore, January
1966. (*U.S. Navy*)

The author outside his quarters at NAS Lemoore, California, April 1966.
(*Author*)

Pilots and ground officers of VA-163 on board USS *Oriskany*, early June 1966. Standing (left to right): ENS Scott Wilkins (air intelligence), LCDR Bill Smith, LTJG Floyd Oakes (aircraft electronics), LT Bob Hofford, LCDR Dick Tulley, LCDR Charlie Wack, CDR Ron Caldwell (XO), Foster (CO), LCDR Marv Reynolds, LT Dale Miller, LCDR John Miles, LT Fred Mitchell, LT John Shore, LT Frank Hughes, and LTJG Jim Taylor (aircraft maintenance). Kneeling (left to right): LTJG Louie Nordby, LTJG Vance Schufeldt, LTJG George "Moose" Lundy, LTJG Wayne Cypress, LTJG Fritz Schroeder, LT Wayne Soliday, LTJG Pete Munro. The author was the squadron's only combat casualty during its 1966 deployment to the Vietnam War. LT Miller died in the tragic fire on board *Oriskany* in October 1966. (*U.S. Navy*)

The author (right) and CDR Ron Caldwell, executive officer of the Saints, during an April 1966 inspection of the squadron's personnel. (*U.S. Navy*)

USS *Oriskany*, launching aircraft on combat missions, Gulf of Tonkin, summer 1966. (*U.S. Navy*)

USS *Oriskany*, steaming in the Gulf of Tonkin, summer 1966. (*Author*)

The author, preparing to board an A-4 Skyhawk on the flight deck of USS *Oriskany*. (*U.S. Navy*)

The author (301) and his wingman in bomb-loaded A-4 Skyhawks, proceeding toward a target in North Vietnam, July 1966. (*Author*)

The author, leading a flight of bomb-loaded A-4 Skyhawks on a combat mission to a target in North Vietnam, July 1966. This photo was taken over the Gulf of Tonkin before the aircraft spread into a loose-goose combat formation. (*Author*)

One of VA-163's A-4 Skyhawks, flying into the rising sun upon returning to *Oriskany* from a night armed recco mission over North Vietnam, 1966. (*Author*)

LTJG Tom Spitzer greets the author (whose hand is at left) upon arriving on board USS *Oriskany* via highline, in the Gulf of Tonkin, July 1966. Spitzer, the author's last wingman, died in the October 1966 fire on board *Oriskany*. (*U.S.Navy*)

The author (left) and the Saints' executive officer, Ron Caldwell, greeting a new pilot, ENS Ralph Bisz, upon the latter's arrival on board USS *Oriskany* via highline from a replenishment ship, in the Gulf of Tonkin, July 1966. Bisz, who narrowly escaped death in the October 1966 fire on board *Oriskany*, was killed in action during a 1967 combat mission. The man in the helmet is the officer in charge of the replenishment operations. (*U.S. Navy*)

The author (left) and Ron Caldwell, greeting ENS Ron "Chico" Tardio upon the latter's arrival on board USS *Oriskany* via highline in the Gulf of Tonkin, July 1966. Tardio, a Bolivian born in the U.S., entered the Navy's flight program under a dual-citizenship rule. He died in the October 1966 fire on board *Oriskany*. (*U.S. Navy*)

CASUALTY RPT SEASIA AREA

A. CINCPACFLTINST. 01771
B. BUPERS MANUAL ART. C-9801
C. USS ORISKANY P 2310512Z   NOTAL

1. AT 230825H CDR WYNN F. FOSTER, USN, 522092/1310 COMMANDING OFFICER ATKRON 163 WHILE ON COMBAT MISSION RECEIVED DIRECT HIT FROM HOSTILE FIRE IN COCKPIT AREA OF A4E BUNO 152100. RIGHT ARM WAS ALMOST SEVERED BY SHELL FRAGMENT AND PILOT WAS FORCED TO EJECT DUE TO OWN CONCERN OVER LOSS OF BLOOD. A/C SUSTAINED HIT VICINITY 18-49N/105-42E. COCKPIT EQU INDICATIONS AND PILOT'S DESCRIPTION SUPPORTS ANTI AIRCRAFT FIRE TO BE RADAR CONTROLLED 57MM. PILOT MAINTAINED CONTROL OF A/C UNTIL OVER SAR DD LOCATED AT VIC 19-03N/105-54E. HE EJECTED AT 0830H USING LEFT ARM TO PULL FACE CURTAIN. EJECTION AND CHUTE DEPLOYMENT WERE NORMAL. PILOT INFLATED LEFT SIDE OF MK 3C AND RELEASED LOWER LEFT ROCKET JET SEAT FITTING DURING DECENT. AFTER ENTRY INTO WATER PILOT UNLOCKED KOCH FITTINGS AND OBSERVED RISERS AND SHROUD LINES TO SINK BELOW SURFACE. PILOT WAS PICKED UP BY WHALE BOAT AND TAKEN ABOARD SAR DD. PILOT WAS LATER EVACUATED BY HELO TO USS ORISKANY FOR SURGICAL COMPLETION OF AMPUTATION BY SHIPS MEDICAL OFFICER. CDR FOSTER PRESENTLY IN GOOD CONDITION AND PROGNOSIS STATED AS GOOD.

2. PERSONNEL CASREP RQD BY REF B SUBMITTED BY REF C.

COPY HUGHES
(RETAIN FOR C.O.)

					O	W	WCM	RAW	VF								MARDET	RELEASED
CDR R. H. CALDWELL								163										CDR R.E. SPRUIT
AOM	C/S	CPER	AIR OPS	SUPL O/C	SPEC V.FFS	CIC	INTEL	SEC	NAV	SUR LOG	MO	WEO	ENG	GEN FLDS	COMM	L.D	B/CM	SS? EAD	SDO	SOPA				
CO	XO	OPER	AIR OPS	NAV CWNZ	SPEC	CIC	INTEL	FLES	COM	SUP	WO	MEO	ENG	GEN FLDS	CONT	SEO	GSO	FC3	AIR	ENG	GUN	BAY	CHAP MED DENT	

USS ORISKANY CVA-34   MRD

CINGPACFLT
BUPERS

ROUTINE

DATE 24 JUL 66	YCN 0830 Z			
	WGTR UP T-54			

2405092

MSG NO. 1

The casualty report announcing the author's combat injury and rescue.

CAPT John Iarrobino, commanding officer of USS *Oriskany*, in 1966. A long-time friend of the author, Iarrobino planted the seed that resulted in the author's successful campaign to remain on active duty after his combat injury. (*U.S. Navy*)

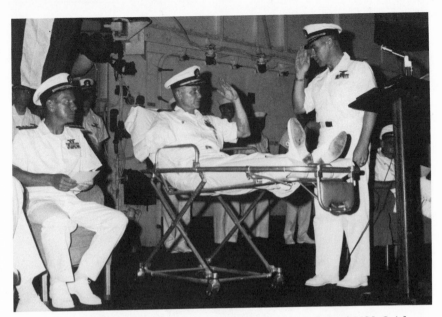

At a 1 August 1966 change-of-command ceremony on board USS *Oriskany*, CDR Ron Caldwell (right) executes the traditional "I relieve you, sir" salute after reading the orders assigning him as the author's successor in command of the VA-163 Saints. (*U.S. Navy*)

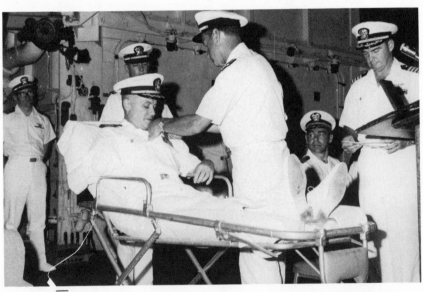

RADM Ralph Cousins presents the Silver Star to the author during a 1 August 1966 change-of-command ceremony on board USS *Oriskany* CAPT John Iarrobino, *Oriskany*'s commanding officer, is at right. CDR Ron Caldwell, VA-163's executive officer, is seated between Cousins and Iarrobino. At far left is LT (later RADM) Dan Lestage, flight surgeon. (*U.S. Navy*)

The author departs USS Oriskany for the hospital at Clark Air Base, Republic of the Philippines, after the 1 August 1966 change-of-command ceremony. CDR Ron Caldwell, Foster's relief as skipper of the VA-163 Saints, is at left. CAPT John Iarrobino, CO of *Oriskany*, is at right. With Foster are the ship's surgeon, CDR Dick Donahue (back to camera), and LT Dan Lestage, air-wing flight surgeon. (*U.S. Navy*)

In January 1967 the author (left) received the Distinguished Flying Cross for leading a successful strike against North Vietnamese port facilities in July 1966. RADM Harold Cokely, commandant of the Oakland naval hospital, presented the award. (*U.S. Navy*)

The author with his family at the Jerome, Arizona, "Wynn Foster Day" celebration. With the author are his son, Scott (white shirt), daughter Corinne, wife, Marilyn, mother, Winifred, a Jerome resident, and daughter Amy. (*Author*)

The author at Naval Hospital Oakland, California, in October 1966, prior to departing on a first trip home to NAS Lemoore. The uniform fits snugly over a twelve-pound upper-body cast that holds the stump right arm immobile during the knitting of the bone graft. (*K. Dennison*)

ADM Wesley McDonald, USN (Ret.), former Supreme Allied Commander, Atlantic. As a captain, McDonald was the author's detailer in the Bureau of Naval Personnel in 1967–68 and played a key role in the author's successful campaign to remain on active duty. (*U.S. Navy*)

The author (right), receiving the Vietnamese Cross of Gallantry from RADM Fred Bennett, at the Pentagon, Washington, D.C., January 1968. (*U.S. Navy*)

The author, March 1988. (*R. L. Lawson*)

ADM Roy Johnson, Commander-in-Chief, Pacific Fleet in 1967, whose letter in support of the author's quest to continue on active duty favorably impressed the Secretary of the Navy. (*U.S. Navy*)

Upon his retirement in 1972 the author was awarded the Legion of Merit and piped over the side through a formation of fellow officers standing as sideboys. (*U.S. Navy*)

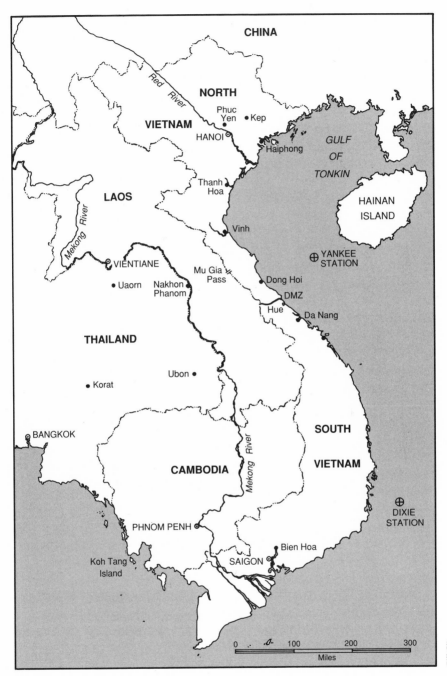

CHINA

NORTH

VIETNAM

Red River

Phuc Yen
• Kep

HANOI

Haiphong

GULF
OF
TONKIN

LAOS

Thanh Hoa

Mekong River

Vinh

HAINAN
ISLAND

VIENTIANE

Mu Gia
Pass

⊕ YANKEE
STATION

• Uaorn

Nakhon
Phanom

Dong Hoi

DMZ

Hue

Da Nang

THAILAND

Ubon •

• Korat

⊕ BANGKOK

CAMBODIA

Mekong River

SOUTH

VIETNAM

⊕
DIXIE
STATION

PHNOM PENH

Bien Hoa

Koh Tang
Island

SAIGON

0   100   200   300
Miles

Bill Clipson

0   100   200
Miles

CHINA

NORTH

VIETNAM

Red River

Phuc Yen

Kep

"Hornet's Nest" Attack Route

Hai Duong

Black River

Son La

Hanoi

Haiphong

Hon Gay

Moc Chau

Qui Hou

Phu Ly

Nam Dinh

Song Ma River

Ninh Binh

GULF OF TONKIN

"Turkey Shoot"

"Hour Glass"

Ha Trung

"Back Door" Attack Route

Thanh Hoa

HAINAN

ISLAND

(CHINA)

Song Ca River

SOUTH SAR STATION

Annam

Vinh

Carrier Operating Area

YANKEE STATION

Mekong River

Mountains

"PANHANDLE"

Required Circuitous Route to Attack Laotian Targets

Dong Hoi

DMZ

SOUTH

LAOS

Da Nang

THAILAND

VIETNAM

Bill Clipson

8 Largest Flak Site

 Some welcome R and R came our way in mid-September. After a brief call at Subic Bay, *Oriskany* steamed to Hong Kong for a six-day visit. The Subic stopover was part of the diplomatic charades that surrounded the Vietnam War and was scheduled in deference to our nonbelligerent British allies, who were nominally neutral in the Southeast Asia conflict. Their Crown Colony was perched precariously on the broad underbelly of China, the "neutral" ally of North Vietnam. Somehow, going to Hong Kong from Subic rather than directly from the war zone had a diplomatic sanitizing effect, cleansing the British of the appearance of supporting the U.S. war effort. Instead, we were simply an allied aircraft carrier popping over from the Philippines for a few days.

It was an odd rationale. British ships regularly transported supplies and materials to Haiphong for the North Vietnamese, as did the ships of other "neutrals," Russia and the Soviet-bloc countries. Alice in Wonderland. The presence of all those "neutral" ships in Haiphong harbor was the principal reason that Washington prohibited us from attacking its docks or mining its waters.

The Hong Kong anchorages immediately off the downtown area of Victoria were convenient to the fleet landing and were vacant. But *Oriskany* had to drop anchor four inconvenient miles farther out to the west, lest our presence nearer to the center of activity present too warlike an image. The remote anchorage was a stark contrast to the welcome we had received upon my first visit to Hong Kong during the

Korean War in 1953. At that time the British were squarely on our side, involved in a free-world fight against Communist aggression in Asia, and USS *Kearsarge* had been assigned a highly visible anchorage in the roadstead between downtown Victoria and the mainland city of Kowloon. Although the enemy had been the North Koreans *and* the Chinese, there had been little apparent concern about Hong Kong's precarious attachment to the broad underbelly of China.

During that same visit in 1953 the French aircraft carrier *Arro-manches* had an equally conspicuous mooring nearby. France wasn't involved in the Korean War because it was coping with a foreign entanglement of its own. *Arromanches* had just arrived from the Gulf of Tonkin, where its planes had been conducting combat operations against the Vietnamese in the French Indochina War.

In 1953 neither *Kearsarge* nor *Arromanches* had been required to make sanitizing stops elsewhere before steaming into Hong Kong, and the simultaneous visits of the two carriers had prophetic overtones for me. During that earlier visit I enjoyed an impromptu reunion with a French pilot friend who had attended U.S. Navy flight training with me. My friend took me on board the French carrier and showed me 8-mm aerial movies that he had taken during some of the bombing missions he had flown over Vietnam.

If *Oriskany*'s presence in the Crown Colony in 1965 was a diplomatic discomfort to the British government, the prospect of receiving a good chunk of dollars from American sailors apparently caused no similar gas pain. Hong Kong was a delightful liberty port, and we at the working level didn't waste time fretting over things diplomatic, especially after thirty-three days on the line.

During my first trip ashore the engine of our liberty boat conked out when we were still about two miles from the fleet landing. Thirty liberty-bound pilots and officers of the ship's company were adrift in the channel, and as senior officer on board, I was looked to for leadership and action. So I stepped into the cockpit of the boat, surveyed the situation, and hailed a passing "walla-walla" water taxi. After stepping ashore at the fleet landing, I notified *Oriskany* that the boat was adrift, then transited the harbor via the Star Ferry to check into the President Hotel in Kowloon. Unrestricted by water hours, I luxuriated with a twenty-five-minute shower, then wrote a long letter to Marilyn. Finally, I turned the air-conditioning control to full cold, put an extra blanket on the bed, climbed in, and slept blissfully for eleven hours. For the next five days I shopped, went sight-seeing, partied with friends, and was almost successful in forgetting about the war.

Oriskany returned to Subic Bay after the visit to Hong Kong for several days of ship and aircraft maintenance and upkeep. The Saints replayed the squadron beer-and-hot-dogs-picnic scenario, and during the afternoon festivities the troops tossed me into the bay once more. In the process I scraped my knee on some coral and for three weeks thereafter had a strange wound that resisted healing. Dr. Dan gave me a lengthy but not-too-clear explanation, from which I learned that coral contains animal protein, and my system was reluctant to develop antibodies. I asked Dan if he thought it would do any good to see a *real* doctor.

While at Subic I completed the uncomfortable chore of writing to Sybil Stockdale. Earlier attempts had ended in the waste can of my hotel room in Kowloon because I couldn't put a positive twist into my words. I knew that Sybil, like any Navy wife, knew the hazards that her man faced in his chosen profession. But I wanted to give her a factual, first-person account of Jim's shoot down, without effusive sentimentality, and to tell her both how much Jim meant to all the pilots in *Oriskany* and how much I missed him personally. Finally, I composed words that satisfied me. At the time I didn't know if Jim was still alive, but I couldn't visualize him as nonexistent. I closed my letter to Sybil by expressing my confidence that one day Jim would walk out of North Vietnam.[1]

Oriskany was back on Yankee Station on 30 September, and CDR Bob Spruit, the new air-wing commander, arrived on board four days later. Bob and I had served together in the Atlantic Fleet several years earlier, and his considerable experience in the cockpit of the Skyhawk was encouraging. Skyhawk pilots were bearing the brunt of the Navy's

---

1. He was alive, although badly injured from a brutal beating administered by the Vietnamese villagers immediately after he landed. Jim Stockdale's remarkable story of seven and a half years as a POW, and Sybil's parallel story of those same years, actively lobbying in the U.S. on behalf of all POWs, are dramatically told in the Stockdale's book *In Love and War*, originally published by Harper Rowe in 1984 and revised, updated, and reissued by the Naval Institute Press in 1990.

air war over North Vietnam, and the brunt of the related combat losses.

My reunion with Bob was brief, however. Paul Merchant and I were slated to leave the ship on the same COD (carrier on-board delivery) utility aircraft that had brought Bob to us. Before departing, I briefed the new CAG on our mission—to fly to Yokosuka, Japan, where we would embark in the carrier *Independence*. While that ship was en route to Yankee Station, we would with other combat-experienced aviators create a tactics annex to Task Force 77's standing operations order. The intended product would document the lessons learned from flying various types of aircraft in the war.

The idea behind the conference seemed sound, but it had generated concern among *Oriskany's* senior combat aviators because it smacked of a possible attempt to standardize combat tactics. The folks in Washington had already meddled too much in the tactical situation. Stereotyped, doctrinal thinking had crept into the strike plans originated by the staff of the Yankee Station commander. An example was the routine and arbitrary northward repositioning of support ships in the Gulf well in advance of Alfa strikes, a dead giveaway to the enemy that something big was about to happen.

From experience, we knew that what was left of local control of the tactical situation often demanded maximum flexibility on the part of our pilots. While guiding those who were to follow us into the air war over North Vietnam, we also wanted to leave room for innovation. In short, we wanted to avoid creating a "combat NATOPS" manual.

As I had learned several months earlier, Captain Connolly was no fan of NATOPS, and he agreed with the thinking of the senior pilots. Before the conference Connolly fired a message to the task-force commander, cautioning against writing canned rules that could inhibit the initiative of on-scene mission leaders.

The preconference homework performed by the *Oriskany's* senior pilots, and Captain Connolly's message, paid off when the conference was convened and the attendees initially tried to design the proverbial camel. Some pilots presented their own combat experiences, and the tactics developed therein, with such pride and zeal that on paper they read as if they were (or should be) established doctrine. On the second day of the conference, disagreement caused us to tear up the first day's draft and start anew. By the time *Independence* approached Yankee Station, we had agreed. The final draft of our jet attack tactics reflected a philosophy of helpful hints while avoiding a "thou shalt" approach. We hoped our efforts would help future prosecutors of the air war get up to speed.[2]

Pressure to find and destroy more SAM sites resulted in a small but perceptible change in the air war in early October 1965. Before, except for an occasional Alfa strike, missions had been arbitrarily limited to the territory south of the twentieth parallel. While I was attending the tactics conference, SAM-hunting efforts via Iron Hand missions were expanded northward, but with new restrictions. Previously, missions against targets near Hanoi and Haiphong simply were not authorized. The mid-October order, however, was accompanied by an outright prohibition: Under no conditions were Navy aircraft to fly within imaginary, sanctuary-providing circles around Hanoi and Haiphong. In effect, Navy pilots were not to be trusted.

On 16 October I sat in my Skyhawk, awaiting the order to start engines, and pondered the red circles drawn around Hanoi and Haiphong on my kneeboard chart. No matter what formidable AAA or SAM defenses the enemy was able to muster, its best defense seemed to lay ten thousand miles to the east, along the banks of the Potomac River.

John Shore and I, ready to launch on an Iron Hand mission, had been accorded the honor of being among the first to penetrate the newly opened territory. Intelligence experts believed that a roving SAM site was operating in the Red River delta, 30–60 miles southeast of Hanoi. It was a moot question whether the intelligence had been the cause of, or justification for, the expanded Iron Hand coverage. In either case, we were the bait in a trolling operation.

John and I launched and proceeded to a coast-in near the "hour glass" area, so called because of the sinuous shape of two fingers of the Red River northeast of Thanh Hoa. We zigzagged across the roads and

2. The tactics conference proved a waste of time. The annex was not kept current as the war progressed. By 1969 it was obsolete and removed from the task force's standing operations order.

byways of the delta, looking for clues. I followed a buttonhook track around Nam Dinh, maintaining a respectful distance from known flak sites, and settled on a northwest course toward Phy Ly. We were flying in a triple-threat area, and the feeling was spooky. My head was on a swivel as I watched for ground fire, SAMs, and MiGs. The parallel railroad-highway link and the surrounding countryside between Nam Dinh and Phy Ly were devoid of activity. Short of Phy Ly, again mindful of flak sites, I turned south in a sweeping "S" turn to intercept the road-rail link running southwest from Nam Dinh to Ninh Binh. There was still no sign of activity on the ground and, curiously, no apparent interest in our presence.

That area of North Vietnam normally generated considerable anti-aircraft opposition. Although there had been no MiG warnings from the snoopers over the Gulf, the absence of flak was a possible indication that we were being set up for a MiG attack. Nervously, I pulled into a tight left turn to reexamine the sky behind us. Nothing.

Returning to a southwest track, I looked beyond Ninh Binh and the road-rail line that swung due south around a karst ridge. As I climbed to a higher altitude to clear the ridge, the calm ended abruptly. The sky erupted with tracers and flak bursts, right at our altitude. I looked below, alongside the railroad tracks, and found myself staring into the blinking barrels of antiaircraft guns. They looked like the detonation of a string of Chinese firecrackers. As the muzzle flashes were visible in broad daylight, there was no doubt as to where the barrels were aimed. The tracers whizzed past me. An impressive amount of gunfire was coming from what apparently was a single flak site.

"Breaking down and left," I radioed to John as I popped the stick over and pulled into a 4-G descending turn away from the flak site.

"Rog."

Jinking, I reversed the stick and pulled hard to the right, toward the flak site. Why such a spirited reaction to our presence? Perhaps the roving SAM unit that we were hunting?

But as I arced back toward the streaming tracers, I could see no worthwhile target—no SAM equipment, no SAM-site pattern, no freshly made access roads, no train or other equipment on the railroad tracks, no vehicles on or off the road, nothing that looked like camouflaged equipment. The only thing worthy of note was the single antiaircraft battery pumping a helluva lot of lead into the air. I turned sharply away from the flak site, dismissing the macho-foolish temptation to duel with the gunners on the ground. Our allotted time over the beach was almost up, so I headed for the coast.

"Did you see anything worth a second look back there?" I radioed to John.

"Negative." But a moment later John became unusually chatty, adding, "That's got to be the world's largest flak site!"

Back on *Oriskany,* having ruled out the probability that the flak was protecting a roving SAM site, I asked John Sloan to recheck his intelligence files. Maybe something around Ninh Binh warranted another look. But Sloan came up blank, and the reason for the gunner's energetic response remained a mystery.

Twenty-four hours later I was preparing for a night armed recco mission. Visibility was marginal in intermittent rain showers, and *Oriskany* pitched substantially in heavy seas. Charlie Wack and his wingman, Dave Small, and John Shore and I were scheduled for the 2100 launch. As that time approached, however, the maintenance chief could promise only two up aircraft. John and Dave had already flown missions that day, so I scratched them from the schedule and substituted Charlie as my wingman. A last-minute radio report from a pilot returning from the beach characterized the weather over North Vietnam as "thick and gooey." I wasn't encouraged and wondered why someone with a little compassion didn't scrub flight operations altogether.

A stinging rain shower pelted Charlie and me as we scurried across the dark flight deck to man our aircraft. The wind-driven rain was moving almost horizontally, and the sea caused the deck to rise and fall beneath my feet. My Skyhawk was spotted on the port catapult. With only my red-lens flashlight for illumination, I did a walk-around preflight inspection, being careful near the deck edge lest a misstep tumble me into the drink sixty feet below.

Strapped into the cockpit, awaiting the start-engines call, I stared joylessly into the black void ahead of the ship. Across the deck, strapped into his bird on the starboard catapult, Charlie Wack no doubt was pursuing the same thoughts. The start signal came, and I quickly went through the prelaunch checklist. At 100-percent power I flicked on the exterior aircraft lights, the nighttime substitute for the salute, the signal to the catapult officer that I was ready to go. Two seconds, three seconds, four seconds. The built-in delay between my ready signal and the firing of the catapult seemed agonizingly long at night. Finally, I was hurled into the dark. Once again busy flying the aircraft, again in charge of my fate, I felt the tension ease, and I was reasonably comfortable.

Charlie joined me at 22,000 feet, on top of the weather. The sky above was clear, with a bright canopy of stars, a marked contrast to the weather below. Tracking via TACAN signal, I headed northwest and navigated to a point overhead the SAR ship, then reentered the heavy clouds and worked us cautiously down to lower altitude. In almost total darkness I located our coast-in point, half by TACAN bearing and half by guesswork.

"Red Crown, Old Salt Three Four Two is feet dry with two, your two two zero at sixteen miles."

The "thick and gooey" weather description was no exaggeration. Charlie and I gingerly grubbed around beneath a ragged 2,500-foot overcast, going in and out of rain showers. Periodically, I dropped a flare that cast an eerie, diffused glow on the countryside through the sheets of rain. There was nothing of interest to be seen except a sudden string of fast-moving white tracers glowing ominously through the clouds. A few more miles. Another flare. More nothing. Forty minutes later time was running out, so I dropped my last flare to illuminate a possible truck-traffic choke point. Still nothing. Charlie and I bombed an embankment to create a mud slide across the road. It was only temporary damage, probably no more than mildly irritating to the dozen or so coolies who would be out to clear the road immediately after our departure. And I was sure that the North Vietnamese below joined the two of us above in questioning the sanity of anyone willing to fly at night in such miserable weather. We escaped to the coast, climbed back into the overcast for another long stint on instruments, and returned to the ship.

We were surprised upon our arrival at marshal, the assembly area from which aircraft are fed into the night carrier-landing pattern. No one else seemed to be there, and we were cleared for immediate approaches. Normally, the fighters were cleared down and taken aboard first because of their higher fuel consumption.

"Childplay, I take it we have no Crew-saders tonight," I queried the ship.

"Negative fighters," the approach controller replied. "They weren't launched because of a pitching deck."

"I'm glad I'm an attack pilot."

Charlie and I separated to make individual instrument approaches, Charlie following me down at a two-minute interval. The weather was solid to 500 feet, and it wasn't until 400 feet, flying in and out of the bottoms of the ragged overcast, that I spotted the ship's lights through the rain-streaked windshield. I leveled off, always a bit worried at night about the low-level accuracy of the radar altimeter and not wishing to become a statistic by flying into the water.

After descending on instruments for several minutes, I was visited by vertigo. The lights of the ship looked as if they were tacked onto two-dimensional blackness ahead, but my inner ears told me that I was still descending. Disbelieving, I asked myself, "What's the ship doing *up there?*"

I cross-checked my instruments and assured myself that I was in level flight regardless of what vertigo was trying to tell me. I intercepted the glide slope, eased off a little power, and began the final descent. The ball was slowly moving up and down, confirming that the deck was pitching as advertised. I reminded myself not to chase the ball but to hold a steady rate of descent. With the deck pitching, there was a 50–50 chance I'd bolter.

But the deck's up-down cycle was in my favor. It steadied momentarily as I crossed the stern, and I slammed down on deck, catching a cable. Glowing hand wands materialized in the rain, coaxing me forward to clear the landing area. I taxied to the aft end of the starboard catapult, where signals indicated that the chocks were in place. I relaxed, moved the throttle aft to cut the engine, and opened the canopy. I heard Charlie's plane touch down behind me, followed immediately by the roar of his engine as he advanced the throttle to 100-percent power in anticipation of a bolter. Then the roar abated sharply. Charlie was down safely.

"Recovery complete," boomed a voice over the fligh-deck loudspeakers from PriFly, the air officer's primary flight-control station located high above the flight deck in the island. I was surprised. That meant that Charlie and I had been the only *Oriskany* aircraft airborne from the 2100 launch! It was still raining as we walked aft, steadying ourselves against the tilted flight deck as the ship turned out of the wind.

Below in Ready Five, Charlie and I learned that *Oriskany* had been the only carrier to launch aircraft at 2100. The other two carriers on Yankee Station had canceled their remaining night schedules *before* our launch. The squadron duty officer told me that the Air Force had scrubbed the balance of its night missions over North Vietnam because of the poor weather. It was an eerie sensation to realize that, for the better part of an hour in nasty weather on an inky night, Charlie and I had been the only two aviators flying over all of North Vietnam! It made me mad as hell, and a little scared.

Oriskany's October line period had been an unusually short nineteen days when we left Yankee Station for another visit to Subic Bay. Our in-port agenda included, among other events, a wetting-down party to celebrate the recent promotions of Larry DeSha and Bob Hofford to the rank of lieutenant. The two demonstrated shrewd economic sense by scheduling their party to coincide with the Wednesday evening happy hour at the Subic officers' club, when all drinks were ten cents apiece.

During the wetting-down party I had a long getting-to-know-you talk with our newest pilot, LTJG Vance Schufeldt, who had recently joined us. Vance was a gregarious, even-tempered young Naval Academy graduate in his mid-twenties. Tall, with a large frame, a baritone voice, a prominent Roman nose, and a serious expression on his face, Vance gave the impression of being several years older than his contemporaries. At six-foot-two he dwarfed "Moose" Lundy and quickly appreciated the humor in Lundy's nickname. Perhaps a bit relieved, Vance admitted that "Moose" had been a nickname given to him by his Naval Academy classmates, and he didn't favor it.

LCDR Don Martin left the squadron while the ship was in Subic. The stress of combat and his forceful approach to everyday chores had coupled to chew up Don's insides. He had developed a bleeding ulcer, and his condition had deteriorated to the point that Dan Lestage recommended surgery. That required a transfer to the Naval Hospital at Oakland, California. Don and I were friends, and I was sorry to see him leave. He had a perceptive wit, was a farsighted planner, and frequently served as a good sounding board for my ideas. But Don's departure meant more than just an interrupted friendship. He was an experienced flight leader, and his absence would mean a larger work load for the rest of us.

We had begun the 1965 cruise with eighteen pilots, three shy of our peacetime allowance. Moose Lundy and Vance Schufeldt had arrived, but the net change had been zero because of the accident that had killed Art Avore and the eye problem that had permanently grounded Russ Weidman. Without Don, we were down to seventeen pilots. Experience told me that, with less than two months remaining in *Oriskany*'s WestPac deployment, the probability was slim that we would see more replacements.

After leaving Subic Bay, *Oriskany* paid a second visit to Hong Kong before returning to Yankee Station, a bonus that had befallen few carriers to date. But we all agreed that we had earned it and managed to keep stiff upper lips as we endured another six days of R and R in WestPac's best liberty port.

Under way from Hong Kong on 29 October, *Oriskany* proceeded directly to Yankee Station. While we were en route, a COD aircraft delivered a load of mail that was a welcome dessert to our second Hong Kong visit. I received three letters from Marilyn, bringing me up to speed on home-front doings and the latest activities of the kids. Another upbeat letter was from my brother Ben, a professor of forestry economics at the University of New Hampshire. Ben described the "Vietnam Perspective" TV program, which had aired early in September. He said that the program had brought him temporary notice as "the brother of the Navy Commander on TV." Alas, he continued, fame had been fleeting. He said that his reputation would be enhanced if I could "arrange another TV appearance."

A blunt missive from my five-year-old daughter, Amy, announced, "DEAR DADDY I AM GOING TO MARY ROBBIE PLEASE SEND ME A PICTURE OF YOUR AIRPLANE." And my four-year-old nephew, Ben's son Daniel, wrote, "Dear Uncle Wyyn why do they cal ships 'shes'?"

I was surprised to receive a copy of a girlie magazine titled *Sir!*, passed on to me by one of our aircraft mechanics. Sandwiched between a story about "world famous" nude models and an exposé called "The Sex Life of the BEATLES" was an article and eleven-photo account of *Oriskany*'s operations on Yankee Station. Surprisingly accurate, the article was well written in a journalistic style more suited to *Time* or *Newsweek*. One of the photos showed me standing beside one of our Skyhawks on *Oriskany*'s flight deck, talking to Don Martin. The photo was captioned, "Squadron commander gives pilot a personal briefing before takeoff." Harry Jenkins kidded me about the magazine article in the presence of the other pilots. "First the Ha Trung bridge was hit on *my* squadron's first combat mission," Harry said. "Then you allowed the CBS thing in *my* squadron's ready room, and now this! Have you executive officers no shame?"

The personal mail enhanced morale, but some of the official mail was irritating. The flag secretary on the staff of Commander Seventh Fleet rejected and returned 250 Air Medal nominations for Air Wing 16 pilots and aircrewmen, submitted when the ship was in Japan some three months earlier. The rejection resulted from our failure to spell out the admiral's *exact* title on each citation. Previously, I had wondered how many people in the Stateside Navy appreciated the fact that there was a war going on. The Air Medal rejections made me wonder how many people in WestPac were aware of the fact. Certainly not the Seventh Fleet commander's flag secretary.

As penance for our bonus visit to Hong Kong, we were assigned to fly the topsy-turvy midnight-to-noon schedule upon our return to Yankee Station. Evening prayer was broadcast in the ship at noon, breakfast was at midnight, and the hours of the ship's convenience store were altered to accommodate the flight schedule. There were some grumbles about "aviator hours" by those few who misunderstood the purpose of the aircraft carrier, but generally the upside-down work routine was accepted as par for the course.

9 Skipper

During my absence for the tactics conference in early October, the Saints participated in an Alfa strike that destroyed a railroad bridge in "Kep country" about thirty-five miles northeast of Hanoi. Bad weather had prevented an immediate follow-on strike against a nearby highway bridge, and a return visit was in the cards as our Halloween trick or treat. In a rare joint effort, large strike groups composed of aircraft from *Oriskany*, planes from Air Wing 7 in *Independence*, and tactical bombers from Air Force units in Thailand were to hit the Kep highway bridge simultaneously.

Harry Jenkins led the *Oriskany*'s strike group, with the *Independence*'s team following close behind. LCDR Trent "Dick" Powers, the operations officer of VA-164, flew a Skyhawk from *Oriskany* to Thailand. There he briefed and led an Iron Hand mission of supporting F-105 fighter-bombers. All told, sixty-five aircraft were involved, the largest single air strike flown against a North Vietnamese target to date.

The enemy was ready with its defenses, and the antiaircraft fire that greeted our planes was fierce. The sky was pockmarked with 37-, 57-, and 85-mm flak bursts in all quadrants, and sixteen SAMs were fired against the American planes. Amazingly, although the SAMs confused matters, none hit their targets, and our aircraft demolished the bridge. *Oriskany*'s Iron Hand element destroyed one of the SAM sites, and the Air Force's F-105s destroyed two others. The successful evasion of sixteen SAMs showed that we were becoming more effective in coping with that threat.

The mission was a success but was not without its toll. Flak hit Dick Powers's Skyhawk, and he was forced to eject directly over the target area in the height of the action. There was a good chute but no way to determine Dick's condition, nor was there any hope of mounting a rescue effort.[1] The loss of Powers colored the mission bittersweet.

The operational tempo and the psychological pressure increased steadily as the days of November ticked by and we edged closer to the end of our combat deployment. *Oriskany* was scheduled to leave the line the day after Thanksgiving, and those of us that survived would be home by Christmas.

In the meantime, Alfa strikes increased in number as we probed deep into North Vietnam against stepped-up defenses. For the first time, pilots were regularly flying two missions a day on Yankee Station. Harry Jenkins led another Alfa strike on 5 November against the Hai Duong highway-railroad bridge, midway between Hanoi and Haiphong. It was our closest approach to Hanoi, only twenty-five miles away. The less-than-expected opposition was a pleasant surprise, but the bombing was inaccurate and the results discouraging.

The intelligence analysts believed the Hai Duong bridge to be still passably intact. That was a certain indication that we soon would be scheduled for another go at it. And the mission was not without its cost. CAPT Harley Chapman of VMF-212, *Oriskany*'s marine fighter squadron, was shot down while flying fighter cover for the strike group. Harley was later confirmed as a POW.

Two days later Charlie Wack earned a Silver Star for his actions during a strike on a SAM complex near Nam Dinh, forty miles southeast of Hanoi. Assigned as Harry Jenkins's alternate strike leader for the mission, Charlie overslept that morning and skipped breakfast to meet the scheduled briefing time. During the launch Harry's aircraft developed a mechanical problem that kept it on deck. Charlie automatically succeeded to the lead position. Heavy flak greeted the strike

---

1. Apparently injured badly by antiaircraft fire or during bailout, Powers died in captivity.

group as it approached Nam Dinh, and Charlie's plane was damaged when an AAA shell burst nearby just as he rolled into his bombing run.

"I didn't haul all those bombs all that way just to jettison them a few seconds short of target," Charlie said later. He disregarded both the damage to his aircraft and his personal safety to continue the attack. The result was the total destruction of six SAM launchers and their associated equipment.

When he pulled off the target after his bombing run and advanced his throttle, Charlie heard rumbling noises from the engine. His aircraft was vibrating heavily, and the engine EGT needle pegged itself on the red line. Yet with AAA fire still zinging around him, Charlie coolly accounted for the other aircraft of the strike group, ensuring that they were all OK and safely clear of the target area. Then he headed for the Gulf. Within seconds, while still over enemy territory, Charlie lost electrical power. Most of his cockpit instruments were inoperative, but Charlie muttered a few silent prayers and managed to nurse his wounded bird out over the Gulf.

Charlie had put several miles of salt water between himself and land before his wingman reported flames burning through the side of the fuselage. When the flight controls went limp, Charlie ejected and plunked down in the Gulf twenty miles offshore. He floated in his life raft for several minutes until an Air Force SA-16 "Albatross" amphibian aircraft touched down and rescued him.

An Air Force flight surgeon on board the Albatross checked Charlie's physical condition. Discovering no injuries, he offered a two-ounce combat ration of medicinal brandy. Charlie accepted. The amphibian set down at Da Nang in South Vietnam shortly after noon. An intelligence officer met Charlie and whisked him off to debriefing. After the routine interrogation, the Air Force intelligence officer allowed that Charlie had probably had a rough morning and offered him another ration of medicinal brandy. Charlie accepted. The crew of the SA-16, by then off duty, corralled Charlie after the debriefing, insisting that he join them for drinks at the DOOM (Da Nang Open Officers Mess). Charlie was the first Navy pilot they had rescued, they said, an event worth celebrating. The earlier slugs of brandy on an empty stomach were having an effect, and at the DOOM Charlie ordered two hamburgers and French fries. A messenger arrived before the food, however. Colonel So-and-so, the base commander, had sent his compliments and invited Charlie to join him at base headquarters. During the ensuing chat, the colonel sympathized with Charlie's rough morning and produced a bottle of scotch and a pair of tumblers from the bottom drawer of his desk. Not wishing to appear unappreciative to our allies in blue, Charlie accepted.

Carrier attack pilots were infrequent visitors at Da Nang, and Charlie managed only a couple of hours of sleep in the late afternoon before Air Force officers again took him to the DOOM and plied him with free drinks.

The next morning Charlie returned to *Oriskany* from Da Nang by COD. Harry Jenkins and I and several other Saints met him on the flight deck to chide him about his impromptu vacation. Charlie's response: "I sure hope I don't get shot down again. I couldn't stand the hangover!"

On 10 November Harry Jenkins received orders directing his detachment from the squadron in December, after our return to Lemoore. Late that evening, when flight operations had been completed for the day, Harry and I sat and talked in the deserted ready room. We discussed the arrangements for the traditional change-of-command ceremony at which I would relieve him as commanding officer of the Saints. Harry kidded about liking his job as skipper of the Saints so much that he might not leave and suggested that I find another squadron in another ship.

Our conversation then shifted to the more somber business at hand. Harry commented on the excellent performance of our pilots and men, how well we had held up under intense operating pressure, and how close we were to the end of our first combat cruise. From the way he talked, I could tell that Harry felt a great deal of pride in his assignment as skipper of a tailhook squadron. Hesitantly, he touched upon the reality of our situation, the daily threat to life and limb. It was a subject almost taboo among pilots. Symbolically knocking on wood, Harry mentioned that the only pilot we had lost so far had been Art Avore. "I hope our luck holds," he said with a sigh. Then he added, "I'm tired, really tired. Not just physically tired, but mentally and emotionally tired. This cruise has taken a lot out of all of us."

The A-1 Skyraider was the only propeller-driven attack aircraft that remained in the Navy's inventory. Its ordnance-carrying capacity made it a formidable weapons platform. The single-engine, single-pilot "Spad" could carry into combat a bomb load greater than that of the famed B-17 Flying Fortress of World War II. The A-1 had a powerful engine and was quite maneuverable at low altitude, but heavily loading down the plane considerably diminished its speed and maneuverability. Because of their vulnerability when carrying heavy bomb loads in the growing SAM environment, the A-1s had been phased out of Alfa strikes except to support rescues.

Paul Merchant had briefed me on an unorthodox rescue role that he was willing to play with his venerable bird in extremis. He showed me how to quickly get into the "hell hole," the ground-accessible maintenance compartment in the belly of the Skyraider. Paul swore that if I got shot down when he was anywhere nearby, he'd land his Spad on the nearest straight stretch of road and pick me up. The display of concern and friendship was encouraging, but the probability of such a dramatic rescue was not great because the Spads and the jets operated in different territories. The Spads' recco missions were generally confined to the southern panhandle of North Vietnam, where the AAA threat was somewhat less and SAMs had not yet been deployed.

The panhandle area was by no means risk free, however, as Paul Merchant learned on the dark night of the day Harry Jenkins got his orders. Paul was on an armed recco mission forty miles southeast of Vinh. Flak hit and badly damaged his aircraft, so Paul jettisoned his bomb load and began to climb, hoping to gain enough altitude to allow him to reach the safety of the Gulf. In short order, however, the engine-oil pressure dropped to zero, the engine quit, and Paul was at the controls of a large glider. In pitch darkness he was faced with a damned-if-you-do/damned-if-you-don't situation. He had enough altitude for a safe parachute opening if he bailed out immediately, but he'd come down on land, and the enemy would almost certainly capture him. The alternative was to stay with the plane and try to reach the water for a dead-stick landing.

Such a landing was dangerous under ideal conditions in broad daylight and nearly unthinkable at night. But Paul rejected the idea of being a willing party to easy capture and stuck with his plane. Several minutes and much sweat later he successfully crash-landed in the Gulf, a courageous feat that was a credit to skillful piloting.

Paul scrambled uninjured from the sinking aircraft into his life raft, and almost immediately he was aware of another problem. The ditching had occurred close to the shoreline, and Paul could hear excited Vietnamese voices drifting across the water from that direction. He quickly contacted a rescue helo via his survival radio, but a successful pickup would hinge upon another crucial judgment call.

To be located by the helo pilot, Paul would have to ignite a signal flare, revealing his location to the enemy as well. The alternative was to be passive, hoping that the enemy wouldn't locate him, hoping that he wouldn't drift toward shore, and taking a chance on a first-light rescue. Always full of nervous energy, Paul was not a passive man. When he heard the sound of rotors close by, he lit the flare. The race was on. The helo won, literally snatching Paul out of the water from under the noses of two boatloads of North Vietnamese. They were within a hundred feet of the life raft when Paul's signal flare created a weird red glow over the scene.

In the same area, south of where Paul was shot down and near the coastal town of Dong Hoi, was a dam and a small reservoir. Near the reservoir lurked a North Vietnamese automatic weapon site that we had nicknamed "One-Shot Charlie," a sobriquet held over from the Korean War. Like his predecessor, One-Shot Charlie was not an overly energetic gunner. Generally, he fired off only a brief burst at any aircraft that ventured near the reservoir. It may have been One-Shot Charlie who had bagged Ed Davis in September.

On the morning of 13 November, three days after Paul Merchant's hairbreadth escape, Harry Jenkins tangled with One-Shot Charlie.

John Shore and I were briefing for an armed recco mission when the strike-operations officer called the ready room on the squawk box. The mission was changed for VA-163's pilots waiting on the flight deck to launch, he said. Dave Small, the squadron duty officer, responded by asking what the new mission was, and the answer was chilling: "Rescue cover for your boss. He's down."

My heart skipped a beat. For several seconds I stared in disbelief at the gray metal squawk box mounted on the bulkhead, as if it had perpetrated a bad joke. Then I told Dave to find another pilot to fly with John and hurried to the ship's strike-operations center to monitor the SAR radio circuit.

Harry and his wingman, Vance Schufeldt, had been flying an

armed recco mission near the Dong Hoi reservoir when they encountered automatic-weapon fire from the ground. Harry radioed that he was going to fly clear of the area. As Vance rogered the transmission, he saw something—perhaps an engine-access panel—fall away from Harry's aircraft. The entire tail section of the plane then became a fireball, and Harry ejected. Seconds later the plane rolled into a steep right bank and exploded. Nine other aircraft were on the scene within minutes in response to Vance's Mayday call, but to no avail. Harry had landed near a rice paddy, and Vance saw a number of people moving toward the skipper's position. Seconds later Vance saw something else—the red flame of a pilot's signal flare on the ground at Harry's position. The flare was a message and was typical of Harry Jenkins's quick thinking. Surrounded and seeing no chance for rescue, Harry had lit the flare to let his fellow pilots know that he was alive.

As I listened to the conversations on the SAR radio circuit, it was soon painfully obvious that Harry was in another "no chance" situation. My head was swimming with confused scenarios as I returned to the ready room. I sat silently for a long time, in a state of mild shock. The news spread, and other Saints, officers and enlisted men, gathered in the ready room to converse in halting, hushed tones.

Absorbed in thought, I was only half aware of their presence or what, if anything, they instinctively expected from me. I struggled to make sense of the circumstance. After sixteen years of working to attain the highly cherished job of commanding a tailhook squadron, it had come to me in a harsh and abrupt manner for which I was not fully prepared. Some thirty-six hours earlier Harry and I had discussed the change-of-command ceremony. I had looked forward to "fleeting up" to the CO's spot with growing excitement, but things hadn't evolved in the traditional manner. Instead, the job was suddenly and unexpectedly and sadly mine. Losing Harry was the wrong way to get it.

Other details of that late-night conversation returned to mind: Harry's joking about liking his job as CO so much that he might not give it up; his playful suggestion that I should find another squadron in another carrier; his prophetic statement about Art Avore's being our only loss; his hoping our luck would hold. That certainly rang with a note of cold irony.

The main reason that I was the squadron's executive officer, the reason that I drew my paycheck, was to take over command if necessary. That was the Navy's system. But that kind of objectivity didn't help. I felt very much alone and inadequate. Also I knew that I couldn't let it show, not for long at any rate. The war would continue as it had in days past, missions would be flown, and the squadron needed leadership. I couldn't wallow in self-pity. The people gathering in the ready room shared the loss and were instinctively looking to me to make the next move, to somehow ease the hurt of losing the head of our official family. The trouble was, I didn't know how to perform that miracle.

We had a strong, well-organized, smooth-working squadron of well-trained and highly competent people. Harry's loss notwithstanding, I knew that the squadron wouldn't suddenly fall apart. We would finish the remaining two weeks of our last line period at the same high level of performance that we had displayed all along. Harry would have settled for nothing less, and I should expect nothing less. But the hurt still didn't stop.

An overflow crowd packed the ready room that evening after flight operations when I briefed the officers and petty officers about the circumstances of Harry's loss. Vance Schufeldt filled in with eyewitness details, and I shared some of my earlier thoughts with the troops, asking for their considerate support as we worked our way through the tragedy and went on to complete the deployment. Normally, at the end of each day of flying I strolled around the ship to visit the squadron's working spaces and chat with the men about the day's activities. But I wasn't up to it that night and asked the petty officers to pass the word to the rest of the men. Paul Merchant came into Ready Five after the meeting broke up and invited me to his stateroom. Dan Lestage, CAG Bob Spruit, and several other pilots joined us. Paul produced a bottle from his stateroom safe, and in what was in essence a quiet wake we chatted and sipped scotch to depress our sorrows.

Four days after Harry Jenkins was shot down we again went after the Hai Duong bridge between Hanoi and Haiphong. We finally destroyed the bridge, but the North Vietnamese threw up a fierce barrage of opposition. Shortly after we completed the attack, LCDR Roy "Hap" Bowling, the squadron's operations officer, was shot down. An antiaircraft shell blew off one of the horizontal stabilizers on the tail of

Hap's Skyhawk as he departed the target area at high speed. Thrown into instant aerodynamic instability, the aircraft executed a series of violent longitudinal rolls. Within seconds it hit the ground and exploded.

LT Larry Spear was flying a few seconds behind Hap and saw a parachute as he zipped past the scene. Making a tight turn at low altitude, Larry next spotted the collapsed chute on the ground but could discern no movement. Hap had landed fifteen miles west of Haiphong in a well-populated area. Larry's presence caused a furious outburst of antiaircraft fire, so he flew clear, broadcasting a Mayday and the location of the downed pilot.

Thirty miles away over the Gulf, flying rescue support in Spads, were banjo player Eric Shade and LCDR Jesse Taylor, the air wing's operations officer. Hearing the Mayday call, they immediately proceeded toward the downed pilot's location. Their first task was to determine if a rescue helo could safely reach the scene. If the helo could get in, Eric and Jesse would suppress the flak. The two spotted the aircraft wreckage but could see no sign of either Hap or his parachute. Intense AAA fire flew up at them, and flak hit both Skyraiders as they beat a hasty retreat toward the Gulf. Eric Shade made it to safety, but Jesse Taylor did not. Before reaching the water, Jesse's plane burst into flames and crashed into the soggy coastal tidelands. Jesse's loss was particularly poignant because he voluntarily flew the rescue-support mission. Formerly a fighter pilot, he was a conscientious air-wing operations officer, wanting to gain as much experience as possible in a variety of combat missions. He had understood and accepted the hazards involved in rescue work and courageously did his best to help a fellow pilot.[2]

The seventeenth of November had been a miserable day. When filing the combat accident report, I listed Hap Bowling as MIA (missing in action), even though the circumstances of his ejection—the low

2. For his unselfish and heroic role in the SAR mission, Jesse Taylor was posthumously awarded the Navy Cross, the second-highest combat decoration. I was privileged to attend the ceremony at which the award was given to his wife and two sons. The Navy's guided-missile frigate USS *Jesse M. Taylor*, launched in 1972, was named in his memory.

level, high speed, rapid roll rate, and high G forces—left little hope that he might be alive. However, as long as there was a remote chance of survival, I couldn't report him as KIA.[3]

Fear in some degree was the constant companion of every pilot. A few vented their fears by outwardly playing macho roles, with bravado and casual disdain of combat hazards. Some were openly frank about their feelings. Others were more stoic, preferring to keep emotions a private matter. Some masked fear with humor. But we all were afraid. I was thankful that not one Saint gave a hint that fear might stand in the way of flying whatever mission he was assigned.

Like most of us, Hap Bowling had had a philosophical attitude about the hazards we faced each day. He was afraid, but there wasn't much he could do about the dangers, and he hoped that his fear didn't show too much. Just before his last mission, Hap Bowling verbally vented his fear in a subtle way. The second Hai Duong bridge strike had been scheduled for each of the four preceding days. Three times we worked late into the night, planning the strike details before grabbing a few hours of fitful sleep. Then we suited up for the mission. But three times bad weather had postponed the strike. As we completed the preflight briefing in Ready Five on the fourth morning, Hap Bowling heaved a sigh and gave me a wry smile.

"I sure hope this mission goes today," he said. "I don't think I can stand another twenty-four hours of this kind of tension."

The mission went that day.

A message from Washington, D.C., received in the evening after Hap Bowling and Jesse Taylor were shot down, brought a bit of pleasant news to an otherwise bleak day. Orders from the Chief of Naval Personnel officially assigned me as the commanding officer of VA-163. For five days I had been acting CO, but in the minds of the rest of the Saints, as well as my own, I was still the XO. Still the number two guy, a temporary holder of Harry Jenkins's job. The message was only

---

3. Hap Bowling apparently died during or shortly after his shoot down. Initially, he was listed as a POW, but that status was never confirmed. He was carried as MIA for nearly eleven years. In 1976, without amplifying details or other explanation, the Vietnamese government returned his remains to the U.S. for burial.

a piece of paper, but it triggered a subtle change in attitude. The system had spoken. Without mention of his name, Harry Jenkins had been detached from duty with VA-163, and I was the new commanding officer. Shortly thereafter, Bob Hofford was the first person in the squadron to address me as "Skipper." The title felt strange at first, but at the same time it gave me a feeling of confidence and reassurance that had been missing during the past several days of sorrow.

10 Homeward Bound

 For political and public-relations purposes, the Johnson administration was by late 1965 trying to place as good a face as possible on the war in Vietnam. From my seat in the cockpit, however, I was convinced that there was no good face. Restraints placed on the conduct of the air war over North Vietnam clearly indicated a deep reluctance to take effective advantage of the air superiority possessed by the United States.

As *Oriskany* approached her date of rotation back to the States, the air war against North Vietnam was entering its second year. But we were no closer to seriously curbing the enemy's real war-making potential than we had been in May when we arrived in the war zone. The sanctuaries, target restrictions, and periodic bombing pauses had badly diffused the effectiveness of Operation Rolling Thunder. Within the Pentagon, determining whether we were winning or losing the strategically static northern air war had become difficult if not impossible. To help with the analysis, someone in the "E" ring of Mr. McNamara's "Puzzle Palace" developed a theory of how to measure the effectiveness of air power quantitatively. One aircraft flying one mission equaled one sortie. A sortie was something that could be measured, assimilated by a computer, reduced to formulae, divided into dollar amounts, and analyzed for cost effectiveness. Never mind about combat effectiveness.

By November 1965 it seemed to me that daily sortie production had become an end in itself, even to the extent of ignoring the practical considerations of unsafe flying conditions and pilot overutilization. Since we had little control over that aspect of our lives, however, pilot frustrations typically found relief in wry, sometimes black, humor. At naval air stations back in the States, posters prominently reminded pilots and other aviation personnel, "Of all our operations, SAFETY is paramount!" In Ready Room Five, the flight-scheduling officer Larry DeSha, after working hours to juggle the availability of the pilots against a frequently amended daily mission plan, posted his own notice: "Of all our operations, GETTIN' THEM SORTIES OUT is paramount!"

The first ten days of our November line period were spent on a midnight-to-noon operating schedule, and another ten days consisted of noon-to-midnight flying. On 21 November *Oriskany* was slated to shift again to the midnight-to-noon schedule. Previously, a carrier was allowed a twenty-four-hour stand down to accommodate the shift. However, for our late-November changeover we were blessed with a modified transition. Someone at the task-force commander's level had become concerned with the gaps that existed in our coverage of the North Vietnamese recco routes. There was a loss of sorties when a carrier was allowed something as unproductive as a twenty-four-hour stand down. Thus, a modification to the schedule extended our flying day to eighteen hours and reduced the minivacation time. Our working day on 21 November began before noon and continued without interruption until after 0600 the following morning. But even the additional sorties gained thereby apparently weren't enough.

During our extended operating day, the A-4 squadrons were assigned additional, "special" night missions. Regular night recco missions involved from 1.9–2.3 hours of flight time, only about 40 percent of which was devoted to hunting and attacking targets. The balance was eaten up in the postlaunch rendezvous, transit between the ship and target areas, and return to the ship. The special missions were designed so that Skyhawks could carry more bombs and remain on station over the beach for longer periods—3.5–4 hours. Dedicated tankers would be provided for each pair of truck-hunting Skyhawks to permit the extra flight time. The additional time over the beach would reduce the gaps in coverage, and voilà!, more truck kills would result.

Staff planners didn't bother to check the theory in advance with the people who did the night recco flying. That was disappointing. The proposal caught CAG Spruit, Skipper Jack Shaw of VA-164, and me by surprise, and we wasted little time in expressing our concerns to the staff operations officer.

There were basic flaws in the dedicated-tanker idea. It could increase the total airborne time of two recco aircraft but not necessarily the productive over-the-beach recco time. Additional fuel wasn't needed early in a mission when recco aircraft were carrying full loads. It was needed later, however, and getting it then would require a time-consuming interruption while the aircraft returned to a safe airspace over the Gulf to meet the tanker. In addition, nighttime aerial fueling was more difficult than daylight. I was thankful the staff hadn't proposed that the night fueling be conducted over enemy territory during the recco mission itself.

But even if the night-fueling hurdle could be successfully cleared, the proposed special mission still would just be tinkering with parts of the overall puzzle. Carrying more bombs meant either carrying fewer flares to illuminate the targets or increasing the weight-drag factor, which in turn would increase fuel consumption. Aircraft availability and pilot utilization also had to be considered. Four pilots and four aircraft would have to be dedicated to each special mission—two "go" birds, a spare as backup, and a tanker. The number of "buddy stores" we had available on board *Oriskany* limited the total number of Skyhawks that we could configure as tankers. Each time we guaranteed fuel for a pair of recco birds, we would have one fewer tanker available for solving fuel-shortage problems around the ship during aircraft recovery.

Finally, we argued, the assumption that double-cycle night recco missions would result in more truck kills was faulty. Except for an occasional lucky find such as our daylight "turkey shoot" in early September, a given pair of recco aircraft seldom discovered large numbers of trucks, day or night. Grubbing around at low altitude and hunting for authorized targets, not attacking them, ate up the majority of any armed recco flight.

The staff operations officer seemed only minimally impressed by our objections. My guess was that he considered us spoilsports, unwilling to try an innovative tactic. Perhaps he was under some career-influencing pressure from upstairs, but most certainly he'd never been in the cockpit of an A-4 over North Vietnam at night. He insisted that the special missions be launched, but he gave in a bit to our resistance. The initial requirement for four sets of special-mission aircraft and tankers was reduced to two, and the missions would be a trial run.

Jack Shaw and I scheduled ourselves to lead the special missions. We didn't want to foist upon subordinates in our squadrons the job of flying half-baked missions we neither invented nor endorsed. The weather in the Gulf was terrible and getting worse when the special mission's 1830 launch time rolled around on 21 November. Jack Shaw's participation turned to worms even as he and his wingman were launching from *Oriskany*. Aircraft returning from other missions were making instrument approaches through the heavy weather. Two aircraft needed extra fuel, and the airborne duty tanker developed a malfunction that prevented fuel transfer. The tanker "dedicated" to Jack Shaw's special mission was diverted as a replacement. Jack and his wingman flew around in the lousy weather at the tanker-rendezvous point for a fuel-consuming twenty-five minutes before being informed of any change in plan. By then the prospect of completing even a single-cycle mission was slim. An irritated Jack Shaw exercised a pilot's prerogative and canceled his mission.

Moose Lundy was my wingman, and at our rendezvous point we darted in and out of the clouds, awaiting our tanker. I had arbitrarily decided to take on as much fuel as possible early in the game rather than playing mission interruptus later. If we waited, we might miss the tanker when we really needed a drink. Anyway, the prospects of completing a double-cycle mission had diminished considerably by the time our tanker made the rendezvous. He was late because his aircraft had been buried in the pack on the flight deck, and his was the last plane to be launched.

We headed for the beach and took on extra fuel as close as possible to our recco area. That took more minutes while Moose and I topped off in the skittish weather. When we left the tanker over the Gulf and descended toward our coast-in point, I mentally translated the extra fuel into extra recco time over the beach. I came up with 12–15 minutes.

The low-level weather was also miserable. Moose and I dodged in and out of rain showers and the low-hanging overcast. Our flares illuminated various roads and choke points, but we found no targets. I spent half my time avoiding mountains, fighting vertigo, and trying not to get lost. Even if we had spotted trucks, there was an even chance that the cloud ceiling would have been too low for safe bombing. I decided that we wouldn't come close to a double-cycle mission and arbitrarily abbreviated the unproductive effort. I illuminated an unimportant small bridge as our target for the night. We dropped our bombs and headed for home.

The weather over the Gulf had deteriorated since our departure. Moose and I separated at the marshal point astern the ship and descended into the clouds on individual instrument approaches. I broke out of the overcast at 400 feet. It was dark, but I could see wave tops whipped white by the surface wind. I wrestled with the controls for a couple of minutes until I spotted the ball. Mustering my very best piloting skills, I got aboard the heavily pitching deck, ringing wet with sweat but still in one piece. I prayed that Moose, behind me, didn't experience another "glad to be alive" night. Thankfully, he didn't.

My debriefing with the staff operations officer was a one-sided conversation. I pointed out the inadvisability of augmenting an already busy flight schedule with any more special missions. Beyond that, I questioned the need for any more flight operations that night because of the lousy weather and the pitching deck.

Back in Ready Five, as the twenty-two-hour transition flying period progressed, it became obvious that even the best efforts of our maintenance crews would not meet the extended demand for aircraft. When we ran out of up birds, the 0130 launch, my second mission of the night, was rescheduled for 0430, and I went to my room to nap. Sometime during my slumber the powers that be decided to cancel all flight operations because of the weather. The subject of special missions was never mentioned again.

Air Wing 16's last major effort of the 1965 cruise was an Alfa strike against the Me Xa (May-Zah) railroad-highway bridge. It was five miles from the Hai Duong bridge that we had destroyed the previous week. Hai Duong had been a hotbed of opposition, resulting in the loss of two pilots, and there was no reason to expect that the reception at Me Xa would be any friendler. The strike had been postponed twice for bad weather, and we were again caught up in that stomach-souring go/no-go tension. When we finally flew the mission on 24 November, the North Vietnamese air defenses hardly reacted at all. A single SAM warning was broadcast, based on the detection of a Fan Song radar sig-

nal, but no missile was fired. Equally pleasant was the lack of antiaircraft fire. The Me Xa milk run prompted John Shore to suggest later
that the North Vietnamese had used up their November allowance of
missiles and ammunition, and perhaps that idea was not too far from
the truth.

Poor weather persisted. In the next few days the night missions
were scrubbed, and only a handful of armed recco missions were
flown in the early daylight hours. Shortly after noon on the twenty-
sixth the last aircraft landed. Captain Connolly turned *Oriskany* to the
southeast, ordered 28 knots, and headed for Subic Bay. We enjoyed
Thanksgiving dinner that evening, a day late, but the timing was
appropriate.

I felt the psychological pressure decrease sharply when the last of
our planes safely recovered. Two weeks had elapsed since I had taken
command of the Saints. Two weeks that seemed like six months. Two
weeks of tragedy and taut nerves, but we managed to get through it.
The adventuresome, beginning-of-the-cruise enthusiasm was gone,
replaced by a sober maturity and a few emotional scars.

En route to Subic Bay, I reread some mail received earlier but only
scanned at the time. CDR Ron Caldwell, with whom I had gone
through the Skyhawk training course at Lemoore, wrote that he would
soon report to VA-163 as my executive officer. The squadron had not
yet received official notification of Ron's orders.

A letter from LCDR Bernie White, who was in training at Lemoore
and was slated to become a Saint, talked about the Skyhawk portion of
the TF-77 Tactics Annex that I had helped write in October. I had
mailed a bootleg copy to the CO of the training squadron and was
pleased to discover that it was a hot item back home, locally repro-
duced and distributed to all of Lemoore's Skyhawk squadrons. But it
was discouraging to learn that my backdoor copy had been the only
tactical information available from the horse's mouth to assist in training pilots for combat. Carrier combat operations from Yankee Station
were almost a year old, yet it appeared that no effective system had
been developed to automatically feed the lessons learned from combat
to the people who needed them for training. An "urgent requirement"
to compile and disseminate those lessons had pulled me out of the
cockpit and sent me scurrying to Yokosuka early in October. For dis-
semination to whom? I wondered. The finished product of the tactics

conference was already a month and a half old, but conspicuous by its absence. I felt smug about my role as a bootlegger. Maybe I had contributed something to the war effort more significant than merely filling in boxes on the Pentagon's great chart of combat sorties flown.

A third letter had done a lot for my morale during the last two hectic weeks on Yankee Station. It was from Bob Hofford's wife, Beverly, who wrote that my wife, Marilyn, had been "a rock for the other wives to lean upon" after the loss of Harry Jenkins and Hap Bowling. I knew that Marilyn would do a good job, but it was nice to read the compliment. Several times I had reread Beverly's closing words: "I guess you know how lucky you are on the home front, but I just wanted to say it. God bless you in your command."

With combat worries behind us, VA-163's pilots looked ahead to the flyoff to Lemoore when *Oriskany* neared the California coast some nineteen days hence. We had expected to leave most of our aircraft at Cubi Point as replacements for other deployed squadrons, transporting only few to the States for transfer to an overhaul facility. At the last moment, however, I was directed to take all fourteen Skyhawks to Lemoore, and that order gave birth to concern about the flyoff.

We'd begun the deployment with eighteen pilots and gained Moose Lundy and Vance Schufeldt but lost Art Avore, Harry Jenkins, and Hap Bowling in combat. Don Martin had been hospitalized, and Russ Weidman was permanently grounded with eye trouble. With fifteen bodies to fill fourteen cockpits, the problem was deciding who would *not* fly off. The married pilots eagerly anticipated going home to their families in Lemoore, but only one of the seven bachelor pilots would be able to ride the ship to San Diego. That Southern California port was a paradise for bachelors compared to Lemoore. Plus it featured major airline service to all points for people on leave. I was amused at the problem—the need to pass judgment on the flyoff concerns of a group of men who only recently had regularly risked their butts in combat. I promised only that the identity of the nonflyoff pilot would be revealed before the ship reached Hawaii, allowing ample time to notify loved ones and make Stateside transportation arrangements.

The 1965 Army-Navy football game was played in Philadelphia on Saturday, 27 November. But it occurred in the wee hours of Sunday morning the twenty-eighth in the Philippines, some nine thousand miles to the west. We held a "thank God it's over and Go Navy" party that night at the Cubi Point officers club, made more festive by the presence of our brethren from the carrier *Enterprise* and Air Wing 9. That ship was also in port at Cubi, bound for Yankee Station and her first combat exposure. As a precaution, the commanding officers of the two carriers had earlier lectured their people on the necessity of avoiding any incidents stemming from the excessive intake of liquor and an exaggerated sense of which ship/air-wing team was the best.

VF-162 had a young pilot nicknamed "Gomer" by his fellow pilots because he reminded them of the awkward but lovable TV character, Gomer Pyle. Our Gomer was a big man with a bull-in-a-china-shop reputation after a few drinks. Following Captain Connolly's admonition, CDR Ken Horn, skipper of VF-162, personally counseled Gomer about his conduct at the *Oriskany-Enterprise* party. Gomer guaranteed that he would behave. And so he did until the early morning hours. During halftime of the Army-Navy game, Gomer visited the men's room. While Gomer was standing at a urinal, an inebriated pilot from *Enterprise* stepped to an adjacent urinal and focused his bleary eyes on Gomer.

"Are you from Rish-kny?" the Big E flyer asked.

"Yes, sir, I sure am," Gomer replied politely. The tipsy officer pondered the answer for several moments, then announced, "Rish-kny sucks!"

A few moments later RADM Hank Miller, the carrier-division commander embarked in *Enterprise*, Captain Connolly, and CAPT Jim Holloway, the Big E's skipper, were interrupted as they conversed at a table. Standing at attention and earnestly trying to appear at least semi-sober, Gomer addressed himself to Connolly:

"Captain, I'd like to turn myself in."

"For what?" Connolly replied.

"Some guy from *Enterprise* said, '*Oriskany* sucks.' I decked him. He's on the floor in the men's john with his face against the urinal."

Before Connolly could respond, Admiral Miller entered the conversation.

"Did he really say that to you, son?"

"Yessir," said Gomer.

"Well, good for you," the admiral continued. "Those guys were told not to bad-mouth *Oriskany*. Sit down, son, and have a drink with us."

The admiral dispatched his aide to see to the sore-jawed officer in the men's room, and Gomer's confession was the only unusual incident of the evening—except for the disappointing score of the football game: Army 7, Navy 7.

Before leaving Subic, I finished and mailed the final monthly "Saints Newsletter" to the squadron's wives, parents, and families. Harry Jenkins began the newsletter early in the cruise and had received many warm and friendly letters of thanks from wives, mothers, and sweethearts who appreciated reading about what their men were doing in the war. For the newsletter of our last and saddest month, I used the notes that Harry had kept for that purpose. Also, I included the remarks that Harry had prepared for the change-of-command ceremony that we had planned for late December. The words told of how Harry felt about the squadron and the folks back home:

> Since I can remember, I have wanted to command a "tailhook" squadron. I could not have been given a finer command. Together we have done things no other squadron in history has done. As a unit we have tasted the sweetness of combat victory and have shared the deep sorrow of losing shipmates and comrades. We have shared our family tragedies and wept for relatives we didn't know because they were part of us. I have never observed an instance where anyone put himself above the squadron and nothing ever made me feel prouder than to be called "Skipper."
>
> This change of command marks an end to my career at the level where I can be identified with a working aviation unit. It also marks a parting with you men, for whom I've gained the greatest respect and admiration. And, I cannot leave without thanking you wives and families of this squadron, who accept and share the long months of loneliness, and whose letters of love, encouragement, and prayers often made it possible for your men to work miracles. Without you we'd have been much less.
>
> To each of you men, thank you, and I hope someday to share with you the memories of this past year.

In a final paragraph, I added, "Thank *you*, Harry, for all you did.

May God watch over you and bring you safely back to us."[1]

Oriskany was underway at 0800 on 30 November 1965, steaming northward through the Balintang Channel of Luzon Strait and eastward toward Hawaii. By the time we reached the quay wall at North Island in San Diego, we would have been deployed for 265 days, spending 210 of those days at sea. Around delightful visits to Yokosuka and Hong Kong, *Oriskany* and Air Wing 16 had made a credible mark in naval annals. In 141 days on the line, we had chalked up 14,750 air-combat missions, more that any carrier had previously logged in American naval history. In Ready Room Five we were proud that the Saints, short-handed in pilots and but one of five squadrons making up *Oriskany*'s air wing, had flown 23 percent of those combat sorties. Air Wing 16's pilots had earned 1 Navy Cross, 5 Silver Stars, 56 Distinguished Flying Crosses, 120 Navy Commendations, 7 Purple Hearts, and 929 Air Medals. But our record was not cheap. Left behind were fourteen pilots dead, missing in action, or confirmed as POWs. In the press releases announcing our homecoming, Air Wing 16 was touted as heroes, but none of us felt very heroic. We were just thankful to be heading home.

The Saints maintenance crews gave us 100-percent availability for our arrival off the California coast, ensuring that all fourteen of our planes were up and ready to launch to Lemoore. There was a special feeling among the crews on the flight deck on the morning of 15 December as the pilots manned their aircraft for the last time in the deployment. Only the fourteen flyoff pilots would arrive at home base that day; the other 126 Saints, officers and enlisted men, would arrive in Lemoore some forty-eight hours later, after riding the ship to San Diego. But there was excitement among all squadron personnel. We were a close-knit unit, and the flyoff was official confirmation that the deployment was over, that we really were going home. I saw the excitement in the face of Henry Baron, my young plane captain from Phoenix, Arizona, as he helped strap me into the cockpit of my Sky-

---

1. He did. On 12 February 1973, after seven years and four months as a POW, Harry was repatriated. He and Jim Stockdale were on the first POW-evacuation plane out of Hanoi. And Harry got his wish. In July 1973 former Saints from all over the country and as far away as Guam converged on San Diego to share their memories at a squadron reunion picnic.

hawk. He was all grin. Before he dismounted from the plane, he patted my shoulder and said, "Welcome home, Skipper." As the ship turned into the wind and I taxied forward to the catapult, I glanced over my shoulder at the island. On every deck and catwalk, spectators crowded every inch of available viewing space.

It was a clear day with excellent visibility as thirteen other Saints rendezvoused with me and headed toward California in a loose-goose tactical formation. It was the first time in almost a year that we'd had that many planes together in the air without having enemy flak awaiting us on the other end.

Hundreds of people—families, friends, and well-wishers—greeted us at Lemoore as we taxied up to the squadron's hangar. A nice pre-Christmas present was the concert by bands from the air station and Lemoore High School. They belted out "California, Here I Come," "Hello, Dolly!" "I'll Be Home For Christmas," and other festive tunes. Huge welcoming banners hung from the hangar's walls, and reporters and cameramen from local newspapers and TV stations were on hand, busily recording us for the next edition of the news. With Marilyn on the ramp was my seventy-four-year-old mother, who had flown in from Arizona for the gala event. My six-year-old daughter, Amy, carried a homemade sign that proclaimed:

W E L C O M
E H O M E D
A D D Y

My fourteen-year-old daughter, Cori, decked out in a new outfit that included high heels and a touch of makeup, looked very grown up, making my seven-month absence from the family circle seem like a lot longer. My son, Scott, was bursting with pride as he enthused about the influence I wielded as commanding officer of a squadron. First, I had arranged to have the CBS program "Vietnam Perspective," in which I appeared, broadcast on 6 September, his older sister's birthday. Then I had arranged to have the squadron fly home to Lemoore on 15 December, *his* twelfth birthday.

Being home was delightful, being in Marilyn's arms again, being able to spend Christmas with her and the children, and having the opportunity to recreate some semblance of normal family life. Unfortunately, circumstances did not permit my thoughts to stray very far from my official family, the squadron.

Although the war was temporarily out of sight, it couldn't be put out of mind. In peacetime a squadron's turnaround between deployments normally lasted nine months to a year. *Oriskany* and Air Wing 16 were scheduled to deploy again to Vietnam in late May 1966. A thirty-day stand down, permitting an official postdeployment vacation for the squadron's personnel, happily coincided with the Christmas holidays. By mid-January, however, the clock would start counting down our preparations for another deployment. In the meantime, the squadron would have significant personnel changes, replace almost all our aircraft, and try to work our way through a lengthy list of training requirements. Deducting the thirty-day stand down, I had a few days longer than four months to get the squadron ready for another trip to WestPac. It was obvious that we'd be operating under pressure during our short stay at home base, and something would have to give. My concern was ensuring that that something wouldn't be the squadron's morale.

With most of the squadron's personnel on leave and only a skeleton crew remaining behind, we transferred four aircraft to other Lemoore squadrons soon to deploy, and four other A-4s were sent for overhaul to the Naval Air Rework Facility in Alameda, California. We were promised a full bag of fourteen planes by the time we deployed in May, including four brand-new Skyhawks fresh off the Douglas production line at Palmdale, California. In the interim, we'd have to make do with six birds, two of which would always be in down status for maintenance and engine checks. We'd have only four planes available for pilot training when the full squadron returned to work in January.

Ron Caldwell had reported on board as the new XO. A cheerful bear of a man with a measured approach to his tasks, Ron quickly relieved me of worry over routine administrative matters. Russ Weidman and Duke Tyler, their tours with the squadron completed, were transferred to new duty stations. Don Martin returned, his bout with stomach surgery successfully behind him, and several Saints-to-be were in the pilot-training pipeline at Lemoore, soon to report for duty.

The initial stability of the pilot ranks was short-lived, however. We'd been home exactly one week when CAG Spruit summoned Jack Shaw and me to his office and related an urgent directive received by telephone from ComNavAirPac headquarters in San Diego. Each of our squadrons was to swap three pilots with an Atlantic Fleet A-4 squadron, and those pilots were to be identified within twenty-four hours. The only guideline was that the pilots must have completed at least five months of the recent combat cruise. That part was easy since it included all of VA-163's pilots except Moose Lundy and Vance Schufeldt, who had joined the squadron in mid-cruise. I asked CAG what he thought the reaction might be at ComNavAirPac headquarters if I submitted my own name for transfer to an East Coast squadron.

Beneath the levity, the directive disturbed me. There was no doubt in my mind that the pilots who remained would view the transfers to an East Coast squadron as a good deal, a longer, albeit temporary, reprieve from combat. Moreover, most of the pilots were away on postdeployment leave, and the three selected for transfer would have to be recalled to Lemoore promptly, disrupting their holiday plans. Most of all, I was disturbed by the absence of clear logic in the directive. The folks at ComNavAirPac knew damn well that the squadron was only one week into a month-long postdeployment stand down and that most of the squadron's personnel were absent on leave. A wish to accomplish the swap quickly to avoid any adverse impact on predeployment training no doubt influenced high-level thinking. But ComNavAirPac's personnel department apparently hadn't talked to the aircraft-assignments people. With only four flyable planes in our inventory, the Saints weren't going to cut a wide swath in the pilot-training business when we returned to work in January.

Personally, the directive was distasteful because it came just before Christmas, casting me in the role of Scrooge. I would decide who would *not* get a temporary reprieve from combat. No matter how carefully made, my selections could have an adverse effect on the attitudes of the pilots who didn't get picked. But making decisions was why the Navy paid me to be a skipper, so I closeted myself with Ron Caldwell to review the options. Ron didn't yet know the other pilots well, but that was helpful. He could apply greater objectivity, a quality I found elusive at the moment.

One choice was easy and, admittedly, influenced by emotion. Unassuming and efficient Larry DeSha was an excellent pilot, and his combat experience would have made him a valuable section leader when we returned to Yankee Station. But Larry was about to bid adieu to bachelorhood, having departed on leave to get married. The promise of a honeymoon a bit longer than his present squadron could afford was the nicest wedding present that came to my mind. The other two selections weren't so easy, and I made them only after Ron and I had had an extended discussion—a mental wrestling match for me—on the subject of reward versus readiness. My mind told me that the Saints should deploy in May in the best possible state of readiness, meaning that I should keep the most qualified men, the combat-experienced pilots. My heart told me that those same pilots had earned top priority for the transfer opportunity.

Eventually, I opted for readiness, transferring the two pilots in whom I had the least confidence. One was a pleasant young man but a weak performer. The other was an adequate performer who had been a problem child since he first joined the squadron, a quintessential rebel who tested authority at every opportunity until it became a game with him. The rebel was being sent to a Skyhawk squadron at Cecil Field in Florida, skippered by CDR Jim Scott, a longtime friend of mine. Responding to a twinge of conscience, I telephoned Jim to explain my reasons for sending the pilot in question. After listening to my long and careful rationale, Jim merely chuckled and said, "Wait until you meet the 'hippie' I've sent to you."

The Saints' pilot ranks were fattened in February when four junior pilots, "nuggets" fresh from flight training, reported for duty. LTJG Pete Munro and LTJG Fritz Schroeder were outgoing, personable young men with good flight records. Except for the newness of it all they had no difficulty adapting to the squadron's routine.

ENS Dan Kapner was the consummate newboy. Hollywood couldn't have done a better job of typecasting the role. Although he was himself a qualified pilot, Dan was somewhat naive and seemed bewildered to find himself in the company of real fleet pilots. Dan was in his mid-twenties, no younger than the other new pilots, but he acted like a kid. With great tolerance and benevolence, the experienced pilots called him "Kap" and looked upon him more as a younger brother than as a member of their peer group. His habit of sucking hard candy during flight briefings contributed to his image and once prompted Larry Spear to chide him gently, "You shouldn't eat so much candy, Kap. It'll rot your teeth."

The fourth new pilot, LTJG Wayne Cypress, was an enigma from the first day I met him. He was polite and militarily proper but seemed uncomfortable in the squadron atmosphere. I couldn't put my finger on the reason, but his face always seemed to hint at a vague unhappiness. He carried out his assignments adequately but tended to remain on the fringe of the daily activity, at a psychological arm's length from the good-natured repartee of the ready room. And Wayne seemed always a little too much in awe of me as the commanding officer.

John Shore, having survived both combat with the Vietnamese and almost a year of flying as my wingman, had graduated to section-leader status, and I was looking for a replacement wingman. Because of Dan Kapner's seeming naïveté, and perhaps with a bit of big-brother instinct on my own part, I selected him as my new wing-man.

The swap pilots came on board shortly after the nuggets arrived. From Atlantic Fleet squadrons came LT Frank Hughes, LTJG Wayne Soliday, and LTJG Louie Nordby. All were well-qualified Skyhawk pilots and quickly fit into the rhythm of the squadron.

Hughes was a graduate of the Naval Academy, intense, energetic, enthusiastic, resourceful. A former football player, he had a physique that called to mind a fire plug, and the other pilots quickly tagged him with the nickname "Buddha."

Wayne Soliday was quiet and reserved, at times seeming almost mousy, but he soon displayed maturity and precision in everything he did, particularly in his flying skills.

"Big Louie" Nordby was the hippie whom Jim Scott had sent to become a Saint. An unconventional individual, not exactly the model the Navy would select to pose for a recruiting poster, Louie nonetheless was gregarious and relaxed. And, to my relief, he was devoid of the authority-challenging traits of the pilot he replaced. Most important, like Soliday, Louie Nordby was an excellent aviator. After observing Louie for a few weeks, I decided that I had come off best in the swap with Jim Scott. Louie Nordby was a much better pilot than he pretended to be.

At three months and counting before deployment we still had only four flyable aircraft. That created a flight-scheduling problem because we then had nineteen pilots on board against an allowance of twenty-one. We kept the planes in the air as much as possible, but I was frustrated that our plans for training the pilots in combat tactics were progressing slowly. The pilots and men got a maximum of the needed ground training, but otherwise I refused to create nonflying busywork. With so few planes, the troops enjoyed a lot of time off.

We received our eight replacement planes in March, putting everyone back to full-time employment. In one week's time, we received seven aircraft, including the four brand-new Skyhawks flown to us directly from the Douglas production line.

We had to do acceptance checks to ensure that the new aircraft and all of their component systems were in top operating shape. Part of the acceptance process was painting the aircraft with unique markings for visual identification. On delivery, each new bird bore the U.S. insignia on its wings and fuselage and the standard Navy markings. Our maintenance crews added large three-digit identification numbers on the nose section, and the "AH" (Air Wing 16) code and a boomerang symbol on the vertical tail sections. The Saints' ID numbers were in the 300 series, and our boomerang color was blue.

Additionally, the name of a pilot and the assigned plane captain would be painted on the fuselage of each plane, just below the cockpit. Putting the names of the plane captains on the aircraft acknowledged their daily hard work, and the association of a plane with a particular pilot was a traditional perk accorded to the fourteen most senior pilots. As skipper, my plane would be AH 301; Ron Caldwell's name would appear on 302, and so on. The symbolic ownership seldom was a consideration when matching planes to pilots on a given day's flight schedule, but a pilot generally could arrange to fly "his" plane if it happened to be available.

Don Martin, the fourth-senior pilot and the head of the squadron's aircraft-maintenance department, came into my office one morning with a cheery greeting and a question. "Skipper, my crews are going to start painting the new birds, and I wondered if you've picked out three-zero-one." I hadn't had the opportunity to fly any of the new planes and hadn't given "my" plane any thought, but Don's question tweaked my curiosity. Was his query merely an RHIP (rank has its privileges) courtesy? He was the overall supervisor of the squadron's aircraft maintenance and no doubt was the most familiar with the relative qualities of the planes we had received.

"Have you got one picked out for yourself?" I asked, innocently.

Don took the bait. "Yes, sir, bureau number 152100."

"Sounds good to me," I replied with a smile. "I'll take that one."

Don's jaw dropped momentarily, then he broke into a broad grin. "Yes, sir, you got me on that one." He went on to explain that bureau number 152100 was the last to be produced in the A-4E series of Skyhawks. Subsequent versions of the airframe would bear the A-4F designation.

Having selected my own plane, I made up my mind always to use 301 if it was available when I was scheduled to fly.

In the midst of my concerns about getting the squadron ready to return to combat, I found time to get embroiled in a minor administrative brouhaha about officers' uniform insignia. I'd seen no evidence among the Saints, but some junior Navy officers had revolted against the system. They'd had their uniforms striped with an unauthorized gold-colored nylon braid rather than the prescribed but more expensive French gold lace. The minirevolt had prompted a missive from the Chief of Naval Personnel (ChNavPers) cautioning against such unauthorized decor.

The prescribed striping material was more attractive than the nylon but tarnished easily when exposed to salt air. Also it didn't fare too well under dry cleaning. The nylon material was more durable, but it had an unattractive, artificial look. At about the same time that ChNavPers issued his warning, the Secretary of the Navy issued a report of the findings of a special board that he had appointed to look into morale-enhancing changes in the Navy. One of the board's recommendations was that more economical and durable uniform insignia should be considered. Earlier, I had seen a sample of a commercially developed, nontarnishing, gold-anodized aluminum braid. The aluminum product had the attractiveness of French gold lace but purportedly avoided the artificial look.

I prepared a letter to ChNavPers, recommending that a synthetic substitute for gold lace "such as the experimental gold-anodized aluminum" be investigated and considered for testing. CAG Spruit gave my letter a favorable endorsement, and off it went up the chain of command.

I had forgotten about the letter when Bob called me to his office several weeks later. He smiled as he handed me a sheaf of papers. The synthetic-braid matter had progressed no farther than the desk of the Commander Fleet Air's (ComFAir) chief staff officer at Alameda, California. ComFAir was the air wing's administrative boss while we were based ashore. Attached to my letter was a personal note to "Dear Bob" from Captain Fuddy-Duddy, the CSO. In a thinly disguised tail-chewing, Fuddy-Duddy pointedly said that my letter "didn't represent the standards we desire." He snootily referred to my "first try at command" and admonished Bob that his job was to help me through my "trial period as commanding officer." And the help was to be provided "in other than a perfunctory manner."

It was obvious that the CSO viewed my recommendation to ChNavPers as some form of heresy. He said that he had "taken the liberty" of removing the letter from the chain of command and returning it, "rather than spreading it [sic] throughout the whole fleet."

No question about it, I had touched a sensitive "old Navy" nerve. But there was nothing in the rejection to indicate why that nerve was sensitive. The CSO made no comment about the merit of my proposal but merely gave it a summary rejection. Since I was busy at my "first try at command," getting the squadron ready to go back to war, I dropped the matter, concluding that Captain Fuddy-Duddy either had misinterpreted my intent or, because of some raging blind prejudice, had completely missed the point.[2]

More pleasing than the return of my official correspondence was a letter from the first-grade class at the Lemoore air station's elementary school. Earlier, I had invited the class, which included my daughter Amy, to visit the squadron's hangar on a field trip. The invitation was accepted, and Ron Caldwell had arranged an excellent experience for the children. The squadron's personnel created fun things to do, as well as to see, and a mound of cookies and five gallons of punch were consumed with gusto. The post-visit letter, probably written by the classmate with the best penmanship, apparently was a collective effort:

A visit to the hangar We went to the hangar yesterday. We visited VA-163. We saw airplanes we saw a one man plane it is a jet. We looked at it. We saw a bunch of buttons and a seat. We saw two planes starting we saw a prop plane they had

---

2. About four years later, after a satisfactory fleet test, ChNavPers approved a durable, nontarnishing substitute for the French gold lace.

orange tails. We saw a parachute pack. We got to ride in it. We liked the ride. A man blew up a life raft by pulling a string. Only one man can get into it. The life raft is in the airplane in case the pilot is shot down or didn't have any gas the pilot can blow up his raft and float. We got cookies and juice. Thank you for letting us come. Signed Mrs. McAuleys class.

The thank-you letter from Mrs. McAuley's pupils had a lot more class than my rejection slip from ComFAir's chief staff officer. I asked Ron Caldwell to have the kids' letter posted where the troops could read it.

In late March and early April carrier-landing practice and coordinated-air-wing predeployment training on board *Oriskany* occupied much of our time. I led one simulated Alfa strike against an "airfield" in the Chocolate Mountains target area, east of the Salton Sea in the Imperial Valley of Southern California. We carried live ordnance. To add maximum realism to the training exercise, I wove a Vietnam scenario into the strike planning by rotating the chart of the Southern California operating area 90 degrees. East became north, and *Oriskany's* position in the Pacific west of San Diego became "Yankee Station." A felt-tip pen and a little imagination converted the eastern shore of the Salton Sea into the coast of North Vietnam, and the adjacent Chocolate Mountain target became Haiphong's Cat Bai airfield.

A marine F-8 Crusader squadron based at the Yuma, Arizona, air station was enlisted as "MiG" opposition. By coincidence, the location of the Yuma air station relative to the Chocolate Mountain training target was about the same as the relative position of Hanoi's Phuc Yen to the Cat Bai airfield. For a bit of levity in an otherwise serious undertaking, I labeled Marine Corps Air Station Yuma as "Phuc Yuma" on the training-mission chart.

A search-and-rescue problem was included in the exercise. To recover a simulated downed pilot, a rescue helo would be launched from the "SAR ship," the nearby naval air station at El Centro, and four Skyraiders of *Oriskany's* VA-152 would provide on-scene rescue support.

The sixteen-plane strike group and our four Crusader escorts launched from *Oriskany* and rendezvoused at 17,000 feet. Because we were carrying live ordnance, we followed a circuitous route to avoid the San Diego area, flying northward to cross over the Marine Corps's

Camp Pendleton and the sparsely populated Cleveland National Forest. Over the Anza Borrego Desert Park east of Pendleton, we descended to cross the Salton Sea on a southeast heading at low level and high speed. The fighters remained at a higher altitude to attract the attention of the opposing "MiGs" from Phuc Yuma.

Flashing over the initial point near the eastern shore of the Salton Sea, I transmitted, "Old Salt One popping up, now." Pulling my Skyhawk into a steep climb, I continued directly toward the target four miles away. Behind me, fourteen of the fifteen Skyhawks began their own climbs, fanning out from one another, gaining separation and maneuvering room for their prebriefed individual dive attacks. At 8,100 feet I rolled into a modified wingover maneuver and spotted the target off my nose at the one-o'clock position.

A movement in the rearview mirror caught my attention, and I was surprised to see Dan Kapner's Skyhawk flying close behind. Damn! He was in parade formation rather than maneuvering for separation as he'd been briefed to do.

"Salt Two, check your interval," I radioed, then shifted my attention back to the dive, the target, and the ground that was rushing up at me at 450 knots. The bombsight reticle slowly crept toward the target. I looked back and forth between the bombsight and the altimeter. The needle wound down to 3,500 feet, and I jammed my thumb against the bomb-release pickle. The plane shuddered slightly as the ejectors kicked the bombs from the wing racks, and I hauled back on the stick in a steady 4-G pullout. While jinking to avoid imaginary enemy flak, my thoughts momentarily flashed back to the previous summer and the "hornet's nest" mission to Kep. The cockpit air conditioner was turned to full cold, but I found myself sweating.

Still jinking, I glanced in the mirror while retiring from the target area. Back at the target, bombs were exploding, but something else, something out of the ordinary, caught my attention. Off target to the south a huge fireball boiled into a cloud of black smoke and dust.

We were dropping live ordnance, so explosions were expected, but bombs didn't create that kind of fireball. I shuddered involuntarily. The black smoke was a sign of burning jet fuel. The third and fourth pilots of my division checked in on the tactical radio frequency with "Tallyho" calls. They were clear of the target area and had me in sight, but two brief radio calls to Dan Kapner went unanswered. I hauled the stick back and to the left, pulling my plane back toward the target.

The voice of another strike pilot on the tactical circuit confirmed what I already suspected: "Salt Lead, this is Magic Stone Four One Four. Looks like someone flew into the target."

Acknowledging the call, I switched to the emergency frequency and broadcast a Mayday to Navy El Centro tower. Then I instructed the alternate strike leader to take charge of the group and return to *Oriskany*.

The planned drill for a simulated aircraft loss had become the real thing, and I felt heavyhearted. The area around the target revealed few clues. There was a scorched area among the sand and rocks, still burning in some places. The rescue helo from El Centro arrived some minutes later and landed at the target site. But there was no "downed" pilot to rescue. For reasons that might never be known and causes that could only be speculated—target fixation, a late bomb release, too low a pullout—the plane had flown into the ground. My wingman, Dan Kapner, had been killed instantly.

The December-to-May turnaround time was hectic, but the Saints emerged in fairly good shape. As the time for our return to the war approached, we had completed a large part of the prescribed conventional-warfare training. I had all but ignored the still-existing requirements concerning the delivery of nuclear weapons, but no one at Com-NavAirPac headquarters had challenged the omission.

By bitching to CAG Bob Spruit, I had engineered a major departure from the peacetime norm—the long-established practice of physically relocating attack squadrons to the naval air station at Fallon, Nevada, for air-to-ground weapons training. Our visit to home base was already too brief, I argued, and was interrupted by necessary periods on board *Oriskany*. An additional two-week absence for a weapons deployment to Fallon would qualify as cruel and unusual punishment. I was concerned about the squadron's morale. My plea was that, with such a short time at home, something had to bend; and the bending shouldn't all fall to the people who were fighting the war.

Lemoore was designated a "master" jet air station, and my contention was that it should try to live up to that advertisement by supporting the necessary weapons training. Most of the weapons we would carry were relatively harmless practice bombs, which could safely be loaded at the perimeter of Lemoore field, away from all buildings and traffic. En route to the Fallon and El Centro targets our planes could fly over sparsely populated areas. Jack Shaw of VA-164 endorsed my idea, and influential support came from CAPT Howard Boydstun, Lemoore's commanding officer. Boydstun liked the challenge, and his support was a key selling point when Bob Spruit presented the idea to ComNavAirPac for consideration.

The departure from established procedure was approved. The Saints, and the Ghostriders of VA-164, accomplished the required weapons training and were still able to go home to mama and the kids at the end of the working day.

On 26 May, five months and a few days after our return to the States, *Oriskany* and Air Wing 16 again left San Diego. As I watched the Southern California coastline retreat in the ship's wake once more, the excitement and sense of adventure that I had experienced a year earlier was missing. I felt a lot older, perhaps a bit wiser, and I wasn't happy to be going back to war. But rather than working myself into a blue funk, I reminded myself that happiness wasn't the issue, and I went below to the ready room to focus my thoughts on the squadron's readiness.

The Saints deployed for a second combat cruise with a full bag of fourteen airplanes, the last one finally arriving two days before we left Lemoore. But replacements had not been identified for Dan Kapner, or for Charlie Stender, who had been transferred to other duty. We were still at nineteen pilots, two shy of our allowance. Furthermore, Charlie Wack had orders and would leave us when the ship put into Subic Bay en route to the war zone. ComNavAirPac's personnel officer had optimistically assured me that the squadron would be up to allowance very soon, but that rosy prediction hadn't materialized by the time *Oriskany* steamed out of San Diego bay.

On the plus side, we'd return to combat with a strong nucleus of experienced pilots—Lieutenant Commanders Bill Smith and Dick Tulley, and Lieutenants Fred Mitchell, Bob Hofford, and John Shore.

Smith had a strong, know-it-all personality that occasionally grated on the nerves of the other pilots, me included; but he was a brilliant and fearless pilot, one of the most knowledgeable Skyhawk drivers in the fleet. Dick Tulley, like Smith, was an excellent pilot with an enviable knowledge of the Skyhawk and its combat employment. Dick had a serious streak but was more laid-back, less intense than Smith. Fred Mitchell was smoothness and polish, a gentle man on the ground and a tiger in the air. A fellow pilot had once accorded Fred a fine compliment: "Mr. Nice Guy, the one you want your sister to marry." A plank owner, Fred had been an air-intelligence specialist and was the first officer to report for duty when the squadron was formed in 1960. Later, he went to flight training and was reassigned to VA-163 upon completion. Bob Hofford rated excellent in my book, as both an officer and an aviator. Along with Art Avore who was killed during the 1965 cruise, I had pegged Bob as a potential future chief of naval operations. And John Shore, my wingman, my friend, my second set of eyes and ears and my airborne alter ego for almost a year, was highly qualified for the combat-section-leader status he'd attained.

Additionally, the newboys of the 1965 cruise, Moose Lundy and Vance Schufeldt, had matured with experience. Both were meeting every expectation. Other recently assigned pilots—LCDR John Miles, LT Dale Miller, and the swap pilots Frank Hughes, Wayne Soliday, and Louie Nordby—had no combat experience but had reassuring numbers of Skyhawk hours in their logbooks. I had no doubts about them.

For personal reasons, Don Martin had left the Saints again, transferring to VA-125, Lemoore's Skyhawk-training squadron. In exchange, we received LCDR Marvin Reynolds. Marv had no combat experience but, having completed a tour as a Skyhawk flight instructor at VA-125, was a veteran in the A-4 cockpit. The only bona fide newboy pilots were Wayne Cypress, Pete Munro, and Fritz Schroeder. ENS Scott Wilkins had replaced John Sloan as the squadron's air-intelligence officer, but the other three ground officers—Jim Taylor, Floyd Oakes, and Dan Lestage—were still with us. Aircraft-maintenance specialists Jim and Floyd were the two jewels on which our maintenance efficiency turned, and I felt more than fortunate to have their experience carry us into our second combat cruise. A cadre of well-qualified senior petty officers, most of whom had the experience of the 1965 deployment under their belts, led the squadron's enlisted ranks.

All things considered, we were in good shape. The most pleasing of all was the high morale. I had asked a lot from the officers and men of the squadron during the previous four months, and they had willingly delivered. The spirit, the belief that the Saints were number one, was still there.

11 Another Crossing

 A variation of Parkinson's Law had taken effect during the air wing's temporary absence from *Oriskany*. The ship's personnel had expanded their work, storage, and living habits so as to occupy some of the vacant spaces assigned to the wing. I had gone through the same drill with regard to the squadron's spaces the previous year and was pleased to leave the settlement of housekeeping flaps to Ron Caldwell.

After a week of shipboard inactivity, the wing flew training strikes against Hawaiian targets during the two days before we entered Pearl Harbor. It had been a month since we had last operated from *Oriskany*'s deck, and some rusty spots in pilot proficiency were revealed. The Saints did well, however, being the only squadron to complete 100 percent of its scheduled flights.

I was quietly pleased and proud, and when I wandered about the ship to chat with the men after the completion of our first day's flying, it was easy to see that they were proud too. Morale was high. The excellent performance of the maintenance crews, giving pilots nearly 100-percent aircraft availability, was a favorable reflection on the leadership provided by Jim Taylor and Floyd Oakes.

The pilots were in good spirits too. On the night before our arrival in Pearl the weather was crystal clear, and the sea was calm. A bright, basketball-size moon beamed the ocean with wavering silver highlights. In Navy vernacular it was a "commander's moon," the implication being that flying on dark and dreary nights was a privilege reserved for junior pilots. Not wishing to spoil a perfectly good naval aviation myth, both Ron Caldwell and I flew that night. For an idyllic hour and a half I absorbed the sight of the moon-washed Pacific from 30,000 feet and pitied the unfortunate folks who never had such an experience.

A special briefing on the WestPac situation was held for squadron COs at Makalapa, the CinCPacFleet complex at the Pearl Harbor Naval Station. The VIP treatment was nice, but the briefing was a disappointment. Restrictions from Washington were still stifling tactical initiative, and little seemed to have changed on Yankee Station.

President Johnson had ordered a December 1965–January 1966 bombing pause, but the only noticeable response to that "peace initiative" had been an increase in the volume of troops and war material flowing from North to South Vietnam. The air war against the north had resumed at the end of January on a limited scale only. By March it had crept back up to about the same level we had been flying when *Oriskany* left the line at the end of November.

I visited the CinCPacFleet operations section after the briefing to review the OpReps (operational reports) of recent Alfa strikes. They were as discouraging as the briefing. I had hoped to find something I could use as encouragement for my pilots as we headed toward combat, but my quest was a failure.

The ship/air wing's operational-readiness inspection (ORI) was the standard three-day affair. We received the standard passing grades and were entitled to the standard all-expenses-paid cruise to the Tonkin Gulf. The Saints' performance was satisfactory overall but was marred by an aircraft accident.

Returning from a training mission, Wayne Cypress made a poor approach, and the LSO was slow to give a wave-off signal. One error compounded the other when Wayne went to full throttle in response to the wave off. His aircraft skimmed a few feet above the flight deck at full power, and the tailhook snagged an arresting wire. Wayne and his Skyhawk were snatched out of the air and slammed to the deck in a sudden, crashing stop. It was a miracle that Wayne was not injured because the aircraft suffered major structural damage as a result of the in-flight engagement.

The damaged aircraft was off-loaded when we returned to Pearl Harbor, and with its loss came renewed concern over Wayne

Cypress's overall flight performance. He'd not been showing the same degree of improvement in flying skills as the other young pilots. For a night flight at Lemoore, he'd accepted a plane with an unintentionally disconnected right-brake hydraulic line. A more thorough preflight inspection of the aircraft by Wayne would have revealed the problem. Lady Luck intervened, and the incident ended with only embarrassment to Wayne. After landing, he had only one wheel brake, and his otherwise undamaged Skyhawk rolled to a stop on the grass adjacent to the taxiway. I had a private chat with him afterward, stressing his good fortune and prior clean record, and cautioning him of the inherent danger of stupidity or dependence on dumb luck.

Wayne's so-so performance was underscored later when Bill Smith and Bob Hofford, the squadron's LSOs, briefed me on the pilot's performance in field carrier-landing practice. Wayne was assessed as a "weak stick," and I added a second item to the Wayne Cypress page in my mental notebook.

The in-flight engagement generated another private but longer and less-fatherly talk with Wayne. I reviewed his performance to date and outlined specific areas where he needed to improve. Wayne seemed genuinely concerned about the criticism and said that there would be improvement.

A mass exodus from the ship to the military recreation facility at Fort DeRussey on Waikiki Beach followed the ship's completion of the ORI. The Saints booked several rooms for the night and settled down on the lanai to divine the contents of that elegant rum concoction, the Mai Tai. The junior pilots waxed eloquent about the parental legitimacy of the Hawaiian fleet air commander's staff. The ORI critique that the staff would conduct was scheduled for the following afternoon—Sunday—effectively lousing up the only free day we had during our visit to the island. Plus, rather than holding the critique on board *Oriskany* at Pearl Harbor for our convenience, it would be held at the fleet air headquarters at Barber's Point, fifteen miles from Pearl Harbor.

By 2000 I was hungry and asked if anyone was interested in taking a trip to the Crouching Lion Restaurant on the east side of Oahu. Paul Merchant and I had enjoyed an excellent meal there during our 1965 visit. John Shore and the two Waynes—Wayne A. Cypress (nicknamed

"Wac" by his fellow pilots) and Wayne A. Soliday ("Was")—accepted the invitation. We launched in a rental car with nondrinker Wayne Cypress in the pilot seat. Twenty-five miles later we were winding our way through small villages and rural Oahu vegetation, with no major signs of civilization and nary a restaurant in sight.

My companions became concerned. Wayne Soliday guardedly suggested that I might be out of my mind. Nostalgically, John Shore compared our outing to a prior combat experience: "I know what's going on. This is all a joke, like Kep. There is no such place as the Crouching Lion."

My suggestion that we continue driving for precisely four more miles temporarily subdued the budding rebellion. If we had not discovered a Crouching Lion by that time, I said, we would turn around and return to civilization. We arrived at the restaurant 3.6 miles later. My navigation prowess and commanding-officer mystique were untarnished, and we enjoyed three hours of dinner and conversation.

On the way back to Honolulu "Wac" was again in the driver's seat. "Was" snoozed beside him in the front seat. John Shore and I talked as we had on many occasions before, but the conversation became unexpectedly somber when John broached the subject of the December pilot swap.

"I was really disappointed at not getting selected for transfer to an East Coast squadron," he said. Worse than the disappointment, he continued, was the resentment he felt over the undeserved selection of one of the swap pilots—the rebel, who had been John's roommate on *Oriskany* during the 1965 cruise.

After flying together for almost a year, John and I had developed a close bond and a large degree of mutual trust. His disappointment and resentment hurt me. I tried to explain my reasons for selecting the other pilot—his unprofessional, chip-on-the-shoulder attitude toward authority, his cocky nature, his occasional personality clashes with fellow pilots. I admitted that selfish reasons had colored my selection. With all the other pressures of flying in combat and running a squadron, I didn't want the additional burden of personal aggravation. I assured John that my intention had not been to reward.

"Yeah, I'd already guessed that was the reason," John said. "Still it was a good deal." Then he sighed: "I was disappointed, that's all."

I sensed that I had backed my friend into an embarrassing corner, so I shifted the conversation to John's performance and attitude. I told him that he was a superb, combat-experienced pilot, recently promoted to section leader with his own wingman. It had been for equally selfish reasons that I had not selected him for transfer.

"The squadron needs your proven abilities," I said. "Your leadership. And I need you, personally—your friendship. I consider you as close a friend as any I've had in my eighteen years of flying."

John sat silent for several minutes as the car rolled down the road through the dark Hawaiian night. Then he quietly said, "Skipper, I wish you had told me that a long time ago." It was both a rebuke and an apology. John was uncomfortable at challenging our friendship, but he was right. In that friendship, I had assumed too much and left too much unsaid. I should have told him earlier, and I was glad my friend finally understood.

The ORI critique was dull, and most of the Saints went out on the town Sunday night. When *Oriskany* steamed out of Pearl Harbor on Monday morning, 6 June, many of the pilots suffered from too much "last night ashore." CAPT John Iarrobino, who had relieved Captain Connolly as CO of the ship in March, was compassionate. On the advice of CAG Spruit, no flying was scheduled that day.

John Iarrobino, a low-key, empathetic man, had been my boss eight years earlier when he was operations officer of the carrier *Forrestal.* Our working relationship had developed into a lasting friendship.

Four days west of Pearl the ship was far enough ahead of track to permit a day's worth of flying. It was good to get back in the air again, but the day ended with yet another discouragement. LCDR John Miles, a competent and quietly gregarious aviator, nicknamed "Mild Man" by his fellow pilots, ran into trouble while practicing aerial fueling. The drogue valve of the tanker's fueling hose, designed to close automatically upon disconnect, malfunctioned and stuck in the open position when John backed out of his connection with the tanker. John's Skyhawk instantly sucked gallons of jet fuel into the starboard air intake. Upon hitting the hot innards of the J-52 engine, the volatile fuel-air mixture exploded with a muffled roar.

The airframe vibrated heavily, the instrument panel's engine-fire warning light glowed red, the EGT needle pegged itself in the danger zone. Miles wasted no time in firing his ejection seat and parachuted into the blue Pacific. *Oriskany*'s helo scooped him up within minutes, and except for a salt-water bath and a souvenir neck abrasion from a parachute riser, John was none the worse for the experience.

The accident was a one-in-a-million freak. Thankful that Miles was safe, I was nevertheless concerned by the recent string of bad luck. The in-flight fire and explosion and Wayne Cypress's earlier crash landing on the flight deck had trimmed the number of Saints aircraft from fourteen to twelve. And we hadn't yet crossed the Pacific! With Dan Kapner's fatal predeployment accident in southern California added to the tally, it occurred to me that my tenure might be in jeopardy. Combat losses were one thing, but higher authority tended to view with concern the qualifications of a CO whose pilots regularly broke or destroyed expensive aircraft during routine operations.

Oriskany's schedule took us to Japan before we headed to the Philippines. Coincident to our arrival in Yokosuka, I moved into a stateroom in a newly air-conditioned area in the forward part of the ship referred to as "skipper's row." At the Yokosuka Navy Exchange I bought a "Saintly" blue throw rug and a matching blue canvas camp chair to brighten up my new quarters. Word of the move and of the new decorations filtered down through the squadron, and shortly thereafter two of the squadron's metalsmiths arrived at my stateroom door—"to brighten up the skipper's room." With obvious pride, they applied an unorthodox coat of paint to the door—blue, to match the boomerang symbol on the tails of our aircraft. When the paint dried, they applied a large squadron decal to the door.

Roberto Lacson, a Filipino steward assigned to the squadron, was proud that the room of "my skee-per" was within his assigned area of room stewardship. The new blue rug had been on the deck for less than thirty minutes when Lacson appeared with a vacuum cleaner to give it a careful going-over. During the remainder of the day he found numerous little things in the room that needed his attention. By the time the evening meal rolled around, he'd given every inch of the room a thorough cleaning. The stainless-steel sink was so highly polished that I was embarrassed to use it.

Our time in Japan was full of the usual liberty activities—shopping, partying, and sight-seeing. However, having the visit occur at the beginning of the cruise, before we reached the combat area, seemed to me an unearned treat. The "show the flag" factor no doubt was a consideration, and perhaps higher authority was showing compensatory compassion for our short Stateside turnaround. I enjoyed visiting Japan again but, at the same time, felt a little guilty.

A letter from LCDR Clem Morisette, under orders to the squadron as operations officer, reached me in Japan. His refresher training at Lemoore was being accelerated, Clem said, and he would join us soon. More good news was the message directing three junior pilots— Ensigns Ralph Bisz, Ronald Tardio, and Tom Spitzer—to join the Saints upon completing their Skyhawk training at Cecil Field, Florida. Another message brought news that two replacement aircraft would soon be on board. One awaited us at NAS Atsugi near Yokosuka, and I directed Fred Mitchell to remain behind when the ship sailed, to fly the new bird to the Philippines. The other plane was waiting for us at NAS Cubi Point. As *Oriskany* steamed south from Yokosuka, it was satisfying to know that we would soon be at our full allowance of both pilots and aircraft. It would be the first time that that had occurred since I had joined the squadron eighteen months and one combat cruise earlier.

Thick clouds and rain-limited visibility canceled flight operations immediately upon our leaving Japan. Twenty-four hours later we were in clear weather under a high-pressure ridge, and a full schedule of training missions was planned.

I had assigned Wayne Cypress as my permanent wingman after his accident off Hawaii so that I could keep an eye on him. Together, we were to fly a long-distance, low-level-navigation mission that would take us the length of the Ryukyu island chain, including Okinawa. Several dry-run "attacks" on simulated targets and new scenery would liven up the mission. I looked forward eagerly to flying again after a long layoff. But the sight-seeing was not to be.

When Wayne was catapulted, the radar scope in his cockpit came loose from the instrument panel. Hurled aft by the G force of the catapult shot, the scope struck Wayne smartly in the chest. The wind was knocked out of him, but he was able to recover just in time to avoid flying into the water. Wayne reported that his chest hurt but thought that he could continue the mission. I was not so certain. I alerted the ship and instructed Wayne to land as soon as possible so that he could be checked out by Dan Lestage. For several concerned minutes I flew as his wingman, following him down into the landing pattern. Wayne trapped without further incident. I remained airborne in the vicinity of the ship because it wasn't smart to go off on a lollygag over the western Pacific with no one to mark the spot if anything happened to me.

For two hours I killed time, orbiting, playing bogey for the fighters, practicing aerial fueling plug-ins with the duty tanker, and mulling over Wayne's near accident. He'd come close to "buying the farm" on that catapult launch, and we might never have guessed the cause. Purely and simply, pilot error caused that incident. Early in his career, every tailhook aviator learned the need to prevent objects from flying around in the cockpit during a catapult shot. The loose radar scope probably resulted from a maintenance technician's oversight. I'd discuss that matter with Floyd Oakes after landing; but that didn't excuse Wayne's failure to make the thorough cockpit preflight inspection that would have revealed the unsecured scope.

What had begun as an upbeat day and deteriorated with Wayne's incident turned to worms when I dismounted from my Skyhawk after landing. I slipped on an oily spot on the boarding ladder and cracked my knee against a rung. In agony, I hobbled off the flight deck and down to sick bay. Doctor Dan eyeballed an X-ray of my knee and announced that nothing was broken, but he trussed me from thigh to shin in an elastic bandage and grounded me for a few days.

When I stiff-legged my way back to Ready Five, I became an object of humor for the other pilots. Bob Hofford muttered an audible reference to "Chester," the gimpy character in TV's "Gunsmoke" series. John Shore castigated me for poor timing: "Skipper, couldn't you at least have waited until you were ready to launch on a combat mission?"

After the movie in the ready room that evening, I invited Wayne Cypress to my stateroom for a stern lecture on the topic of conducting a thorough preflight inspection of the cockpit.

During a twenty-four-hour stopover at Cubi Point, we received the two replacement aircraft, but the new pilots were nowhere to be seen. Ashore, I joined the others of the squadron for drinks, wishing a fond farewell to Charlie Wack and "wetting down" the stripes of our newly promoted lieutenant, Wayne Soliday. But my mind was preoccupied with what lay ahead. After a quiet dinner at the officers' club with Ron Caldwell and Fred Mitchell, I went back to the ship. I stopped by the intelligence center to review the current OpReps from the carriers on Yankee Station, but they didn't provide much cheer. Later, alone in my room, I reflected a long time on the task before us.

In September 1952 USS *Kearsarge* had steamed out of Yokosuka toward the Sea of Japan, heading for combat in the Korean War. At the time I was an eager young fighter pilot with romantic ideas about aerial combat, nurtured by war movies seen in the 1940s. Thirteen years later in 1965, when *Oriskany* left Subic Bay for my first exposure to combat in Vietnam, I was less eager. War was no longer a romantic idea, yet there had still been a tinge of adventure about it. I had expected that U.S. military might would be quickly applied with the object of winning. That pipe dream had disappeared with the misplaced resolve of America's civilian leadership. We were immersed in a no-win war.

Memories of the past year were still fresh—the missions flown, the SAMs and flak, the fellow pilots dead, missing, or captured. Apprehension and uncomfortable resignation had long since replaced my sense of excitement and adventure. Yet, as I sat in my stateroom, I felt a sense of relief. I was always uncomfortable with long layoffs from flying, and the lengthy Pacific crossing had given us little flight time. My second deployment in a year's time was already a month old, but the war was still out there beyond the horizon. Maybe I was bored. I wanted to get on with it and get it behind me.

Thunderstorms churned the skies as *Oriskany* plowed through the South China Sea toward Vietnam. Clouds, driving rain, high winds, and a pitching deck interrupted our full flying schedules for the two days that we were en route.

The evening of 28 June I manned my plane for a warm-up training flight. The rain fell intermittently as I seated myself in the cockpit, but shortly thereafter it began to pour down. "Find yourself a dry spot if you can," I shouted to Baron, my plane captain. He scooted down the boarding ladder and disappeared under the wing as I pulled the canopy closed against the wet.

The cockpit of an A-4 was far from roomy. A joke among the pilots was that you didn't get into the cockpit, you put it on. Strapping in without Baron's assistance was a struggle, and without the engine running there was no air-conditioning. I sweated as if I were in a sauna. The Plexiglas canopy protected me from the drumming rain, but I was damp all over from perspiration by the time I finished strapping in. When I was finally ready to start the engine, the air officer's voice blared over the announcing system, "All missions except for the two Skyhawk tankers are canceled. Pilots may return to ready rooms."

Briefly, I pondered the options—stay in the steam bath or deplane and get even more soaked in the pouring rain. I rubbed a clear spot in the condensate on the canopy and peered into the torrential downpour. Water was flowing two inches deep across the flight deck beneath my plane. It completely overwhelmed the deck-edge drain gutter and cascaded Niagara-like into the catwalk. A blurred figure materialized on the deck and reattached an access ladder to the side of my plane. Loyal Baron, back on duty. I figured I could take it if he could and opened the canopy. It was a bit cooler outside, but I was soaked to the skin by the time my foot touched the flight deck. There was no need to hurry, so I strolled casually aft, feeling the clean rain. A smiling Jim Taylor met me outside the ready room. "Skipper, I know our planes need fresh-water wash downs," he said, "but this is ridiculous."

The torrential downpour was giving airborne pilots fits in their attempts to make visual contact with the ship at the end of their instrument approaches. Some were nearing low fuel state, and an order came to launch the tankers. Pete Munro was one of the tanker pilots, but his aircraft developed a hydraulic-system malfunction when he started the engine. He, too, was soaking wet when he strolled into Ready Five. One fellow pilot chided Pete for "chickening out because of a few sprinkles." Another needled him for "not understanding the benefit of added engine thrust from water injection." Embarrassed and perhaps feeling a bit guilty about downing his plane, Pete was not amused and responded with a deletable expletive.

"The night is not fit for man nor beast," I whispered to Pete. "I'm glad my flight was canceled." Pete broke into a broad grin.

The downpour continued unabated. Visibility was limited to yards. The remainder of the flight schedule was canceled, and the aircraft still in the air were diverted to Cubi Point for the night. Included were Bob Hofford and his wingman, Fritz Schroeder. Their diversion generated sarcastic remarks from pilots envious of the additional night of liberty, but envy quickly turned to sympathy when someone discovered that both pilots had left their wallets in the ready room.

On 30 June we would be at Dixie Station, and the flight schedule for that day prompted unusually high pilot interest. At the time, federal-income-tax regulations automatically exempted the wages earned by enlisted personnel in the designated Vietnam war zone. The rule did not apply to officers, however. Later in the war, Congress would enact legislation to make things more equitable, but in 1966 officers were required to participate in some combat evolution to gain the tax exemption. In the case of a pilot, flying at least one combat mission met the requirement. John Shore, who inherited the collateral duty of writing the flight schedule upon the departure of Larry DeSha, was hassled by his fellow pilots as he tried to rough out the following day's schedule. Suddenly and without comment, John gathered up his paperwork and stomped out of the ready room, to complete his schedule-writing chores in private.

Concerns over income-tax exemption evaporated when flying commitments put each pilot in the air twice on 30 June. As usual, morale took an upturn as soon as we got busy doing our thing as aviators. Another upbeat note that day was the arrival of LCDR Clem Morisette, via COD aircraft from Cubi Point. I was pleased that the squadron's operations-officer billet was filled again. Clem had the balance of a relatively easy week on Dixie Station to get up to speed on operational matters. Things would be considerably more hectic when we moved to Yankee Station.

Clem, a fast learner, responded admirably to his challenge. He flew one mission per day for the next four days and spent the balance of his waking hours familiarizing himself with every aspect of the squadron's, air wing's, and ship's operating procedures. He devoured combat intelligence reports and OpReps and held probing discussions with the combat-experienced pilots. He was businesslike and had a quick grasp of details. He was also easygoing with others and displayed the sense of humor so necessary for survival in a carrier ready room.

On his fifth day on board, Clem announced that he was ready to be operations officer in fact as well as in name. He called an all-pilots meeting after the flying was done for the day. I'd been in his shoes five years earlier as the new operations officer of VA-76 in the Atlantic Fleet and sensed the purpose of Clem's meeting. He would stake a firm claim as boss of things operational and dispel any notions that he was just another newboy. Ron Caldwell and I stayed away from the ready room as Clem, in his quiet way, established his position in the squadron's pecking order.

While down south, I spent a lot of time studying the OpReps from Yankee Station, hoping to make sense of what we soon would be doing. But it was apparent that little had changed. American peace initiatives and targeting restrictions had accomplished nothing toward effecting a negotiated settlement to the hostilities. I had a hollow feeling, thinking of Jim Stockdale, Harry Jenkins, and other American POWs. How discouraging the bombing pause must have been for them.

Our Dixie Station warm-up was complete, and *Oriskany* steamed north to Yankee Station. While we were en route, planes of Air Wing 14 from USS *Ranger* struck a POL target near Haiphong. It was the first Navy strike north of the twentieth parallel in several months. The strike reports showed that the flak and SAM threats were still there, as thick as ever. Not much had changed since we had left, seven months earlier.

12 Back to War

 While *Oriskany* was en route to Yankee Station, I called an all-pilots meeting in the ready room for a discussion of combat tactics and philosophy. Normally, I enjoyed such meetings and the opportunity to give a pep talk. However, the witless war we were joining made it tough to think of what kind of pep I might inject. There was an air of tension among the pilots. A natural reaction, I guessed, since a majority of them had no combat experience.

In my own gut I felt deeply concerned about again being a target for flak, SAMs, and MiGs. Of late I'd been more than a little apprehensive about my second exposure to those threats. As had happened before during my flying career, I found comfort in literature. I particularly liked a passage written by English author Nicholas Monsarrat in his memoir *Three Corvettes.* Discussing his early–World War II experiences as a Royal Navy sailor in small ships on the North Atlantic, Monsarrat wrote:

> ...you seem to be moving in a bad dream, pursued not by terrors but by an intolerable routine....you think: My God, I can't go up there (on deck) again....But you can, of course; it becomes automatic in the end. And, besides, there are people watching you.

The air war over North Vietnam was in its second year and long since had been teetering somewhere between an intolerable routine and a bad dream. And people were watching me. Seniors in the chain of command, of course, watching my performance as a squadron CO. But that was a given in any competitive career, no different in the military, and it didn't bother me. The real pressure came from below, from the pilots who were watching me for clues about how to react to combat—to the certainty of being shot at, the possibility of being injured, killed, or captured. There was no yardage to gain by pretending to the other pilots that war was fun, but I had to avoid giving the impression of being unwilling to "go up there again."

The briefing began with a discussion and review of several technical matters relating to our planes, weapons systems, and tactics—a general review intended to get the pilots thinking in a combat mode. Among other things, Floyd Oakes briefed us on project Shoehorn, which was retrofitting three new pieces of electronic equipment into our Skyhawks. A black box called the ALQ-51 would provide the pilot with a visual alert to any activity by the SAM-associated Fan Song radar. A blinking red light would indicate that the aircraft was being illuminated by a Fan Song in the search mode. A steady red glow would mean that the radar was locked on preparatory to firing a SAM. The second piece, the APR-27, would simultaneously generate a tone through the pilot's helmet earphones—sounding a low pitch during the search phase and increasing to a higher, more frantic pitch at lockon. Eventually, a third component, the APR-23, would provide a visual indication, relative to the nose of the aircraft, of the direction of the threat. But the latter component wasn't available yet for our birds.

To help counter the SAM threat, the new gear was a step in the right direction. But without the APR-23 to determine the direction of the threat, cockpit aural and visual alerts were merely something else to promote adrenalin flow. The real problem in dealing with a SAM lay in not knowing where it was coming from. Without that piece of the puzzle, evading SAMs would remain primarily a matter of solid head-on-a-swivel cockpit discipline.

When the technical matters were disposed of, I took center stage and delivered my monologue. I touched on fear and aggression. None of us, I reminded the pilots, had been drafted to fly. Each of us was a volunteer. We had been aware from the start that our chosen occupation might eventually require us to do exactly the sort of work we'd be doing the following day. That work required courage—courage being not a lack of fear but the ability to carry on in spite of fear (that was another literary reference, clipped and filed in memory years earlier).

I admitted that in every combat mission I'd flown, over Korea and Vietnam, I'd felt fear. There had been occasions, such as the Kep debacle in 1965, when I had come close to pissing in my flight suit. That comment brought supportive nods of affirmation from Bill Smith and John Shore, veterans of that mission. I cited Charlie Stender's courage when he returned from the Kep mission in a badly damaged, burning plane. Facing combat hazards every day wasn't going to be a picnic, I said, but it might be easier to take if each pilot realized that he didn't have a corner on the fear market.

Aggressiveness, an inherent and necessary element of every mission in the bomb-dropping business, was a more difficult subject to broach. I stressed that if each pilot was to do an effective day-to-day job in the face of flak and SAMs, each had to recognize and respect the narrow line that separated combat aggressiveness from foolhardiness.

Bill Smith was in the back of my mind at that moment. A superb pilot, Bill was seemingly fearless in combat. But he could be overly aggressive. Like a modern knight on a quest, Bill seemed to view military aviation as an exciting challenge in which he had to regularly prove his abilities—to himself as much as to others. He was not foolhardy. I doubted that he'd do something as stupid as dueling with a flak site. But if he had, I wouldn't have been surprised, and he probably would have won.

My concern about Bill was not what he would do to himself but the example his own actions posed for the junior pilots who flew with him. Bill could do things at the controls of a Skyhawk that an aviator of lesser experience might not be able to handle. In fact, during the 1965 deployment while Harry Jenkins was absent from the ship, I temporarily grounded Bill's wingman for flying recklessly. The young man had nearly killed himself trying to emulate his leader's flight skills by making a "hot" rendezvous at an altitude of 20,000 feet. Momentarily forgetting that he was carrying nearly a full load of fuel and four thousand pounds of bombs, the young pilot threw his wing up in a steep turn to slow the relative motion between the aircraft. The plane stalled and snapped into a violent spin. The pilot barely managed to regain control of his aircraft at 1,500 feet above the water, after jettisoning his bombs and external fuel tank.

The Vietnam War was eighteen months old, I told the pilots, and had already proved to be a no-win situation. We were faced with target restrictions, and Washington was calling the tactical shots and making no real attempt to cripple the enemy's war-making potential. The war wouldn't be won with "John Wayne" aggressiveness. The assigned missions were to be accomplished as efficiently and quickly as possible with no unnecessary risks. I stressed that there were few, if any, targets in North Vietnam worth the loss of a pilot or a plane. Unless there was some compelling reason to stick around a target, the already-established "one pass and haul ass" maxim was still the operative principle.

There was no room for bravado. At worst, a pilot who foolishly endangered himself or his wingman in combat might not come back. At best, he'd face my wrath and possibly lose his wings. And there was another important consideration that each pilot should keep in mind. Mr. McNamara's peacetime budget had allowed the procurement of A-4 Skyhawks to fall behind the need. Even as we steamed to Yankee Station, the war was costing the Navy an average of six A-4s per month. In comparison, Douglas Aircraft was producing only ten Skyhawks per month, and they had to suit the needs of both the Atlantic and Pacific fleets and the Marine Corps. Thus, I concluded, the real hero would be the pilot who did his job and brought his plane back to fly again.

Dan Lestage followed my presentation with a medical briefing. He made a few quasi-serious remarks about health hazards and sanitary conditions in Hanoi and handed each pilot a two-ounce, combat-ration bottle of medicinal brandy. If consumed immediately, Dan said reassuringly, the medicine would provide temporary immunity from concerns about the aforementioned hazards. The brandy was promptly consumed, and we all enjoyed the promised reprieve from worrying about the next day's duty on Yankee Station.

As the meeting broke up, John Shore made my day by whispering, "Good words, Skipper."

In short order, our days on Yankee Station became carbon copies of those experienced during the prior year. Each one was not much different from any other—the "intolerable routine" spoken of by author Monsarrat. My principal interest in the first several days was to observe the performance of pilots new to combat, particularly the three nuggets. As for Pete Munro and Fritz Schroeder, their section leaders reported that they were doing well. My own wingman, Wayne Cypress, continued to be an enigma, however. I was certain that he was wrestling with a personal problem, the nature of which was vague and worrisome to me. Wayne was courteous and respectful, on time and attentive at briefings. He hadn't displayed any obvious aversion to flying in general or combat in particular, but his attitude was not positive. He seemed unable to relax, not even to the extent of enjoying the brief, after-mission, thank-God-I'm-still-alive euphoria.

In addition, he seemed to be maintaining a psychological distance between us, intentionally keeping our leader-wingman relationship cool. In that relationship, the leader was responsible for navigating and hunting targets, keeping his attention focused on the ground. The wingman functioned as a second set of senses focused on the rest of the combat environment. A wingman and his leader had to think alike, with harmonious and complementary reactions. That interplay hadn't developed between Wayne and me. In the vernacular, we didn't click. I wondered if it was my fault for expecting too much. After all, I'd been spoiled by the nearly ideal relationship John Shore and I had enjoyed for eleven months.

Wayne had a college degree in engineering and postgraduate training at the prestigious General Motors Institute. His flight-training record was unexceptional but contained no black marks. But compared with that of his contemporaries, Pete Munro and Fritz Schroeder, and of Moose Lundy and Vance Schufeldt during their first cruise, Wayne's flight performance was static. He showed little growth in flying proficiency.

During the week we flew at Dixie Station, the pressure had been minimal, and Wayne's standoffish attitude was lower on my list of concerns. I thought, or hoped at least, that he'd grow into the job. The first couple of days at Yankee Station brought me to an uneasy edge, however. Wayne was flying in the same sky with me but not as part of the same team. He frequently seemed not to be quite where he was supposed to be, not to be doing quite what he was supposed to do. I found myself distracted, spending too much time worrying about whether Wayne would be there at any given juncture.

The warning signals that Wayne had been displaying preoccupied my mind. His performance in night carrier-landing practice at

Lemoore: marginally acceptable. His carrier landings since: the same. The incident with the defective hydraulic line at Lemoore. The in-flight engagement off Hawaii that had cost us an airplane. The radar-scope incident after we left Japan. By itself, each incident could be explained logically and rationally; but they had all happened to the same guy.

After my third mission on Yankee Station with Wayne, I instructed Clem Morisette to fly him with the other senior pilots for a few missions. Ostensibly, the reason was to allow me to fly with and observe the performance of the other junior pilots. That evening I called Wayne to my stateroom for another private talk. I told him the reason for the change and reminded him of our earlier conversations. Then I outlined my concerns about his most recent flying. Wayne reacted with mild resentment and volunteered little information to shed light on the dilemma. Tensely and tersely, he responded to my questions. He denied the existence of any personal problem. Crisply and without emotion, he apologized for his "so-called poor perfor-mance" and assured me that he could improve. I told Wayne that the other senior pilots weren't aware of my reason for rotating wingmen and left the matter there.

In the next several days Wayne flew with Ron Caldwell, Marv Reynolds, and Bill Smith. Ron and Marv expressed a general uneasi-ness similar to mine about Wayne's flying, noting that he was less than helpful as a good wingman should be. Bill Smith, with an analytic approach to every aviation endeavor, was more blunt. He outlined sev-eral specific shortcomings in Wayne's performance, including an apparent aversion to flying over the beach. Bill questioned the wisdom of allowing the young pilot to continue flying combat missions. The opinions of the senior pilots, particularly Bill Smith's blunt evaluation, fanned my flame of concern. The problem was serious, and a solution couldn't be postponed much longer.

Calling Wayne for another private talk, I apprised him of the opin-ions and specific criticisms of the other senior pilots. I tried not to sound threatening as I outlined the limited options available. Either there had to be an immediate bootstrap improvement in his flight per-formance or I'd be forced to consider terminating his flight status.

Further training and possible assignment to another squadron might have been an option if we had been Stateside. But they were unaffordable luxuries in combat, where each pilot had to carry his share of the load. Wayne cautiously asked about the worst-case scenario, and I replied, "ComNavAirPac won't react benevolently to the news that a pilot with a combat squadron is either unwilling or unable to cut the mustard."

Surprisingly, even with that ominous possibility coming from my lips, a threat to the wings he wore, Wayne relaxed a bit. We talked further. Some of his prior resentment and psychological distance seemed to melt away, but he was still on guard. At one point, however, a damaging admission slipped out: "Once in a while during flight training I had sort of a lack of self-confidence—in my flying abilities." He quickly covered the admission, though, by insisting that the problem was history and well in hand.

I became hypothetical: "Have you ever thought you might be in the wrong business? That earlier flying challenges were easier to overcome but are less manageable now that we're in combat?" I mentioned that pride was often a stumbling block in any self-evaluation of one's capabilities and limitations.

Wayne didn't respond directly, so I returned to basics and backed away from playing amateur psychologist. We were at the fish-or-cut-bait juncture, I said. The rest of us would help as best we could, but he had to be the principle architect of the solution. The next few days would be critical.

Still reserved but more relaxed than earlier, Wayne said that he understood the problem and wanted to try the bootstraps, the self-improvement route.

When Wayne left my stateroom, I was momentarily relieved but wary. The problem at best had only been postponed. Eventually, I might have to recommend that Wayne be removed from flight status. Also, I knew a lot of guilt would be added to heartache if Wayne should be lost in combat before I found a solution to my dilemma.

After Wayne left my stateroom, I picked up the telephone and called Bob Spruit. "CAG, I've got a problem. Have you got time to talk?" A few minutes later I was briefing CAG about Wayne Cypress.

Oriskany's return to Yankee Station coincided with a general lifting of the restriction on attacking targets north of the twentieth parallel. I found little reassurance in arriving on station just as the privilege to probe deep into the Red River delta was once again ours. Intelligence reports indicated that the enemy was quick to respond, redeploying their SAM assets to the north of Thanh Hoa. However, although those weapons were physically relocated, the North Vietnamese were niggardly in using them. We encountered only light antiaircraft opposition in the delta for several days. The heightened anticipation made me wonder if the enemy was playing a game, trying to spook us.

I was assigned to lead an Alfa strike against the Phu Ly highway-railroad bridges, twenty-five miles south of Hanoi. While planning the mission, I pondered the stereotypical approach—practically a straight line from our launch point to the target—that had become a routine in our Yankee Station thinking. My group was to be of medium size—twelve Skyhawks, eight Saints and four "Magic Stones" of VA-164, with four Crusaders as fighter cover. Instead of the stereotype, I decided to play a game with the enemy. I planned a circuitous back-door approach to the bridge targets, hoping to gain the element of surprise.

After rendezvousing overhead the ship, the group descended on a westerly heading toward a coast-in point forty miles south of Thanh Hoa. We went feet dry seventy-five miles south of the target at treetop level and continued west. We roared across the sparsely populated territory at 300 knots, using the ridge lines for radar masking. Four minutes later we were twenty miles inland. I turned the group north and, still at low level, proceeded to a point thirty miles west of the target. There, I turned east, nudged the throttle forward, and let the airspeed settle on the prebriefed 360 knots. Armament switches on.

The day was clear, and the scenery rushing past was idyllic as we skimmed over the karst formations and rich green vegetation. At four miles from the bridges I radioed my first words to the group since leaving rendezvous: "Salt One popping up, now."

Twelve Skyhawks climbed and fanned out for the attack. The ruse worked. Out in front, I saw no sign of opposition. Bright sun bathed the countryside as I did a wingover into my bombing run at 8,000 feet above the target. The westernmost of the targets, the highway bridge, drifted under the cross hairs on my bombsight, and I pickled my bombs. Pulling out and jinking, I retired west at low altitude, back-tracking on the inbound route. I hadn't seen a single shot fired at us.

The other three pilots of my division made "Tallyho" off-target calls, indicating that they were clear and had me in sight. A few seconds later, as the last four Skyhawks entered their runs, the enemy responded. The Magic Stone leader, number nine in the group, reported flak bursts north of the target. Moments later I heard chilling but calm words from the number eleven pilot: "Magic Stone Three, missile away. Two SAMs north of target. Heads up."

I was several miles away by then and relatively safe, but I cringed and involuntarily held my breath.

Then the good news came: "Magic Stone Four, off and clear." Tail-end Charlie had completed his attack, and we were all on our way home! Both of the SAMs fired went wide of the mark, and the enemy had time only to toss up a moderate flak barrage, too late to be effective.

The backdoor tactic had worked better than expected, and I decided to try it again when the opportunity presented itself. But I harbored no illusions. Not many targets in North Vietnam lent themselves to such a maneuver.

Poststrike photography showed our bombing accuracy to be less than perfect. The Phu Ly bridges were damaged but not destroyed, and we, or some other carrier wing, would be ordered back into that area soon.

The next day we flew another Alfa strike, against the Ninh Binh highway bridge, twenty miles south of the Phu Lai target. It was near Ninh Binh that John Shore and I had encountered "the world's largest flak site" during the 1965 cruise. In the prestrike briefing I had stressed the possibility of receiving a lot of AAA opposition.

The Ninh Binh target was only fifteen miles inland and offered no opportunity for surprise, so I led the group in a straight-in-and-out shot designed to keep the aircraft over land for the shortest possible time. Surprisingly, our strike attracted little attention. No SAMs were fired, AAA was light, and we destroyed the bridge.

A third Alfa strike in as many days targeted an electrical power plant thirty miles east of Hanoi. CAG Spruit assigned himself to lead the strike and gave me a "day off." I was scheduled for only two armed recco missions that day. The strike on the power plant was the closest probe the air wing had made to North Vietnam's capital city since the fateful Hai Duong mission in late 1965. Although heavy opposition was expected, flak was uncommonly light for a target so close to Hanoi, and no SAMs were fired. All of the attack planes returned safely, but there was a close shave.

One of the "Superheats," an escorting VF-162 fighter jock, LTJG Rick Adams, had an exciting morning. Flak hit his F-8 Crusader as the strike group retired from the target area. The aircraft became uncontrollable, and Adams had to eject over mountainous terrain northeast of Haiphong. Pursued by North Vietnamese, he spent forty-five tense minutes on the ground before a rescue helo snatched him to safety.

The attention we were focusing on targets in the Red River delta hadn't stirred up the expected ground-to-air opposition. But it did arouse the interest of North Vietnam's Russian-built MiG fighters. Our supporting VAW-11 crews in their E-1B Tracers intercepted MiG-associated radar signals during the 12 July and 13 July Alfa strikes. Airborne MiGs had been sighted in the distance on both days but had made no attempt to oppose the strike groups. The presence of the MiGs probably accounted for the lack of SAM activity.

For reasons obscured by the mental fog bank along the Potomac River, the ROE under which we operated were overly cautious when it came to air-to-air combat. The enemy was considered a bad guy only if he was airborne and initiated a scrap. Our fighters were not allowed to seek air-to-air engagements, and attacking MiGs on the ground was prohibited. It had been a disappointment to our fighter boys when the enemy aircraft had elected to stay clear of the two Alfa strikes.

During the planning of yet another Alfa strike, CDR Dick "Belly" Bellinger, skipper of the VF-162 Superheats, groused about the lack of air-to-air combat opportunity for his pilots. "It's been a long dry spell," Belly said, "and my guys are itching for a hassle."

The target was the Red River storage facilities at Nam Dinh, forty miles downstream from Hanoi. The location, in the middle of flat delta a few miles inland from the Gulf, offered little chance for tactical surprise. We'd be strapped to the stereotypical approach from seaward, but to spice things up I suggested to Belly that we bend the ROE a bit. Because conditions seemed right for drawing out MiGs, I suggested that we include a MiG trap in the mission planning, an attempt to sucker the enemy into combat. Belly offered no objection.

Simultaneously with *Oriskany's* strike at Nam Dinh, Air Wing 14 in *Ranger* was to strike the Phu Ly bridges that we had damaged four days earlier. By secure radio I talked to a long-time friend, CDR Fred Palmer, the CAG of Air Wing 14. We agreed on a coordinated effort, with the two strike groups launching at the same time. *Ranger*'s planes would approach and retire from their Phu Ly target on a north-south track, flying over the "hourglass" territory northeast of Thanh Hoa. At the same time my group would cross the coast forty miles farther north on a track toward Hanoi. The simultaneous approaches would appear on North Vietnamese radar scopes as a massive, two-prong strike aimed directly at the capital city. If that didn't stir MiGs into action, nothing would.

The fourteenth of July was a clear day. I led sixteen bomb-loaded A-4s toward the coast-in point twenty miles south of the port of Haiphong. To bait the MiG trap with the impression that Hanoi might be the target, I kept the flight at 20,000 feet as we crossed the coast. Belly Bellinger had gone feet dry about two minutes ahead of the strike group and led his fighters to a position halfway to Hanoi.

The North Vietnamese took the bait. By the time Belly reached the halfway point the air was alive with electronic signals and MiG-warning broadcasts. And Belly's fighter boys got their hassle.

Meanwhile, back with the strike group, I led the bombers two minutes past the coast-in point. At ten miles inland I turned 90 degrees left to the planned southwest heading for the Nam Dinh attack and let down rapidly. The time from the turn point to the roll in was only sixty seconds, and I hoped that surprise was on our side. Like a lot of good plans, ours almost worked.

I peered down and ahead as the group approached the roll-in point and was appalled to see four Skyhawks from the *Ranger*'s group streaking southeastward at low altitude, directly over the rooftops of Nam Dinh. Instead of retiring on the agreed southern track after striking their Phu Lai target, the *Ranger*'s Skyhawks were some 30 degrees and ten miles off course.

So much for surprise. The Nam Dinh gunners were wide awake for our arrival, and all prior speculation about a possible North Vietnamese ammunition shortage was dispelled a few seconds later.

The sky erupted like the Fourth of July fireworks. Passing through the roll-in point, I saw muzzle flashes from three separate antiaircraft batteries, disquieting confirmation that the gun barrels were pointed in my direction. My bombsight pipper tracked steadily to the target as I dove through the flak. There was no crosswind drift to complicate the bombing problem, thank Heaven for small favors. The flak temporarily disappeared from my mind as I concentrated on the target rushing up at me—rows of buildings along the Nam Dinh riverfront. The pipper crossed the aim point. I felt the airframe shudder slightly as I pressed the pickle and released my bombs, then I pulled my Skyhawk into a hard left climbing turn. I looked over my shoulder to see flak bursts pocking the sky. Dust and smoke from the bomb explosions boiled up from the target. Then flashes and visible shock waves created another display as the bombs dropped by the second division exploded.

I pulled into a reverse turn and looked over my other shoulder. More explosions. Twenty-four tons of high explosives had ripped apart the storage buildings in the long, narrow riverfront corridor. Every bomb appeared to have been on target—a surgical operation.

Simultaneous with the attack, Fred Mitchell had been busy with his Iron Hand division. No SAMs were fired, so Fred led his four Skyhawks against the flak sites, obliterating one of those that had been firing at me. In three minutes, the attack was over, and all planes were safely back over the Gulf.

While we were attacking Nam Dinh, Dick Bellinger's fighters were engaging MiGs over the Red River, twenty miles from Hanoi. But the result of their hassle was not the major air victory that the fighter jocks might have envisioned. In a brief good-guy/bad-guy mix-up, one MiG was damaged, and Dick Bellinger's Crusader was shot up by an aggressive enemy pilot. Dick's crippled F-8 was leaking fuel as he flew to a waiting tanker over the Gulf, but the Crusader's in-flight fueling system had been damaged and was inoperative. Unable to reach *Oriskany* or the nearest friendly airfield at Da Nang in South Vietnam, Dick punched out when his Crusader ran out of fuel. A rescue helo scooped him from the Gulf.

All in all, it had been a good day. *Oriskany's* aircraft destroyed the Nam Dinh waterfront complex, and the *Ranger's* group completed the destruction of the Phy Ly bridges. Dick Bellinger came through his narrow escape unscathed but later chided me about the precise mission planning that included having the fighter cover's leader shot down. The errant Skyhawks from *Ranger* had ensured that the Nam Dinh gunners were not napping when we arrived, but we all made it home safely, so even that navigational boo-boo was forgivable. But I did wonder what the *Ranger*'s division leader would have thought had my group been a minute earlier over the target—or he a minute later—and he found himself in the midst of a rainstorm of bombs.

The Saints' daily routine had a pleasant interruption on 16 July when we welcomed the three new pilots who had trekked halfway around the world to join us. Tom Spitzer, Ralph Bisz, and Ronald Tardio arrived on board *Oriskany* unannounced. After a five-day Florida-to-Philippines trip, they had spent a like period at Cubi Point, awaiting onward transportation, and another three days on board USS *Hassayampa*. The Task Force 77 replenishment ship brought them to Yankee Station and transferred them to *Oriskany* by highline. The three travel-weary nuggets were glad to find a permanent home at last and were eagerly in need of laundry service.

Tom Spitzer was pleased to learn that I was familiar with his hometown of Baldwin, North Dakota. During my first year in the Navy I had been assigned to a training unit at the State Teachers College in Dickinson, ninety miles to the west of Baldwin. The two towns were mere dots on the map of the vast, open remoteness of the North Dakota plains. A smiling Tom said, "You're the first person I've met in the Navy who's even *heard* of Baldwin. A lot of people claim they've never heard of North Dakota."

I kidded Tom about being out of uniform and owing us a wetting-down party. He was still wearing ensign bars, and the paperwork for his promotion to lieutenant junior grade had arrived while he was en route to Yankee Station.

Ralph Bisz was a pleasant, quiet man, seeming a little introverted. He had a good flight-training record, but it would be eight months before I would get to know him well.

Ron Tardio ("Chico to my friends") was a thoroughly outgoing and gregarious young man. Handsome almost to a fault, he had dark, wavy hair, sparkling brown eyes, a flashing smile, and a ready wit. A Bolivian, Ron was an American citizen by birth, born in Oakland, California, where his father had been the Bolivian Consul in the late 1940s and early 1950s. Ron had lived most of his life in La Paz, Bolivia, and spoke Spanish and English beautifully. He had taken advantage of his dual citizenship to gain entry into the U.S. Navy's flight-training program. As a teenager, he'd become hooked on aviation, and his father's friend, a Bolivian Air Force colonel named Ortuno, had taught him to fly. The former flight instructor subsequently rose to head the Bolivian air force and, in November 1964, led the political coup that deposed Bolivia's President Estenssoro. A few days before Ron joined the Saints, Ortuno had been elected as the new president of Bolivia. The young pilot had a cryptic evaluation of Ortuno: "He's a nut, but he'll probably make a successful president."

Ron was an engaging storyteller and soon had Ready Five in hysterics with stories about "those crazy people, the Bolivians." Tom Spitzer told me later that the Chico charm had left a trail of brokenhearted ladies throughout the Navy's flight-training command.

After greeting the new pilots, I sat down with Clem Morisette to review their personnel and flight records. One especially impressed me, so I told Clem to assign Tom Spitzer as my new wingman, replacing Wayne Cypress. In a sense, I was relieved by the decision, but my motivation was only indirectly related to Wayne's problem. Newboy pilots were traditionally assigned to fly with the most experienced aviators. Even without Cypress's problem, the arrival of Bisz, Spitzer, and Tardio would have meant reconsidering who would routinely be flying with whom.

Stomach acidity had been plaguing me off and on for several months, no doubt caused by job pressure, frustration with the no-win war strategy, and too much Navy coffee. Euphemistically labeled "combat stomach" by Dan Lestage, it was the same malady that had eventually put Don Martin under the surgeon's knife the previous year. My discomfort had increased since our return to Yankee Station, and Doctor Dan's handouts of disgusting, chalk-flavored antacid concoctions were only partially effective in calming my innards. At Dan's insistence, I reluctantly agreed to take a few days off to undergo an upper-GI series and consult with the internal-medicine people at the Cubi Point naval hospital.

We'd been on the line only nineteen days, and I met the idea of a minivacation with mixed emotions. The time off would be nice, and Ron Caldwell was fully capable of managing the squadron in my absence. But my conscience nagged a bit at the thought of abandoning the squadron even temporarily. More to the point, I was concerned that an examination might disclose a problem that could permanently wrest me away from my assignment as skipper.

I flew for six hours as a passenger on a COD. The C-1 "Trader" was one of the twin-engine utility planes that daily hauled people and priority cargo across the one thousand–mile expanse of the South China Sea, between Cubi Point and Yankee Station. My mid-July trip turned out to be a waste of time, however. Upon my arrival at Cubi I learned that the naval hospital's fluoroscope had gone out of commission the previous day, with no immediate prospects of repair.

My return flight to Yankee Station was scheduled for four days later. I had a three-day holiday in hand, but my conscience wouldn't let me savor the idea. I sent a message to a friend serving on the Yankee Station commander's staff in USS *Roosevelt*, asking his assistance in getting "a wandering Skipper back to his flock." The response was prompt. Less than twenty-four hours later I was "priority cargo" on another COD flight and spent another six hours winging back to *Oriskany*, chewing my antacid tablets.

The squadron's mice had been up to mischief while the cat was away, and the pilots gleefully greeted my return to Ready Five on 21 July. The mischief focused on my flight boots. During the visit to Japan in June, Dan Lestage and John Miles had made a late-evening excursion into Yokosuka and discovered a bottle of "Skipper Blue" shoe dye in one of the many side-street retail stalls on Thieves Row. Since blue was the squadron's color, the Dan-John team decided that it was both logical and practically mandatory that their skipper's flight boots be dyed "Skipper Blue." My dressing habits had temporarily thwarted the boot-dyeing project—I kept my flight gear locked in my air-conditioned stateroom. But the plotters were patient. When I left the ship for Cubi, the wheels of the COD aircraft had hardly cleared the deck when Operation Skipper Blue was put into effect.

Dan and John conned Lacson, my room steward, into giving them temporary access to my stateroom, and soon the whole squadron knew of the project. Particularly enthusiastic in support of Operation Skipper Blue were the pilots who recalled my slave-driving days as "Bluefinger" during the 1965 rehabilitation of our ready room. Ready Five was packed with an unusual number of people when I walked in after my return from Cubi, and I was immediately suspicious. But my "What's going on here?" netted only Cheshire-cat grins. Then I spied the pair of brilliant blue flight boots hanging conspicuously from a hook on the overhead above my chair. I grinned, and the rest of the people in the ready room burst into harmonious laughter. I was genuinely touched, and my eyes misted. Morale was obviously high as, in common delight, the pilots had manufactured yet another way to help relieve the tension. In our close-knit squadron/family environment, Operation Skipper Blue was a gesture of unspoken love and camaraderie.

My return to *Oriskany* was doubly happy because Wayne Cypress's problem had been resolved. Late the night before my COD flight to Cubi, the telephone in my room had jangled just after I had turned out the light and was dozing off to sleep. The caller was Wayne.

"Skipper, would it be convenient for me to stop by your room for a talk?"

I was dead tired and tempted to ask if the matter couldn't wait until the morning. But a sixth sense brought me wide awake. Wayne was a confused young man in need of help. I didn't want to do anything that would be a turnoff. It occurred to me that the request for a private late-night audience wasn't so that he could tell me that he was going to stick with the program. I crawled out of bed, pulled on my flight suit, and splashed some water on my face.

Wayne was dressed in freshly laundered khakis when he arrived a few minutes later. He looked happy, a picture of confidence, and he came directly to the point: "You were right, Skipper. I'm over my head in the wrong business. I've just been kidding myself. I want to turn in my wings."

The announcement was not unexpected but still came as a mild surprise. Wayne said he'd given the matter considerable thought and had done some heavy self-analysis since our last talk. He openly admitted that his problem had been long-standing, dating back to the beginning of his flight training. Only recently had it come to a head. Always uncomfortable flying planes, Wayne said, he'd never been able to make himself face the real reason for the discomfort. Pride had kept him from accepting the obvious solution, and he thanked me for helping him face reality.

The step Wayne was taking was serious. We'd covered the ground in a prior conversation, but I reviewed the matter to ensure that he realized the full import of what he was doing. Then I outlined the necessary follow-on steps and what the future might hold for him. I repeated my earlier warning that higher authority would not receive the news favorably and that action to remove him from his present assignment would probably be swift. And there was another concern. I remembered Bill Smith's comments and told Wayne that, true or not, other pilots might view his action as cowardly.

Still Wayne maintained his composure and stuck with his decision. He appeared to be a new person—cheerful and relaxed, quite different from the withdrawn and unhappy man whom I had known for several months. In that wee hour of the morning I got to know Wayne Cypress better, and I gained respect for him. He had finally opened up, and I thought of the lecture on courage that I had given to the pilots as we were steaming toward Yankee Station two weeks earlier. In his own way, Wayne had mustered the necessary courage to face himself and to make what probably was the most significant decision of his young life. He had swallowed his pride and come to grips with self-honesty. It couldn't have been an easy decision, and arriving at it must have been a terribly lonely process.

When Wayne left my room, still the picture of confidence, he stopped at the door and turned back toward me. "Thanks, Skipper," he said. "I feel a lot better now."

It was the first time that I had seen Wayne Cypress with a real smile on his face. He was free of a tremendous burden.

On the morning of 23 July I carefully briefed Tom Spitzer on the attack mission against the petroleum-storage facility at Vinh. It was Tom's first combat hop, and I wanted to ensure that he was mentally ready, particularly for the antiaircraft fire that I knew we'd encounter. Vinh would surely have a reception committee waiting.

When I appeared on the flight deck and headed for my aircraft, the air boss bellowed a message over the loudspeakers. He directed everyone's attention to the blue flight boots that I was wearing.

1 3 Decision

 The upward thrust of the ejection seat drained the little blood that still fed my brain. Though I had blacked out, I was vaguely aware of a tumbling sensation and of hearing a series of snaps and pops.

I opened my eyes to find myself suspended in midair as if in a weird dream. It was a beautiful day. The sun shone brightly, and there were puffy white clouds painted against a light blue sky. Below me was the deeper blue of the water. I had no sensation of movement. All was calm. The war was a million miles away. The space in which I was floating was a far more pleasant environment than the confusing cockpit that I had just departed.

With no sense of urgency, I removed my oxygen mask and felt for my right arm with my left hand. It was not there. I was not dreaming. The events of the past few minutes came back into focus. Strangely, though, I felt euphoric and unconcerned. I squeezed the stump of my right arm, thinking the bleeding somehow should be stopped, and wondered what I should do next.

Looking down, I saw my legs and feet dangling toward the blue water. They didn't seem to belong to me. My life vest came to mind. *Oh, yes,* I thought, *I'll need flotation when I hit the water.* I released my grip on my stump arm and grasped the toggle of the left CO_2 cartridge. I tugged it, and the cylinder-trapped gas rushed into half of the flotation bladder built into the waist of my torso harness. It caused a slight pressure against my midsection. I groped for the right toggle, but the

184

half-inflated life vest was in the way. A few more gropes and the pursuit became frustrating, so I lost interest in the vest.

I returned to the easier chore of stump-squeezing and stared blankly at the sky for a few seconds. Then a faint alert signal rang in my brain. Something about the seat pack. I concentrated on the clue, and it grew into a procedure. The life raft was stowed in the seat pack. To release it, the snap on the left side had to be undone. I grasped the fitting and pressed the spring-loaded levers. The seat pack popped away and hung behind my right thigh just as it was supposed to do. I reached across my body with my left hand and awkwardly groped for the lanyard on the seat pack that would release and inflate the life raft. I couldn't find it. I kicked at the seat pack a couple of times, trying to move it within reach of my left hand. But that didn't work. Again, the procedure became too complicated, and I returned to stump-squeezing.

A movement below me to the right grabbed my attention. I watched a Skyhawk crash into the Gulf, and it created a sizable geyser. *That was a stupid thing some pilot just did, flying his plane into the water like that.* I thought about my own plane and looked around, wondering what had happened to it. Another Skyhawk was flying an orbit around me. *Can't be mine,* I thought, watching it for a few seconds. Then it came to me: *Oh, yes, that's Tom, doing what a good wingman is supposed to do.*

What is a good wingman supposed to do in a situation like mine? I couldn't remember and was miffed with myself for being forgetful. Was there something I was supposed to do? Some sort of a signal, perhaps? I couldn't remember. Frustration was strong.

My flight glove was still on my left hand, and another faint alarm bell rang. Did I need the glove? I concentrated again and the message surfaced: *Flight gloves are slippery when wet.* I pulled the glove off with my teeth, spit it out, and went back to stump-squeezing. The glove floated lazily a few feet from me. I watched, fascinated, as it descended only a little faster than I. The SAR ship was below—USS *Reeves.* I studied her carefully. She seemed much closer than when I saw her from the cockpit, and she wasn't moving any more. A boat was suspended from davits on her starboard side.

Tom Spitzer's plane made another orbit, sweeping across the arc of my vision, then disappearing behind me. I was bored. Just hanging there, squeezing the stump of my right arm, seemed pointless. Boredom vanished a few seconds later, however, when I recognized movement. The water was rushing up at me. I crossed my legs and held my breath and plunged into the Gulf.

The half-inflated life vest bobbed me back to the surface. I was floating comfortably in the gentle swell of the warm water. *Concentrate,* I told myself. *Mental checklist. What should I do next?* The parachute came to mind. It had collapsed somewhere behind me, and as I twisted to look around, I could see nothing but a few shroud lines draped over my left shoulder. I disconnected the riser fittings from the shoulders of my torso harness and tossed the metal attachments into the water behind me. Then I thought about the wind and shuddered involuntarily. The sea was calm with only a gentle swell. But if the wind had been blowing, could I have disconnected myself if the parachute had dragged me through the water?

Reeves was close by, perhaps one hundred yards away, dead in the water. The whaleboat, free of the davits, was heading in my direction. As it neared, a khaki-clad figure pointed toward me. The coxswain throttled back the engine and turned the boat sharply away.

"Drive right in, cox'n." I shouted. "I'm bleeding badly and need help."

The coxswain responded by reversing his rudder and bringing the boat directly alongside me. Several pairs of hands reached out.

"Be careful of my right side," I said to no one in particular. A dozen or so hands scooped me out of the water. My head came to rest, cradled in someone's lap. I remembered the elapsed-time clock in the cockpit of my Skyhawk. It was later determined that seventeen minutes had passed from the instant shrapnel ripped through the cockpit until the whaleboat crew pulled me from the water. But at the time those Dali-esque minutes were misshapen, with no beginning or end.

Free of the ocean and safely in the hands of the sailors, my physical condition suddenly became a concern to me. From the moment I was hit I had felt no pain, only a mild stinging sensation in my right elbow. But once I was in the whaleboat my brain seemed to tell my nervous system that it was OK to start hurting. My stump became excruciatingly painful. I was aware that someone had removed my helmet, but I didn't remember that happening. Above me, silhouetted against the bright sky, was a figure holding a bottle with a tube extended toward me. Apparently, there was a corpsman or doctor in the boat and I was receiving something intravenously. But I'd felt no needle puncture.

The pain in my right arm was fierce, and I gritted my teeth to keep from screaming out. I remembered that there were two morphine Syrettes in a plastic case in the left sleeve pocket of my flight suit, part of my survival equipment. There were several people in the boat, but flat on my back, I was only vaguely aware of their presence. But the sailor cradling my head in his lap was real.

"There are morphine Syrettes in my left sleeve pocket," I said to the sailor. "Get one out and give me a shot."

"S-s-sir," he stammered, "I've never done that before."

"That's OK, son, I'll teach you."

I muttered the step-by-step instructions: take a Syrette from the plastic case, remove the plastic protective cap covering the needle, and throw it away; push the wire-loop plunger all the way down into the Syrette, then pull it out and throw it away; then....

The nervous young sailor followed the instructions. He pushed the wire plunger into the tube and removed it. Then, holding the plunger securely in one hand, he casually tossed the morphine Syrette over the side into the water. He paused, then grinned sheepishly.

"I guess I didn't do that right," he said.

I agreed and told him to try again with the second Syrette. Once more I spelled out the procedure as if we were doing a training exercise in a classroom. The sailor went through the drill a second time with the remaining Syrette and gave me a shot, being hesitant only about stabbing the needle into my left arm through the fabric of my flight suit.

Part of a long-forgotten World War II training film flitted through my mind. "Tell the doctor about the morphine," I said. "In case I pass out." At the time I didn't realize that my demand for morphine was nearly suicidal. In my state of shock, the anesthetic-sedative was a potentially fatal medication.

We came alongside *Reeves.* In a single motion the whaleboat's bow and stern hooks were attached, and the boat was hoisted rapidly to the deck level. More hands reached out. I was placed in a stretcher and rushed below to sick bay, where the ship's doctor began to work over me. I took his presence for granted. After all, I had radioed earlier and told whoever was listening that I would need medical attention. But I was fortune-blessed. At the time *Reeves* was the only American ship north of Yankee Station with a doctor on board!

Conscious but in a trancelike state, I lay on what had to be an operating table. Faceless figures moved about the room, muttering quiet words to each other. I watched the proceedings with detachment, as if viewing a TV program with partial interest. One phrase clearly came through the haze of my mind: "About an hour ago," someone said.

I tried to decipher the significance of the remark. Was it in reference to my accident? I tried to reconstruct my morning thus far, focusing on the elapsed-time clock on the instrument panel of my Skyhawk. *What time was I hit? What was my take-off time? Did I remember to start the elapsed-time clock before my cat shot? What was my time over target?* Panic welled up as I drew blank answers. Why couldn't I remember? *Has it been only an hour? An hour from when? Did I eat breakfast? Did the folks in* Oriskany *know that I had been hit? Who told them?*

I had no sense of feel. *Am I still alive? What's it like to be dead?*

I moved my left hand and was surprised to find my arm taped to a board. A tube attached to the board rose from my arm to a bottle hanging on a stainless-steel rig above me. *When did that happen?* I moved my arm and felt my stomach. I was naked. Someone has taken away all my flight clothing and equipment, but I couldn't remember that happening either.

"Don't do that," the doctor said, as if I were a little boy caught playing with himself. He placed my arm back at my side.

Another face loomed into view directly above me. "Hi, Commander, I'm Dr. Pennington from *Ranger*."

Another flush of panic. *What will happen to me?* Ranger? *No, not* Ranger. *My ship is* Oriskany. *I want to go back to* Oriskany. *My personal gear is in* Oriskany. *My squadron is in* Oriskany. *My friends are in* Oriskany. *Why should I go to* Ranger?

"My carrier is *Oriskany*," I announced with authority. "I want to go to *Oriskany*, not to *Ranger!*"

A reassuring Dr. Pennington quieted me down. I would be returned to my own ship.

Another dark thought sprung into my consciousness. A one-arm aviator wasn't much good. I probably wouldn't stay on as skipper of the Saints in my condition. *Where will I go? Will I get to say good-bye to the Saints?*

I was lifted from the operating table and placed on a stretcher. Four sailors carried me along a passageway. I rolled my head and looked at my right arm. The stump was wrapped in a monstrous wad of bandages. *When did that happen?* I had no bodily sensation, and I seemed to be floating between the husky sailors as they maneuvered the stretcher through the crew's mess decks. Groups of other sailors lined the stretcher's route, standing silently, watching. I moved my hand to sneak another "feel." The board with the intravenous tube was still taped to my arm, but I was wrapped in a blanket. I couldn't remember that happening either.

The stretcher floated into another passageway, and I thought of my blue boots, the ones given me as a wonderful surprise in Ready Room Five. I panicked again. Tape, board, and intravenous feeding tube notwithstanding, I reached out with my left arm and grabbed the nearest solid object, a stanchion. The floating stretcher and the four husky sailors came to an abrupt halt.

"I'm not leaving without my blue boots," I announced. Dr. Pennington was familiar with the idiosyncrasies of tailhook pilots. He calmly assured me that all my flight gear would be returned to *Oriskany.* The men on *Reeves* no doubt wondered if I had been hit in the head as well as the arm.

The helo flight to *Oriskany* seemed short. Dr. Pennington spent most of the time with his fingers on my pulse. Twice he asked if I felt cold, if I wanted another blanket. Then he asked if I wanted a cigarette. The thought of smoking didn't excite me, but I was bored again and a cigarette was something to do. I nodded affirmatively. Pennington lit a cigarette and held it to my lips. I took a few puffs while Doc kept his fingers on my pulse, talking to me, insisting on answers. At the time the significance of the doctor's actions escaped me. Only later would I learn how bad off I was. Dr. Pennington thought I might check out at any moment.

The helo touched down on *Oriskany,* and I heard a familiar sound—the voice of the assistant air boss, CDR Jerry Hammil, booming out over the flight-deck announcing system: "One Sixty-Three, returning." It was a variation of the traditional announcement made as a commanding officer returned to his ship—a nice touch, I thought. The sky was bright above, and I closed my eyes to the glare as the stretcher was pulled from the helo. I felt good with my eyes closed.

My mission was complete. I was suddenly very tired. I was home. I wanted to go to sleep.

"Boy, some people will do anything to get out of a little combat." The voice shouting into my ear over the noise of the helo's engine and rotor swirl was familiar. It brought me back from the edge of sleep. I looked up into the face of Dr. Dan Lestage. Maybe I smiled.

"With friends like you, who needs enemies?" I muttered.

Dan kept his fingers on my pulse as I was carried below to sick bay. Soon, the X-ray machine loomed overhead. Then I was lying on a table in the operating room.

"We're going to put you to sleep now, Skipper," Dan said.

I drifted off into an idyllic dream in which my right arm was being bathed in warm, running water. I instantly recognized the location. I was submerged in the gently trickling stream that ran outside my room at the beautiful Fuji Hotel in Miyanoshita, Japan.

When I opened my eyes, I was alone in the small, dimly lit room that served as SOQ, sick officers' quarters. For several seconds I was confused. The stump of my right arm was bundled in bandages and throbbed. I studied the bandages for a moment and everything came clear in my mind. *I'll be damned,* I thought. *I'm alive.*

A corpsman came in to check on me, and I asked the time. It was late afternoon, 23 July. I complained that my stump hurt. The corpsman disappeared for a couple of minutes and returned with a syringe, and a shot of Demerol quickly stopped the pain.

For the next fourteen hours I slipped in and out of groggy sleep, periodically receiving comforting shots at the hands of the corpsman. When Dan Lestage visited me the next morning, I felt chipper and pronounced myself "ready for some action." I conned Dan into permitting me to shower. With my bandaged stump encased in a waterproof plastic bag, and supported by two corpsmen, I stood in the shower for two or three minutes. The water washed away the stickiness of my earlier saltwater bath, and I emerged feeling refreshed if not entirely clean. Afterward, Ron Caldwell came down to act as scribe, writing a letter to Marilyn as I dictated. Then, exhausted from all my action and feeling no pain, I drifted off to sleep.

My stump had been packed open—left as an open wound, treated only to stop the bleeding, and protected in sterile bandages. That was a necessary preparation for the surgery to be performed elsewhere. Dan

Lestage and Dr. Dick Donahue, the ship's surgeon, had done what they could, but my condition required attention that could be given only at a proper hospital, and medical evacuation was warranted. But that meant sending me to Cubi Point via a COD flight. That worried Donahue and Lestage. There was the possibility of hemorrhage if I was subjected to the strain of a catapult shot. And if anything happened during the six-hour flight to Cubi, it could be fatal.

Oriskany was scheduled to leave the line within the week for a visit to Subic Bay, and the doctors decided that I should remain aboard until then. When Dan informed me, I was in complete agreement. My reason was selfish, however, related to my psychological, not physical, well-being. When Harry Jenkins was shot down the prior November, I was executive officer at 0800 and CO by 0900. The war went right on, and the change-of-command ceremony that Harry and I had talked about didn't occur. Eight months later, my cherished squadron command was about to be prematurely terminated, and I wanted to have at least one ceremony. Bob Spruit consulted with Captain Iarrobino, and a change-of-command ceremony was arranged for the morning the ship arrived at Cubi Point.

Forty-eight hours after my accident the doctors' fears came true. In the serenity of SOQ, with little apparent strain, my stump arm hemorrhaged, and I was rushed to surgery a second time. After awakening from that bout and shaking off as much drowsiness as possible, I tape-recorded a letter to Marilyn, detailing my recent experience. RADM Dave Richardson, the commander of our carrier division, would soon leave Yankee Station for a trip to Washington, D.C., and he agreed to expedite my communication by mailing the tape to Marilyn from San Diego.[1]

---

1. A "casualty call" team visited Marilyn at Lemoore and informed her of my accident. She was in the bedroom of our quarters when our daughter, Cori, entered and said, "Mother, there are some men in uniform at the front door." Marilyn knew immediately the significance of those words, and her mind went numb. She doesn't remember going from the bedroom to the door. Later, she received a confirmation telegram from the Chief of Naval Personnel, but neither the casualty-call people nor the telegram shed much light on the details of my accident. The tape that Rear Admiral Richardson mailed from San Diego arrived before the letter I'd dictated to Ron and was the first detailed news she received.

Although pretty well doped up during my time in sick bay, my waking hours were anything but boring. I received many messages of support and encouragement.

From Commander-in-Chief, Pacific Fleet, ADM Roy Johnson: "The determination and courage demonstrated by you have the utmost admiration of all hands back here. Best wishes for a speedy recovery."

From VADM John Hyland, Commander Seventh Fleet: "I am proud to join ADM Johnson in noting your heroism and will to survive. Well done and God speed."

From Rear Admiral James Reedy, Commander Task Force 77: "Your courage, determination, and devotion to duty are an inspiration to all of us. Your example will not be forgotten by your fellow aviators. Well done."

And from my old buddy, CDR Fred Palmer, the CAG in *Ranger*: "CAPT Harnish, all A-4 types, and I join in our concern and prayers for Wynn."

Bob Spruit and Ron Caldwell visited me daily to chat about events in the air wing and my squadron. Other pilots made encouraging visits. My former wingman, John Shore, spent many hours "baby-sitting" me in SOQ.

An important visitor was *Oriskany*'s skipper, John Iarrobino. We talked at length about good times shared several years earlier when we served together in *Forrestal*. Then I spoke of a matter that had been nagging my brain for several days—my desire to remain on active duty. I had a gut feeling that the odds might be against me in that regard, considering my physical condition. But I needed an assessment from someone with a more objective slant. John reminded me that I was a regular officer whose career was guarded by federal legislation. Even though I had lost my arm, there would be nothing automatic about my separation from service. John mentioned my fine service reputation and said that he was convinced that if I chose to take the case to court, to fight for the right to remain on active duty, there would be a lot of support from friends who were senior naval officers. The mechanics of how a pilot missing an arm could go about such a fight were not clear to me at the time. Certainly, if I chose to make it, the fight was still a long way off, but John's words were encouraging.

One pilot whom I wanted to see, but who hadn't voluntarily come to sick bay, was Tom Spitzer. With the squadron for only a week, Tom had had a traumatic introduction to combat as an eyewitness to his skipper's getting shot out of the sky. I was concerned that Tom might somehow think that my getting shot down was his fault. Both Bob Spruit and Ron Caldwell had told me that Tom's performance after my hit had been cool-headed and professional, and he had been of like stripe on the missions flown since.

Ron passed the word, and a few hours later Tom dropped in to see me. It was immediately apparent that he was uncomfortable, and our conversation was a bit strained. Trying to allay any feelings of guilt that Tom might have, I made light of my situation: "Hey, it was just one of the breaks of naval air. I zigged when I should have zagged. It wasn't your fault."

Tom smiled when I told him of the flattering comments that Ron and CAG Spruit had made about his performance. But he was still uncomfortable. The conversation lagged, so I shook his hand, wished him well, and he departed. In our brief professional relationship, I had noted an air of quiet confidence in Tom. I was sorry that we wouldn't fly together again, that we wouldn't get to know each other as a team as John Shore and I had.

In a lucid moment during my seemingly perpetual Demerol haze, I remembered a piece of unfinished business—an unopened bottle of Courvoisier brandy locked in the safe of my stateroom. It had been purchased for a special occasion, and my predicament and pending departure from *Oriskany* sure qualified on that account. When Bob Spruit dropped by, I presented him with my last tactical plan for the air wing: a "briefing" for squadron COs, XOs, and the CAG staff, with the main agenda item being how best to dispose of the Courvoisier. Bob spread the word. The following evening about a dozen of my air-wing contemporaries crowded into the telephone booth–size SOQ. A corpsman provided a generous supply of paper pill cups "for your medicine" and discreetly disappeared. The Courvoisier was passed around several times with each pilot taking snorts. Except me. Already doped up with Demerol, I dozed off to sleep halfway through the first round. The other pilots performed the trick of making the Courvoisier disappear.

Oriskany moored at the Cubi Point carrier pier at about 0900 on Saturday morning, 30 July. At 1000, dressed in my tropical white uniform and semireclined on a gurney stretcher, I was wheeled to the hangar deck for the change-of-command ceremony. RADM Ralph Cousins, who upon learning of my accident a week earlier had rushed Dr. Pennington by helo from *Ranger* to *Reeves,* was on hand to present me with the Purple Heart and Silver Star medals. The Purple Heart was no surprise; my injury was an entitlement for that. But the Silver Star, the third-ranking combat decoration, was unexpected.

"For conspicuous gallantry and intrepidity in aerial flight...."

I suspected that the award was primarily the doing of Bob Spruit because of a running jest that we had enjoyed. Regularly, after each Alfa strike, I'd say to Bob, "Any air-wing commander worth his salt should be able to qualify a squadron skipper and good friend for at least one li'l ol' Distinguished Flying Cross."

Just as regular was Bob's good-natured response: "Well, skipper and good friend, try to do some *distinguished* flying for a change, and I'll see what I can do!"

As Admiral Cousins pinned the prestigious Silver Star on my shirt, I glanced at Bob Spruit. He was grinning from ear to ear.

Still feeling no pain, I made farewell remarks to the air-wing officers and enlisted personnel assembled in formation on the hangar deck, but primarily I was addressing the Saints of VA-163. In the middle of the previous night I had assembled a rough outline of the remarks I wished to make. I hoped they made sense. Ron Caldwell then read the orders from the Chief of Naval Personnel assigning him as commanding officer of VA-163. He saluted me and spoke the traditional words, "I relieve you, sir." I returned the salute, and the ceremony was over. I was no longer skipper of the Saints.

A hollow feeling came over me, but it was quickly gone as a long line of people formed near my gurney and began to shake my hand. I didn't count, but I was certain that every one of my official family, every Saint—officer and enlisted—was in that line. The pilots were last. Some mumbled good wishes; others muttered the single word "Skipper." Many had tears in their eyes and didn't say much. I didn't say much either, probably because of the tears in my eyes. Two handshakes I held longer than the rest, those of my first and last Saints wingmen, John Shore and Tom Spitzer. It was the last time I would see Tom.

John Iarrobino accompanied me to the quarterdeck, and after another emotional good-bye I left the ship. It didn't seem cricket to depart horizontally, so I got off the gurney and walked unsteadily down the access brow, formally piped ashore through a row of side boys.

After a two-hour stop at the Cubi Point hospital, where I telephoned and talked to Marilyn, I was flown to Clark Air Force Base, north of Manila. Two days later I was in the belly of the giant C-141 Liftmaster, on my way to the States. The medevac plane made a brief fueling stop in Japan before heading east on a long transpacific flight to Travis Air Force Base near San Francisco.

Staying strapped into a bunk for hours on end was boring, so I conned the flight nurse into asking the pilot of the Liftmaster if I could visit the cockpit. The answer was yes, and I weakly maneuvered around the three-tier racks of bunks occupied by other wounded men and carefully scaled the short ladder leading to the cockpit door. For a half hour I sat perched on a jump seat in the cockpit, chatting aviator talk with the crew. As the ache in my stump arm worked its way up to a pounding throb, I realized that the limited activity was more tiring than I had anticipated. Thanking the flight crew, I gingerly worked my way back down the ladder and to my bunk and ordered another shot of pain-killing Demerol.

There was a lot of time for reflection during the transpacific flight. After I'd mentally replayed my last combat mission for the umpteenth time, I accepted the fact that a one-arm pilot was not a hot-selling commodity. After an exciting sixteen years, my career as a tailhook jet-jockey was over.

My mind drifted back to my early aviation experiences. My first close-up sight of a barnstorming "Jenny" in a pasture outside Flagstaff in 1931. I was four and a half years old, but that impressive old biplane was forever etched in my memory. A Martin B-10 bomber at the Army Air Corps dirt strip in Albuquerque in 1938. The crew let me crawl all through its cavernous interior and "fly" it from the cockpit. And my love affair with naval aviation that began when a friend of the family gave me a set of pot metal cast toy Navy ships for my tenth birthday. I flew a lot of imaginary missions from the decks of the two toy aircraft carriers, no doubt setting the stage for my enlistment in naval aviation at age seventeen during World War II.

Returning to the present, I weighed the encouraging words that John Iarrobino had spoken a few days earlier and the messages of friendship and encouragement that I had received. I tried to comprehend their significance. So far I hadn't had much opportunity to investigate the prospects of staying on active duty, but John had said that there would be a lot of support if I chose to fight for that privilege.

The future kept parading through my mind. My bunk seemed more comfortable than it had earlier, and I was drowsy. Before drifting off to sleep somewhere over the blue Pacific, however, I decided that I would not voluntarily retire from active duty. I wasn't ready for that. If "they," whoever they might be, wanted to get rid of me, they would jolly well have to chuck me out, for I intended to fight. After all, what more did I have to lose?

14 Fighting the System

 From the first emergency efforts by the personnel of USS *Reeves* in the whaleboat in the Tonkin Gulf, to the tender care provided by Dan Lestage and others in *Oriskany,* to my interim stay at Clark Air Base, and through the transit across the Pacific in the Air Force medevac aircraft, my medical treatment was superb. Marilyn met me upon my arrival at Travis AFB north of San Francisco. For about an hour after the C-141 landed, she was with me in a comfortable private room at the base hospital, where, among other amenities, a duty doctor paid me a courtesy visit.

In contrast, my introduction to the Stateside medical organization of my own service was painful and proved that it was disorganized and embarrassingly inept. When Navy transportation arrived at Travis to take me to the naval hospital at Oakland, my care began to resemble that accorded to a side of beef. The Navy had been notified of my arrival as a litter patient with a packed-open wound, and there were only two other customers destined for the Oakland hospital, both ambulatory marines. Yet someone at Oakland had dispatched a monstrous, forty-passenger, "cattle car" bus to collect the three of us at Travis. I was placed aboard first, my stretcher suspended from "meat hooks" located over the rear wheels. The bus then made a bumpy half-hour tour of Travis while the driver tried to find the baggage belonging to the two ambulatory patients.

The fifty-mile trip to Oakland coincided with afternoon rush-hour traffic and took two hours and fifteen minutes. Since I had an open wound, regular doses of pain medicine had been prescribed for comfort. A flight nurse aboard the Liftmaster had administered the most recent shot of Demerol about two hours before our arrival at Travis. The effects of that shot wore off well before the bus reached Oakland. The Navy corpsman striker, an apprentice under training assigned to ride the bus, had nothing to administer for pain relief, not even aspirin. Even if aspirin had been appropriate for my condition it would have made little difference. There was no drinking water on the bus.

Upon our arrival at the Oakland hospital, I was dehydrated and in agony. Marilyn, who accompanied me on the bus, was in tears. My stretcher was removed from the bus and placed on the floor of the admissions office, where I lay unattended and ignored, except by Marilyn, for another forty-five minutes. At quarter past six in the evening a uniformed doctor poked his face through the door of the admissions room and peered somewhat disdainfully at me. He neither spoke to nor examined me but merely directed that I be transferred to the orthopedic clinic. Twenty minutes more passed before an ambulance and driver arrived. Another twenty dragged by as I rested uncomfortably at the orthopedic clinic without the benefit of wifely consolation. Another doctor, he at least not being mute, arrived and honored my request for a pain shot. A few minutes after 1900 the morphine took effect, the pain began to subside, and I found drowsy relief as I was transferred to the officers' orthopedic ward.

Thank Heaven for friends. While I was still at the Clark air base hospital in the Philippines, I had received a telegram from CAPT Harry Zenner, a friend since flight training sixteen years earlier. Harry and I had long enjoyed a friendly rivalry about various career accomplishments as we moved up through the ranks. Thus, it was not surprising that Harry, upon learning of my accident, sent a telegram asking, "But, what do you do for an encore?"

Harry was attached to the fleet air staff at nearby Alameda Naval Air Station. He had met Marilyn after her drive to the Bay area from Lemoore and accompanied her to Travis. Harry arrived at the Oakland hospital about thirty minutes after I did, expecting to find me resting comfortably in a clean hospital bed, and was shocked and furious to find me indifferently stashed on the floor of the admissions room. He used his rank to get matters off top dead center with an artful tail chewing that enriched the lives of several of the hospital's personnel, including the duty medical officer who finally directed my removal to the orthopedic clinic. The following day, Harry wrote a stinging three-page letter to RADM Harold Cokely, the commandant of the hospital, outlining his observations and icily questioning if improvements might be made. If nothing else, Harry's letter made me an instant celebrity of sorts at the naval hospital. Thereafter, my medical treatment was excellent. Both initially and later, however, it was my impression that the administrative, nonmedical aspects of patient care at U.S. Naval Hospital Oakland suffered from a well-entrenched and burdensome bureaucracy. The premise seemed to be that patients were commodities, not people.

On my first morning in the officers' orthopedic ward, an otherwise personable young corpsman breezed into my room and said, "Hey, Foster, how y' doin', dude?"

Chagrined that the young man had apparently slept through the class on military courtesy, I instructed the corpsman to shut the door. I pointed out that I was an experienced cowboy, not a dude, and that he had my permission to address me as "Commander."

"There is no rank among patients," he answered, less confident. Strike two.

I refuted his theory that patients were nonpersons but explained that I was a reasonable man. As a compromise, if he and his fellow corpsmen found it awkward to address me as "Commander," they should feel free to call me by my nickname, "Sir."

Word spread rapidly among the corpsmen. There were no further incidents of sloppy protocol, and the Foster Program of Patients' Rights and Military Courtesy began to take root in the officers' orthopedic ward. The Mr. Gruff act gained me a reputation as a bear among the corpsmen, but it cloaked me with minor folk-hero status among the other patients.

The first order of medical business, a few days after my arrival at Oakland, was the surgical closing of my wound. The process involved a skin graft and a painful postoperative period of healing for my right thigh, the source of the grafted skin. After that bout of surgery, to my own consternation, I recognized that I was hooked on Demerol. I enjoyed it, not for the relief of pain but for the high it provided, and looked forward to the next shot. Two days after the surgery I quit

Demerol cold turkey and suffered through another two days of headachy withdrawal symptoms.

Through August and September, while my wound healed before further surgery could be done, I kept busy. Three separate press interviews splashed the story of my shoot down across the country via the wire services. I received a deluge of letters and cards from friends and well-wishers. After thirty-nine right-handed years, I produced an awkward and childish scrawl when writing with my left hand, so I borrowed a typewriter from the nurses' station to answer the mail. While the machine was available, I branched out into writing some short stories that had been kicking about in my head for several years. Not wishing to become totally dependent on a machine, however, I took advantage of a longtime crossword-puzzle addiction to improve my left-hand penmanship. A hundred or more puzzles, alternately done in block print and cursive letters, and my handwriting became passably legible. And somewhere in the agonizing process I gave a special thanks to that unsung genius, the inventor of the clip board.

Round two of surgery came in early October when Dr. Robert Colgrove, head of the orthopedic service, transplanted five inches of fibula from my right leg, attaching it to the remaining four inches of my humerus, the upper arm bone. The added length of the humerus would give me better leverage when I got a prosthesis.

The surgery was successful, but a minor postsurgical complication resulted from the choice of my right leg as the source of the fibular bone. Neither Dr. Colgrove nor I had visualized the lopsided awkwardness of trying to ambulate with only a left arm, a left leg, and a crutch. Using a wheelchair was an option, but that struck me as conceding to an invalid status. Besides, it wasn't easy to maneuver a wheelchair with only one hand. I stuck with the crutch and after a few days of experimentation was able to hobble around in fair fashion.

While I recuperated from the bone-graft surgery I struck another blow in my private crusade for patients' dignity and freedom from bureaucratic hassle. One morning a corpsman informed me that I was scheduled for a session in OTC, the occupational-therapy clinic. I asked the purpose of the visit and who had scheduled it, but learned only that it had been ordered by "the doctor." Being of limited mobility, I elected to ignore the summons. For a second scheduling several days later, the messenger was a nurse. Again, I asked the purpose and the source of the order. My challenge to the system frustrated the nurse, who provided a partial answer by saying that OTC was where patients learned "to do things normally."

My next question—"What is normal?"—went unanswered. I explained that I was already doing things normally. One of my normal pastimes was writing, which I was pursuing with part-time use of the borrowed typewriter. Normally, I did a lot of reading and crossword puzzles and was doing just fine in those departments. Briefly, I considered being even more of a smart ass by asking if OTC had any airplanes in its inventory but decided that that might be a bit esoteric. The nurse interjected that occupational therapy was required. My reply was that the only therapy my occupation required was for me to get back to it.

When the third call to visit OTC came, it was delivered by the ward doctor as a plaintive request rather than a summons. The doctor said that he was getting pressure from upstairs about my nonappearance at the clinic. That, at least, was an honest answer, so I went to the OTC the next day.

Miss Amazona, the muscular female therapist in charge of OTC, showed me an array of busywork tasks, from belt beading to wallet making and from weaving to wood carving. She changed the subject when I insisted that I had learned those skills some years earlier as a Cub Scout. Amazona requested and received a sample of my handwriting, which was not much better that second-grade quality, shaky and vertically stroked but legible. I neglected to confess that I had been practicing my own brand of occupational therapy with crossword puzzles back at the ward.

"Very good," Amazona purred, "but we must practice so we can get a nice, normal slant to it."

I ignored both the patronizing "we" and the temptation to ask why normal handwriting had to slant. Instead, I said politely that I saw nothing in the clinic that captured my fancy.

There were two skills that did interest me, however—how to employ a solo left hand to unbutton the cuff of my left shirt sleeve and how to cope with one-hand shoelace tying. Beyond those immediate needs, I said, I had already adjusted to a one-arm existence and saw no pressing need to learn new physical skills until my arm was healed and I was fitted with a prosthesis. Amazona didn't have immediate answers to the skills I had requested but promised to look up the information.

I had invented those two skills on the spot. Pajamas, robe, and slippers were the uniform of the day at the hospital, and I had little need for either shoes or long-sleeve shirts. But having hurled the challenge, I returned to my ward and began exploring the possible solutions. The task of unbuttoning the left-sleeve cuff was a messy failure. The only technique that I could think of was to use my teeth, but that was impossibly awkward and resulted in a soggy cuff. I decided that it was better if I wore short-sleeve shirts. Similarly, I could elect to wear loafers, but the tying of shoelaces with one hand presented an interesting challenge.

Time was plentiful, so I spent the better part of the day fumbling with the laces of my uniform shoes. Eventually, I fumbled my way into discovering the trick. Abandoning a technique ingrained during childhood, I reeved the lace through the last (upper) shoelace holes from the top rather than from the underside. The first overhand knot, awkward but not impossible, then drew the sides of the shoe snugly against the lace. That held the laces taut, snug, and immobile while I fumbled to create the bow knot. By dinner time I had become quite adept with the technique. In the process, I realized that I was learning to be more patient with myself, if not with others.

Amazona called two days later to report no success on shirt-cuff unbuttoning, but she said that she had discovered a shoe-tying method. Would I care to drop by the clinic for a demonstration? No, thanks, I said. My subsequent ignoring of all preprosthesis summons to the OTC went without penalty. I continued typing, reading, and improving my handwriting by doing crossword puzzles, alternately in block and cursive letters, without worrying about the slant.

During the lengthy period required for the grafted bone to complete the knitting process, there was no medical reason for my daily presence at the hospital. Encased in a twelve-pound upper-body cast that held my stump arm immobilized, I was allowed to travel to Lemoore to be with my family. Thus began five months of biweekly visits to the hospital for X rays and cast changes.

On Thursday morning, 27 October, I wandered into the lounge of the orthopedic wing to await a ride to Alameda Naval Air Station where I would catch the "Top Flight," the twice-a-week air transport flight from Alameda to Lemoore. It was shortly after 0800. The lounge was vacant, but the TV set was on with the volume turned down. A picture on the screen stopped me in my tracks. It was a profile I had seen hundreds of times: USS *Oriskany.*

I twisted the volume knob and stood in a daze as the announcer reported a disastrous fire on board and told of many people dead or missing, of aircraft destroyed, of *Oriskany's* limping to Subic Bay for repairs. My heart sank.

Forty-five minutes later I arrived at the fleet air headquarters building at Alameda and went to Harry Zenner's office. The staff rooms were buzzing with intense activity, but Harry found time for me. He steered me into the men's room, at the moment the only place where there was any privacy. He cautioned me that next of kin had not been notified, then handed me a slip of paper. Written thereon were four names: LT Dale Miller, LCDR Clem Morisette, ENS Ron Tardio, and LTJG Tom Spitzer, the confirmed dead of the VA-163 Saints. I felt sick.

"The total is a lot more," Harry said.

Within hours, casualty figures were made public, and they were mind-numbing—forty-three dead. A forty-fourth victim died of burns four days later. The fire had started not far from my former stateroom, in a ready-service storage compartment at the forward end of the hangar deck. The compartment housed the parachute flares we carried on our armed recco missions at night. The burning of hundreds of flares, composed principally of magnesium and sodium nitrate, caused a holocaust until the nonextinguishable magnesium burned itself out. Flames, dense smoke, and acrid fumes had swept through *Oriskany's* forward "officers' country" at an early-morning hour when many were still sleeping or just stirring. Thirty-six of the dead were officers; twenty-four were pilots.

I was in a grim mood when I arrived at Lemoore that afternoon, shattered by the loss of so many shipmates, particularly the Saints who had been close to me. Dale "Batman" Miller, a sharp aviator, personable and gentle of wit, whose nickname stemmed from his habit of sleeping curled up in a prenatal position. Clem Morisette, the Saints' quietly efficient operations officer, who had joined us at Dixie Station three weeks before I was shot down and whom I had come to admire and respect. Ron "Chico" Tardio, the engaging Bolivian bombshell.

And Tom Spitzer, my last wingman. Dear old *Oriskany*, her innards charred and twisted and her air wing devastated, was no longer an effective weapons system. She would return to the States for major repairs.

A few days later I met the plane carrying several of Air Wing 16's pilots home to Lemoore. On board were Marv Reynolds, John Miles, Wayne Soliday, and Vance Schufeldt. Our reunion in the operations terminal was emotional and comforting as we discussed the details of the fire. It was as if we were back in the ready room, recounting a combat mission. Fire is a terrifying thing to a sailor, and the four pilots told agonizing tales of the losses of friends and uplifting stories of the near-miraculous survival of others.

Fall 1966 brought a variety of activities to occupy the time between my biweekly trips to the hospital. Marilyn, the children, and I spent Thanksgiving at my mother's home in Jerome, Arizona. Perched on a mountainside, Jerome was a former copper-mining center turned ghost town, slowly resurrecting itself as a tourist attraction and inexpensive artsy-craftsy mecca. After the death of my father, my mother had moved to Jerome in the mid-1950s and bought a five-bedroom house for $1,100. Eventually, she became a grand dame of the hillside, actively engaged in a variety of local causes and activities.

Jerome was not my hometown, but that mattered little to the folks who knew my mother. By association, I was a local hero and was honored by the townspeople with a "Wynn Foster Day" parade. I rode two or three blocks through Jerome's narrow, winding streets, perched atop the rear seat of an open convertible. The marching band from Verde Valley High School played martial music. In a sometimes comical but sincere ceremony, the mayor gave me a key to the city. Afterward, a local civic leader, ignoring my nonresident status, earnestly pleaded for me to run for Congress against the locally unpopular incumbent.

The December 1966 issue of *Approach* magazine, a publication of the Naval Aviation Safety Center, included comments that I had written about my shoot down. The article and a simultaneous nationwide press release generated another spate of cards and letters from friends and well-wishers. The best of the lot was the following:

Dear Friend: When I was 2 1/2 I lost my right arm too. Now I have an artificial one and can do everything with it. I am 6 1/2 now. I can ride a bicycle too. Love, Sonja Peterson. St. Paul Minnesota.

After receiving Sonja's letter, I was never again able to feel depressed by my own condition.

The publicity for the *Approach* article also resulted in the gift of a framed, 18 x 24 inch oil portrait of me, painted by Roger Wetmore of Chicago. Mr. Wetmore had sent the portrait to the safety center, which forwarded it to me. It showed me in uniform against a background of the sea and the island structure of a carrier. The painting was both a kind gesture and a remarkable artistic effort, considering that Mr. Wetmore had had only a black and white newspaper photo from which to work.

In January 1967 Bob Spruit struck again. I was summoned to Admiral Cokely's office at the hospital and presented with a Distinguished Flying Cross. It was for planning and leading the 14 July 1966 surgical strike against the Nam Dinh riverfront storage area, the mission during which VF-162's skipper Dick Bellinger was shot down.[1]

In the same month I was honored by an invitation to speak to the workers at the Koch Industries plant in Marin County, north of San Francisco. The Koch company made the hardware fittings that connected hundreds of naval aviators to their parachutes around the world. The occasion was the kickoff of a "Zero Defects" production campaign, and I was pleased to tell the workers that, in my case, their product had worked as advertised when I needed it.

Hardly a week went by that didn't include an invitation to speak to a San Joaquin Valley service club, school assembly, or church group. The speaking engagements helped make time pass more quickly and gave me the opportunity to meet many of the wonderful people of all ages who lived and worked in the valley. Throughout much of the country, particularly on college campuses, the military had become a convenient scapegoat for the failures of civilian leadership in the conduct of the Vietnam War. But the San Joaquin Valley's population was unabashedly patriotic and highly supportive of the mil-

1. In a subsequent hassle on 9 October 1966 Dick Bellinger avenged himself by shooting down a North Vietnamese Air Force MiG-17.

itary. Twice I received honoraria—two crates of oranges from local groves—and most engagements included a barbecue or potluck supper. But there was one notable exception.

The invitation to speak to the ladies auxiliary of a national men's organization specified an 1830 gathering time. Marilyn and I assumed that a meal would be served and ate only a light lunch that day. Darkness was setting in at 1815 when we arrived at the designated location in the eastern reaches of the San Joaquin Valley, an hour's drive from Lemoore. There wasn't a soul around the meeting hall, and after a ten-minute wait we wondered if we had the right place. Then, as if in an episode from "The Twilight Zone," an elderly gentleman materialized from somewhere in the growing darkness, unlocked the door to the meeting hall, and turned on the interior lights. Relieved, I introduced myself and asked if I had the right meeting hall.

"I don't know what's going on," said Mr. Twilight Zone gruffly. "I just open up. They say, 'Open up,' and I open up."

Having opened up, the gentleman dematerialized as mysteriously as he had arrived. Three minutes later automobiles began pulling into the parking lot, and with little fanfare or self-introduction, about thirty elderly ladies filed in and seated themselves in the hall.

One lady, presumably the president or grand matron, arose and addressed the assembly: "Commander Foster has come to talk to us about VEETnam."

Madam President abruptly returned to her seat, and I realized that that was all the introduction I would get. I went to the front of the hall and gave my presentation. There were a few seconds of polite applause, then the hall emptied as fast as it had been filled. Madam President quickly thanked me for coming and disappeared out the door, following the rest of the ladies. Marilyn and I didn't dally, but we were the last ones to leave the parking lot. Presumably, the old gentleman rematerialized somewhere in the darkness behind us to "close up."

It was 2000, and we were starved. A fifteen-mile drive later we found a restaurant, ordered dinner, and giggled all the way through a second round of martinis.

I hitched a flight to San Diego for *Oriskany*'s return and rode a helo to meet the ship a few hours before she docked at North Island. I had long talks with John Iarrobino, Ron Caldwell, most of the Saints, and other shipmates. The ship had been cleaned up, but the scars remaining from the fire were sobering evidence of the magnitude of the disaster. My old room, which Ron Caldwell had occupied after my departure, was thirty feet forward of and one deck above the flare locker where the fire began. Ron had been awake when the fire started, fortunately aroused by a telephone call only minutes before. He made a hairbreadth escape to the ship's forecastle just before the contents of the stateroom were incinerated. The electricity had gone off shortly after the fire began. During his escape, Ron had experienced both near suffocation in the acrid smoke and near panic, thinking himself trapped in pitch darkness in the steel maze of the ship's interior. Many who were still asleep nearby weren't so lucky. They never left their bunks.

To keep myself professionally occupied during my days in Lemoore through the early months of 1967 I signed on as a volunteer, part-time assistant to CDR Chuck Hathaway, the skipper of Lemoore's Skyhawk training squadron. I sat as the senior member of a special court-martial, presented operational-training lectures, supervised critiques of training problems, and performed tasks that freed other officers to concentrate on the flight aspects of VA-125's instructional course.

Chuck Hathaway wore a second hat as Commander Fleet Air Detachment, Lemoore, the on-scene representative of Commander Fleet Air, Alameda. He was responsible for operational and administrative support of the twenty-seven fleet attack squadrons home-based at Lemoore. As Chuck's "chief of staff," I acted as a liaison with the fleet squadrons, occasionally soothing tempers, and here and there putting out minor administrative fires before they escalated into major problems.

In March 1967 Ron Caldwell invited me to represent the Saints at a posthumous awards ceremony for Tom Spitzer to be held in Fargo, North Dakota. Accompanying me on the trip was LTJG Ralph Bisz, who had reported on board *Oriskany* with Tom. I didn't get to know Ralph well in the week he was with the squadron before my shoot down, but we made up for it during the trip to Fargo. As we flew to the cold Midwest via commercial airline, we small-talked our way through families, backgrounds, experiences, and goals.

Ralph and Tom had met during flight training, become close

friends, and been roommates in *Oriskany* at the time of the fire. His tale of survival was harrowing. He had awakened Spitzer and led him out of their room when the fire alarm sounded, but they became separated when power failed and the forward section of the ship was plunged into darkness. Holding his breath against the thick, choking smoke, Ralph became disoriented, unsure of his direction. He walked headlong into a bulkhead, did a dizzy turn, and bumped into someone he couldn't identify. In desperation, nauseated, his lungs screaming for air, Ralph broke into a groping trot. Just when he was about to give up, unable to hold his breath any longer, he saw a grayish area in the pitch black. He dove at the gray and tumbled out into the fresh air of *Oriskany*'s forecastle. In the confusion, he had unknowingly retraced his steps, passed his point of departure, and found safety. Ralph had been a competitive swimmer in high school and college and thought that it was breath control that had made the difference in his survival. But his experience had planted a recurrent nightmare in his mind. He said that in his dreams the person he bumped into in the confusion of a dark and smoky passageway was his roommate, Tom Spitzer. If he hadn't panicked, Ralph wondered, might he somehow have been able to save the life of his friend?

As our airliner approached Minneapolis for landing, Ralph stared incredulously downward. "What is that?" he asked, referring to the white ground cover stretching as far as the eye could see.

"Snow," I said with amusement.

Ralph was born, raised, and educated in Miami, Florida. His post-college days were spent with the Navy in Florida, Texas, southeast Asia, and balmy southern California. He was a stranger to snow. In twenty-five years on the planet he'd never seen it in the amount offered by the Minnesota countryside.

Several members of the local Navy League chapter were on hand to greet us at the Fargo airport. LCDR Art Binsfield, the commanding officer of the Fargo Naval Reserve Training Center, arranged pleasant quarters in a local motel. The next day dawned bitter cold in North Dakota. The awards ceremony was held in the relative comfort of a large field house. On hand were several hundred members of the Naval Reserve, a large turnout of local dignitaries, and a representative of North Dakota's Governor Guy. I presented Tom's awards to his parents and made a few remarks to the assembled reservists.

Perhaps preaching to the choir, I lauded Tom as a good example of dedication, commitment, and patriotism in the current confusing times. To emphasize Tom's sacrifice, I cited opposing examples—the angry young men who used the security of college campuses as a stage for antiwar protests and draft-card burnings, activities that were publicized by the press and television out of all proportion to their significance.

After the ceremony Ralph and I visited privately with the large Spitzer family. I was a bit spooked upon meeting Tom's teenage brother, whom I had not seen earlier. The boy was a spitting image of Tom. The family meeting was serious but not sad. There was no bitterness voiced toward the war or the Navy, and no recriminations or demands to know the why of it all. Rather, the family members merely wanted to talk with the two of us. We were special people to them, people who had been closely associated with their Tom during his brief career in a somewhat mysterious Navy, and in faraway places. I assured them that Tom was a first-rate officer and pilot and had done a good job, that they could be proud of him.

Ralph Bisz and I saw each other occasionally thereafter, but duties routed us in different directions. He deployed to Vietnam with the Saints again in June 1967. On 4 August of that year, while he was flying a mission over North Vietnam, a SAM hit his aircraft, and Ralph Bisz was killed in action.

Reentry to the "normal" world began in March 1967 with the fitting of a prosthesis, an artificial arm. I watched, fascinated, as technicians constructed the arm. And I learned a strange new terminology. The *upper socket,* handmade at the hospital around a plaster-cast replica of my stump arm, consisted of multiple layers of flesh-colored, plastic-impregnated fiberglass. The *elbow unit, forearm unit,* and *terminal device* (hook) were procured from commercial sources, all custom-made to match the measurements of my good left arm. With my stump in the upper socket, the prosthesis was attached to me by a nylon-strap, figure-eight *Northwestern harness,* named for the university where it was originally developed.

The harness ran across my upper back and looped under my left *axilla,* the polite name for armpit. The movement of the forearm, pivoting at the elbow unit, and the opening of the hook were achieved through the mechanical advantage of the stainless-steel cables and the harness. The hook was *voluntary opening,* its *fingers* normally held closed by heavy rubber bands. Opening the hook required me to move my stump arm and flex my shoulders.

At first, operating the arm seemed complex, but the newness soon wore off, and the actions became second nature. The prosthesis weighed less than four pounds. But after seven months without an arm, it felt as if it weighed a ton. Following its creation, I began the long process of *change of dominance,* reorienting my thinking and developing new habits. Change of dominance means developing a new life-style, a new way of thinking, and doing with my left hand and holding with my right everything I'd been doing the other way around for the prior forty years. The transition was in opposition to messages from my nervous system. Since my accident, I had continued to experience strong phantom sensations. The arm was gone, but the nerves still sent strong right-arm signals. My missing right hand still "held" the grip of the control stick. By concentrating, I could "move" my nonexistent right forearm and fingers.

A minor incident occurred shortly after I first wore the prosthesis, my new toy. I accidentally dropped my cigarette lighter and instinctively grabbed for it with my right "hand" as it fell. The lighter and the hook collided in midair, the lighter bouncing off and slithering across the linoleum floor to the far side of the room. That was my first practical step in adapting to the prosthesis, an adventure both fun and frustrating. It was like learning to ride a bicycle, drive a car, or fly an airplane all over again—awkward at first and frequently uncomfortable, but eventually successful. In the process, I came to appreciate the complaints of the lefties of the world, my older brother for one, that we live in a society designed by and for right-handed people.

With the fitting of the prosthesis, Amazona of the occupational-therapy clinic reentered my life, and I surrendered willingly. An occupational-therapy report card was a necessary step toward my eventual escape from the hospital. But the formal training I received at the OTC notwithstanding, the most practical advice for one-armed existence in a two-armed world came from another, experienced amputee.

Corbet Ray, an ex-marine who had lost his right arm during the Korean War, was an employee of the hospital. I saw him regularly.

When Corbet learned of my intent to fight to remain on active duty, he became interested in my case and provided me with extracurricular coaching. One afternoon with Corbet taught me more practical one-arm survival tactics than had been offered in a series of sessions with the more academically qualified occupational therapist. Corbet's advice focused on everyday situations—practical and substantive, theory and style be damned. I'd already figured out how to cope with shoelaces and long-sleeve shirts, but Corbet had additional advice: "If a long-sleeve shirt is necessary, have your wife sew the left cuff together with a piece of elastic tape, so your good hand can slip in and out easily." That helpful hint was not included in the curriculum at occupational therapy.

Corbet also had advice on restaurant etiquette: "When you eat steak, never mind politely cutting and eating one piece at a time. Cut it all as fast as you can, then eat—unless, of course, you *like* cold steak."

In response to my question about automobile driving, Amazona of the OTC had given me a slick *adaptive-equipment* catalog that featured a circular-handled, ball-bearing-mounted, automobile-driving device that could be installed between the hub and the outer ring of a steering wheel. The freely rotating handle of the device permitted positive control of steering without removing the hand from the wheel. The retail cost of the device in 1967 was $250. Corbet Ray's advice: "Go to an auto-parts store and buy a buck-fifty 'necking' knob that the kids like for one-armed driving."

My aversion to Miss Amazona stemmed primarily from her over-solicitous, do-gooder attitude toward the handicapped. She lacked Corbet Ray's pragmatism. She had a degree in psychology, knew all the academic theories of handicapped adaptation, and seemed too anxious to press me into a preconceived mold. Frequently, she alluded to the "normal" world, something I had already accepted as gone forever. Corbet Ray recognized, accepted, and talked about his handicap. He knew how it felt to be an amputee. Miss Amazona never bothered to ask. She didn't seem able to say, as Corbet could, "Look, you might as well get used to the fact that, for the rest of your life, you're going to be different. Now, let's get down to the business of learning to cope with that difference."

In fairness to Miss Amazona, her function was to assist in the relearning process, and I did absorb a few handy hints that earlier I hadn't given much thought. But some of the occupational-therapy training bordered on the inane.

Amazona was not amused with my response when she asked me to pick up a coin from a table. I saw no sense in employing my prosthesis terminal device for that task. (Amazona didn't favor the word "hook.") I picked up the coin with my good left hand. Coolly and without humor, Amazona instructed me in the proper procedure: use the terminal device to carefully position the coin so it overlapped the edge of the table, then pick it up by gripping the edge of the coin with the stainless-steel fingers. I did as she instructed, successfully accomplishing that bit of prosthetic dexterity, but then I didn't know what to do with the coin clamped in my hook. So I removed the coin with my good hand and put it in my pocket. Miss Amazona frowned disapprovingly.

Final-exam time came in May 1967. Having achieved proper prosthetic proficiency, I was qualified to go through a drill with the formidable title *Achievement Record, Upper-Extremity Prosthesis*. Of the fifty-nine manual-dexterity skills tested, I was rated excellent in forty-eight, merely good in nine, and poor in door knobs and can openers. More used to me at that juncture, Amazona was mildly amused when I told her that I had done quite well flying complex aircraft off and on aircraft carriers for many years but never was much good at operating manual can openers. I could always use an electric can opener, I explained. As for door knobs, Amazona was not dissuaded from the low mark by my insistence that I operated them quite well with my left hand.

In *Overall Vocational Skill* I received a mark of very good, even though the overall test had not touched upon either of my principal vocations—being a naval officer and flying airplanes.

15 Friends

 With the *Achievement Record, Upper-Extremity Prosthesis* exam successfully behind me, I then faced a Physical Evaluation Board (PEB). The hearing, at which I could present evidence and call witnesses, would be the first in a series of legal hurdles I had to clear if I was to remain on active duty. After the PEB there would be a case review, a closed-door consideration of the record by a Physical Review Council (PRC). Beyond that lay an open hearing before the Physical Disability Review Board (PDRB) in Washington, D.C. The Navy's Judge Advocate General (JAG) would then review my case, and the Secretary of the Navy would make the final decision.

In cases in which the individual offered no objection, the recommendation of the first body, the PEB, generally settled the question of fitness for active duty. The actions of the PRC and the JAG were then pro forma, and the granddaddy PDRB didn't enter the picture. If I took the path of no resistance, the PEB would surely find me unfit for duty, and I would face immediate disability retirement in my current rank of commander.

On the other hand, if I availed myself of every legal right in the review process and lost, my fate would be the same—disability retirement in the rank of commander, but at a later date. I had already decided that my case was not routine, and the appeal system's regulations made it illogical not put up some sort of fight. I had little to lose and much to gain.

As expected, the finding of the Oakland PEB, made in closed session without my presence, was "unfit for duty." The board's decision was not binding, however, and I exercised my first legal option, requesting a formal, open hearing before the board. The starting gate was open, and the race was on. I went home to Lemoore to prepare my case.

I was uneasy, having challenged the system of which I'd been a willing part for so long. The onus was on me. Any battle with the bureaucracy was bound to be an uphill fight. The PEB's decision reflected the fundamental position of the medical side of the Navy— my missing arm automatically disqualified me for active duty. To succeed in my quest, I would have to work within the system and play by the same rules that the system was using to get rid of me.

I dove into my homework. The "bible" for such matters was the Navy's *Disability Separation Manual.* The very title of that publication conveyed the notion that separation from service was the expected consequence of an incurred disability. In legal syntax the manual stated that an individual was "not fit for active duty" if he was "unable to perform in a manner to reasonably fulfill the purpose of his employment" in that capacity. With the help of CDR Bill Hitchcock, the Navy legal officer at Lemoore, I dug into several law books to find legal opinions on the question of disability versus fitness for duty. One, a 1908 ruling by the JAG, was both interesting and pertinent. It offered a "back door" of the kind that I had liked to put into tactical mission planning. The case concerned two officers actively seeking retirement based on physical disabilities incurred while on active duty. However, each of the officers had demonstrated his ability to perform the duties of his rank in spite of his physical disability, and the JAG had disallowed disability retirement. Mine was the opposite case. I was trying to avoid immediate disability retirement, but the same principle applied. If I could prove my ability to perform so as to "reasonably fulfill" the purpose of continued active duty, there was a chance for success.

Another case of more recent (1963) vintage bolstered the 1908 JAG opinion. The later ruling held that fitness for duty depended on the nature of the duties and whether the individual concerned was capable of performing them. The PEB's initial finding left no doubt that medical opinion would be a strong factor in my case. But others, line officers and aviators, would judge the question of reasonable fulfillment of the duties of my rank. I banked on those individuals' carrying more weight. John Iarrobino's prophetic words of almost a year earlier returned to mind. If I chose to fight, he said, there were a lot of friends who could help.

Back to the typewriter. I requested and received testimonials from the *Oriskany*'s commanding officers under whom I had served, Captains Bart Connolly and John Iarrobino; and from Rear Admirals Ralph Cousins and Dave Richardson, who had been Yankee Station commanders during my combat employment as a squadron CO. All were friends and were supportive of my quest. More to the point, they were line officers and aviators who had recently served in the kind of operational assignments that I most likely would be given in the future if I was retained on active duty.

Additionally, my friend Harry Zenner discussed my case with his boss, RADM Fred Bakutis, the fleet-air commander at Alameda. Bakutis sent a supportive letter on my behalf to his friend, VADM Robert Brown, the Navy's surgeon general. The response was not encouraging, however. Admiral Brown stated that the medical side of the Navy had "not yet reached the stage where we can recommend a man with amputation of his dominant arm be found fit for duty." Brown's reply referred, without amplification, to an ongoing study that would establish a new Navy policy concerning amputees. Even in the negative tone, however, I saw a glimmer of hope. Brown's letter reinforced the contention that line officers' opinions would strongly influence the ultimate decision as to fitness. He acknowledged, "Occasionally in the past, the return of an amputee to duty has been justified on an administrative basis when we have been unable to so recommend from a medical or physical standpoint."

My PEB hearing was held on 20 July 1967. I presented a statement that discussed the legal precedents I had discovered and introduced the testimonials that I had received from senior officers. The hearing was over in less than an hour. The three-man panel reversed its previous finding and unanimously recommended that I be found fit for duty. The next day I was released from the hospital and temporarily assigned to VA-125 at Lemoore, pending the final outcome of my case.

I had won the first round, but I had no illusions. Admiral Brown's letter had already raised a red flag. The system—the medical side of the Navy at any rate—was not going to fold its tent because of the PEB's decision. Among other things, the battlefield shifted to Washington, D.C., and I was stuck at Lemoore, 2,500 miles to the west. It appeared that, for the most part, the rest of the fight would have to be conducted on paper.

The gears of one element of American bureaucracy ground slowly but methodically in the summer of 1967. The Selective Service System notified me that my draft status had been reclassified to category 5F. My thirteen-year-old son, Scott, dug into the Foster family encyclopedia to discover that 4F—not physically qualified for military service— was the most lowly of SS categories. Intrigued at being of apparently even lower status, I telephoned the Selective Service Office in Hanford, California, and learned that 5F meant that I was *too old for military service*. Having served in three wars, fought in two, and been wounded in the last one, I was considered a military has-been at age forty. "*Now* they tell us!" was Marilyn's reaction.

I got a big boost when ADM Roy Johnson, still Commander-in-Chief, Pacific Fleet, made a surprise visit to Lemoore that summer. The admiral's arrival came on short notice when his original destination was socked in by bad weather. But it posed a dilemma for CAPT Howie Boydstun, Lemoore's commanding officer.

Protocol dictated that Boydstun host a reception to honor the arrival of the Pacific Fleet's commander, but the officers' club was already booked that evening for a squadron's change-of-command party. Postponing that party twenty-four hours to accommodate a reception for the fleet commander was an awkward alternative for Boydstun. The club was also booked the next evening—for a reception following the wedding of his own daughter!

Admiral Johnson was a perfect gentleman about the situation. He said that he was tired of official receptions and would prefer the informality of a squadron party anyway. "If I'm invited, of course," said the unpretentious admiral.

Admiral Johnson and I discussed my situation at length during the party. Surprisingly, he was well informed of my efforts to remain on active duty, in spite of everything about the Vietnam War that had competed for his attention during the previous year.

"If I can be of any help in your case, let me know," Admiral John-

son said. I thanked him but was not inclined to press the four-star officer to make good on what may have been polite party talk.

The next day, however, I changed my mind. I wrote to the admiral, saying that his offer of support was most welcome. A letter from
the Commander-in-Chief, Pacific Fleet to the PRC, the next body to
consider my case, certainly wouldn't do any harm. Several days later I
received a copy of an impressive personal communiqué from Admiral
Johnson to the senior member of the PRC. It presented a convincing
testimonial of my past performance and future potential, as well as an
unqualified recommendation that I be retained on active duty. Help-
fully, Admiral Johnson forwarded copies of the letter to both the Chief
of Naval Personnel and the Secretary of the Navy.

Even so, the three-member PRC was not persuaded. By the time
that group reviewed my case, the study earlier referred to by the Navy
Surgeon General in his letter to Rear Admiral Bakutis had been completed. A new amputee policy, agreed to by the Navy Surgeon General
and the Chief of Naval Personnel, was nearly on the street. Citing the
yet-to-be-released policy, the PRC overruled the action of the Oakland
PEB and found me "permanently unfit to perform the duties of his
rank in an unrestricted capacity."

I was discouraged but remained determined. Buried in the paperwork justifying the PRC's finding was the phrase "...loss of an upper
extremity involving the major [sic] hand." The words "major hand"
were interesting because they focused on a specific part of the
anatomy. The current rules in the *Disability Separation Manual* contained no such limitation. I thought of "Pegleg" Pete Hoskins, a Navy
captain who had lost a leg during a Japanese attack on his carrier in
World War II. Hoskins subsequently waged a successful campaign to
remain on active duty and was later promoted to admiral. Twenty plus
years later my case had apparently stirred a bit of long-dormant political dust. At the time I was the only person in the Navy who, having
lost an upper extremity involving a "major hand," was making waves
to remain on active duty. As much as anything, the PRC's comment
seemed to be an attempt to patch up a perceived weakness in the existing rules regarding amputees.

The Chief of Naval Personnel sided with the opinion of the medical people in his recommendation to the Secretary of the Navy: "...it
would not be in the best interests of the service to relax the *present*

[emphasis added] physical standards," he wrote, by permitting amputees to remain on active duty. It was a rather convoluted remark. In spite of the negative recommendation, the personnel chief's statement was encouraging. The *present* rules were the ones on which I based my case, and I hadn't asked for any relaxation of standards. But at the same time I was distressed because there was a nail in the coffin.

Under Secretary of the Navy Robert Baldwin had already approved the new amputee policy, and the only pap it offered was an undefined new program that would permit selected amputees to remain on limited active duty for a maximum of one year.

In effect, I had lost round two and perhaps lost altogether because of the new amputee policy. If I chose to stay in the ring there was still the legal option of a full hearing before the Physical Disability Review Board in Washington. But to get around the PRC's ruling, I had to find a loophole in the new amputee policy. Otherwise, it appeared that a final hearing would be little more than a formality, and an expensive one at that.

The rules of the game required that attendance at a hearing of the granddaddy board in Washington be at my own expense. In a temporary funk after receiving the PRC's decision, I wondered about the part of valor called discretion.

I wanted to stay on active duty for many reasons. Having commanded a tailhook squadron, I'd been to the top in the stick-and-throttle business. I wouldn't fly again in my one-arm condition, but I could rationalize that disappointment. There was only a relative handful of exciting cockpit jobs beyond that of squadron CO even under normal conditions. But I could still be part of the naval aviation that I knew and loved. Psychologically, I wasn't ready to quit and find solace in some less-exciting occupation.

On the other hand, it would be easier on the checkbook if I backed away from the fight, found my retirement village somewhere, resettled my family, and got established in a second career. But that sounded like dullsville. The much-to-gain/little-to-lose aspect was still there. I wasn't ready to quit.

I sent an official message to the PRC, stating that I disagreed with its finding and that I would avail myself of the legal option of rebuttal.

Automatically, that message would toss my case to the PDRB in Washington. I pondered the least-cost way to finance what could be a prolonged visit back east. Maybe I could boondoggle a temporary duty assignment. I called CAPT Wes McDonald, the detailer in the Bureau of Naval Personnel who arranged assignments for aviator commanders.

Wes was a friend and a combat-experienced tailhook pilot who had commanded both a Skyhawk squadron and a carrier air wing. He had been following my case since before the PEB at Oakland, and I figured that Wes would be a good sounding board if nothing else. If a continued fight to remain on active duty held little chance of success in view of the new amputee policy, Wes would tell me so candidly. If so, I would focus my energies in other directions.

I was elated when Wes asked if I would accept immediate PCS (permanent change of station) orders to Washington, D.C. "Yes," I replied quickly. The *Disability Separation Manual* said that I was supposed to remain assigned to VA-125 at Lemoore until a final decision was reached in my case. But if Wes wasn't worried about that detail, neither was I.

"Just guidelines," Wes said. He admitted that nothing in the rules specifically permitted him to issue PCS orders in my case. On the other hand, nothing specifically prohibited them. My friend's willingness to interpret the regulations flexibly erased my growing pessimism, born in the wake of the PRC's decision.

Wes McDonald knew how politics were played at the high levels of the Navy. He knew that it would be important for the influential Navy hierarchy to see me before and during the PDRB hearing in Washington. The orders not only would place me conveniently at the hub of political power, but meant that my family would accompany me east. The next day, even before I had scratched out a good outline of a rebuttal to the PRC's findings, orders arrived directing my transfer from VA-125 at Lemoore to duty at the headquarters of the Chief of Naval Operations (CNO) in the Pentagon. I found the orders interesting. My transfer from the Tonkin Gulf to the Oakland naval hospital in August 1966 had been on a temporary status, as were the orders that sent me to VA-125 at Lemoore. Technically, during the twenty-one months before the orders to Washington were issued, I was still CO of the Saints. That evening, I wrote an upbeat letter to Ron Caldwell, telling him that I had quit as the senior commanding officer and that he had the squadron all to himself at last. Then I got down to serious work on my rebuttal.

The PRC's finding was based on the new amputee policy that had not yet been officially promulgated. And it appeared to be aimed at me specifically, changing the rules in the middle of the game. The PRC had neither addressed nor negated the existing amputee policy and regulations as set forth in the *Disability Separation Manual*. The governing criterion was still the "ability to perform those duties normally expected." In fact, the manual went further. It pointed out that it was not necessary that I establish my ability to perform *as well as* an individual without a disability. I merely had to demonstrate that I was able to perform. This statement would help my case. I knew that line officers, not doctors and lawyers, were the best judges of my fitness to perform. Another encouraging element was the manual's requirement that the majority of the PDRB's membership be of my military occupational specialty—unrestricted-line officer-aviators.

The apparent weakness of the "major hand" argument, on which the PRC's decision was based, brought to mind an earlier incident. While I was still in the Oakland hospital, Paul Merchant visited me. During our conversation we disagreed on a subject unrelated to my medical problem. When I stubbornly stuck to my point of view, Paul said, "Wynn, if only you had been hit in the head instead of the arm, you wouldn't have sustained any injury." Paul's retort underscored my conviction that the loss of my arm had diminished neither my knowledge nor my experience as a naval officer-aviator. In my rebuttal to the PRC's finding, I emphasized my ability to perform such duties as might be assigned by poking fun at the degree-of-amputation theory. I wrote, "I was hit in the arm, not in the head." It was a somewhat irreverent inclusion in an official document dealing with my career, but I hoped that it might appeal to the human side of whoever happened to read the rebuttal.

Marilyn and I left Lemoore with our children on 31 August, beginning our twelfth cross-country move in an eighteen-year Navy career. We stashed the kids with Grandma in Arizona, for later air delivery after we found a home in the east. Two weeks later we were comfortably settled in a rental home in Vienna, Virginia, several miles west of

Washington proper. Once our household goods arrived and the children were enrolled in local schools, I reported for duty at the Pentagon. It was 25 September. My hearing before the PDRB was scheduled for 8 November.

I was assigned to the general planning and programming division of the office of the CNO. CAPT Bart Connolly, former CO of *Oriskany*, was my immediate boss. My job wasn't difficult, and in many ways it was interesting. I was one of several officers who maintained point papers, documents that outlined the salient details of every Navy project and program. The Secretary of the Navy and Chief of Naval Operations used the papers for reference during their rounds of Congressional testimony. My job put me at the seat of Navy power, well situated for the "see and be seen" strategy engineered by Wes McDonald.

Obtaining support for my case was not difficult. In short order I had more offers of assistance than I could effectively use. Support came from ranking naval aviators in the Pentagon, from members of the influential Navy League of the United States, and from the Deputy Secretary of Defense for Public Affairs, Daniel Heinken, who, I was thankful, never asked me for an opinion of his former boss, Mr. McNamara. One influential statement of support, unsolicited on my part, came from Senator Ernest Hollings of South Carolina in a letter addressed to the Secretary of the Navy. I never discovered who prompted that gratuity.

LT Nick Calise, a Navy law specialist, was assigned as my counsel for the November PDRB hearing, and together we assembled a dossier and a list of witnesses. To avoid overkill in the staging of my case, Nick suggested that we limit the number of in-person testimonials to three experienced officers—RADM Dave Richardson, a former Yankee Station commander who was then stationed in Washington; Bart Connolly; and Wes McDonald. They represented the two ranks immediately above mine and were showcase witnesses, Calise said, each having an impressive record as an officer and as an aviator. Each was familiar with my career, and their collective experiences represented the types of duties that I might be expected to perform if retained on active duty.

The eighth of November dawned clear and cool in Washington, D.C. The hearing began shortly after 1000 with Nick Calise smoothly presenting my case.

Rear Admiral Richardson was a picture of confidence as he testified to my usefulness to the Navy and fitness for duty afloat or ashore.

"Would you have any hesitations having Commander Foster serving under you in any type of duty assignment?" one member asked.

"Quite the contrary," Richardson responded. "I would not only have no hesitations, I would be most pleased to have him."

Another member asked: "...if Commander Foster were assigned to sea duty...possibly a department head, member of a staff, or possibly commanding officer of a ship...do you think he would have any difficulty fulfilling any assignments?"

"None whatsoever."

"...in your opinion...is Commander Foster fit for full and unrestricted duty?"

"In my opinion, he most certainly is," Richardson said.

Bart Connolly responded to similar questions and detailed our professional relationship and my performance while serving with the Saints on board *Oriskany* in 1965 and in my present assignment. He was almost too flattering, making me sound like Jack Armstrong, the All-American boy.

"He has exhibited...top-notch performance here in Washington," Connolly testified. "His overall performance has been in the top 10 percent of the officers I have encountered."

Not unexpectedly, Wes McDonald received the toughest grilling from the board members. His testimony was crucial because he was my detailer, the individual responsible for my assignment to active-duty jobs. In effect, he was an official spokesman for the Chief of Naval Personnel. Board members asked detailed questions about senior-aviation-officer assignment practices, promotion policies, and career opportunities and about my continued usefulness in the aviation program.

"If the Secretary of the Navy were to find Commander Foster fit for duty, would this present any detailing problems?"

"None," Wes replied.

Strongly supportive of my quest, Wes said that he had no qualms about assigning me to any kind of active duty ashore or afloat. He brushed off the question about the possibility of my flying again, saying that it was academic until the larger determination was made— whether I would remain on active duty.

Finally, there were questions about the recent policy statements regarding the retention of amputees on active duty. One of the two members who were medical officers tried to toss a ringer at Wes: "I wonder if you could explain—you're here officially from the Bureau of Naval Personnel—why you are endorsing the departure from the established policy of Admiral Semmes [the Chief of Naval Personnel] in July of this year in regard to amputees?"

"It also says that each case will be judged on its own merits," Wes replied coolly. "This is the exception...we would like to see him retained on active duty."

Another hypothetical ringer: "If Commander Foster was found fit for duty and (subsequently) was not physically qualified on an annual physical exam or promotion physical, where would we stand then?"

Wes hesitated momentarily, and Nick Calise interrupted, almost as if he had expected the question. "Barring other developments," Calise said, "I don't think he would be found not physically qualified by virtue of his loss of arm after the Secretary of the Navy had already determined that he is fit for duty."

The response sounded strange to me—a bit too much like lawyer double-talk—but it apparently made sense to the doctor because the matter was not pursued.

The kinds of jobs that I might be assigned at sea brought a few more questions for Wes. But they seemed more for the enlightenment of individual board members. Wes was thanked for his appearance and excused, and the board turned its attention to me.

Nick Calise led me through a series of prearranged questions about my past and present performance, career, and family life. He also asked how the prosthesis affected my driving a car, my performing handyman tasks, and my daily swimming, and how I was otherwise adapting to a one-arm existence.

"Would you have any difficulty functioning aboard ship?" Calise asked.

"No," I responded and gave details of my activities when I visited *Oriskany* at sea in late 1966.

Finally, Calise touched on the "biggie": "Could you function in an emergency?"

"I'm confident I could," I replied. "I did at one time in an aircraft for ten or twelve minutes with only one arm after the other was blown off." I told of my accident, the ejection, the use of my survival gear, and I described how I had assisted in my own first aid after I was in the whaleboat.

"As far as abandoning ship or something like that, I don't think I'd have any difficulty."

When it was the board's turn, their questions reflected curiosity about my prosthesis and about the tax implications of disability-retirement pay versus continued active-duty pay. The central issue, my fitness to perform, wasn't mentioned. When one board member, an aviator, asked about my medals and decorations, I sensed that we were almost through and that the majority was leaning in my direction.

I cooled my nervous heels in an adjacent office while the board debated my case for thirty minutes. The two medical officers followed the Navy Surgeon General's position, voting against retention on unrestricted active duty. The three line officer-aviators reasoned differently, opting for a simple finding of "fit for duty." After the decision was announced, one of the medical officers privately apologized for his nay vote, saying that my case had favorably impressed him but that he felt obliged to follow the party line.

My six-month quest was nearly over, but it had gone down to the wire. The three-member PEB at Oakland had voted in my favor. The PRC had cast the same number against me. With the 3-2 decision at the final hearing, I had won by a single vote.

Still, the Secretary of the Navy had to make the final decision after the Judge Advocate General reviewed the case. But with the legal hurdles successfully behind me, and with the mass of political support that had been generated, I was confident of secretarial approval. Unless, of course, some adverse development intervened to throw my case off track. And it did.

Two days after I won the battle of the boards, I was trying to turn a single-bed mattress with the help of my mother, who was visiting from Arizona. My mother steadied the mattress while I moved my good left hand for a better hold, but she lost her grip, and a corner of the mattress flopped smartly downward, striking the elbow of my prosthesis. It was not a hard blow, but the mechanics of it were not in my favor. The prosthesis twisted, and I felt a snap in the stump of my right arm.

Something had broken. There was only a slight twinge of pain, but anguish flooded through me. After six months of maneuvering and politicking through the complex, multitiered disability-retirement system to a favorable conclusion, my future was suddenly in doubt again. Had I won the battles only to lose the war to a freak accident? My morale had plunged to new depths as Marilyn drove me across the Potomac River to the Bethesda naval hospital in Maryland.

X rays showed a fracture of the fibular bone that had been transplanted from my leg and grafted to the humerus in my stump arm. Fortunately, the graft itself was solid and unaffected. The only treatment possible was to immobilize the stump so that the fracture could heal. I spent two hours in the hospital cast room while two corpsmen and a doctor experimented and agonized over how best to apply the immobilizing plaster. Meanwhile, Marilyn and my mother fidgeted in the waiting room, uninformed as to what was happening and imagining all sorts of dire consequences. Marilyn later admitted to being really depressed. At the same time, however, she tried to maintain a buoyant facade to keep from further depressing my mother, who thought the whole thing was her fault.

The experts initially ignored my suggested cast design, but eventually I convinced them that I had some expertise in dealing with my condition. We created a carbon copy of the upper-body cast that had been my familiar companion for five months in California. They wrapped plaster-soaked gauze around the stump arm, then across my chest and back and over both shoulders. That gave me the desired support and immobility.

The next morning I called Captain Connolly at the Pentagon to report what had happened. I was deeply worried. "I may have blown the whole thing," I said to Bart. "I may have put myself back in the clutches of the medical people." If it was merely suggested that my one-arm condition or the presence of a prosthesis made me accident-prone, the entire issue of fitness for duty could easily be raised again.

"Hell," Connolly snorted, "anybody can break an arm. I'll see what I can do." Knowing Bart, I was sure that he was already thinking about what strings he could pull to keep my problem low key. And what he could do was substantial. Bart discussed the matter with his boss, ADM Fred Bennett. Bennett then discussed the matter with CAPT Frank Johnston, the legal adviser to the Under Secretary of the Navy. Johnston was familiar with my case and stated that there was no need to rush things. He agreed with the anybody-can-break-an-arm philosophy and said that further action should await the outcome of my present hospitalization.

After the Judge Advocate General's review, Johnston said, he would merely hold my case in his bottom drawer. The JAG précis was delivered to the under secretary's office in early December, and true to his word, Johnston kept it in the drawer until the following May.

Corrective surgery to repair the transplanted bone was scheduled, and I returned to work at the Pentagon as an outpatient. My contemporaries were supportive, but after a while the jokes about what I had been doing on a mattress to cause a broken arm got a little old.

On 7 December, the day after my forty-first birthday, I underwent surgery on my stump arm for a third time. The fracture was located in the lower portion of the transplanted fibula bone. Dr. Ken Spence, the orthopedic surgeon, did what he called "a carpentry job," splicing the fracture with a piece of my iliac crest (pelvic bone). That would preserve the leverage offered by the full length of the transplanted bone.

I spent another twelve weeks in an upper-body cast while the bones knitted. Technically, I was still the property of the hospital, but I went back to work to avoid going stir crazy. Besides, I wanted to show the powers that be that a little thing like a broken arm didn't affect what had been the cornerstone of my case argument, the ability to perform.

By early March 1968 I was out of the cast, and I was back to wearing my prosthesis in the third week in April.

There was a sticky point about my release from the hospital. Recovered patients were normally released with an entry in the medical record that read, "Fit for duty." My fitness status still rested in Captain Johnston's bottom drawer, however. I spent a couple of sleepless nights concerned that I might again be subjected to the tedious process of disability review. With the new amputee policy in place, there was a strong possibility that a second round of hearings would work against me.

Dr. Spence held the trump card because he would write the clinical record of my case. I had a long talk with him, outlining my quest and reviewing its history. Ken Spence was an understanding man.

"I have to admit your case is establishing precedents faster than answers can be found 'in the book,'" Spence said. He was impressed with the high-level interest that the case had generated and added, "I'm just a mere doctor in the chain of command and don't care to play a villain role. I'll just limit my concern to the healing of the recent injury and leave the rest to the Secretary of the Navy."

In the narrative summary of my recent hospitalization, Spence artfully tiptoed around the fitness issue by certifying that my physical condition was "equivalent to that which existed" before the fracture occurred. He simply discharged me from the hospital with a noncommittal "to duty."

On 6 May 1967 I walked out the door of Bethesda Naval Hospital into a balmy spring day. My troublesome fight to remain on active duty was over. That afternoon, the paperwork in my case was resurrected from Captain Johnston's bottom drawer and sent to Under Secretary of the Navy Charles Baird, recently appointed to that position by President Johnson. Even that change in the civilian management of the Navy had worked in my favor. It was *former* Under Secretary Robert Baldwin who had approved the new amputee policy, the primary weapon used by the Physical Review Council to sidetrack my case.

Under Secretary Baird signed a memorandum addressed to the Judge Advocate General, the brevity of which was anticlimactic. It read: "The recommended findings of the Physical Evaluation Board and the majority of the Physical Disability Review Board are approved."

I was fit for duty, period. The secretary's decision ignored both the negative recommendation of the Physical Review Council and the newly approved amputee policy. Those nineteen words concluded the quest begun in the belly of a C-141 Liftmaster somewhere over the Pacific Ocean twenty-one months earlier.

Shortly after signing the memo, Mr. Baird was kind enough to telephone me at my desk in the Pentagon, saying that he was pleased to have ruled in my favor and wishing me success in the future. The under secretary confided that he was impressed by the favorable comments and recommendations included in the record, the most convincing of which was the testimonial from ADM Roy Johnson, former CinCPacFleet.

"You have a lot of friends in the Navy," Baird said.

Amen, I thought.

After the secretary hung up, I called home to share the good news with Marilyn. Then I placed another phone call, to Virginia Beach, Virginia—the home of ADM Roy Johnson, retired. There weren't enough words to express my gratitude, but I tried.

Epilogue

Not long after this episode in my life I was promoted to the rank of captain. I was then the only officer on active duty in the U.S. Navy with an artificial arm, and with the promotion came a special sobriquet straight out of J. M. Barrie's story of Peter Pan. From that point on I was referred to as Captain Hook.

Before the promotion list was formally approved, however, I imposed upon my friend Wes McDonald one more time. The war in Vietnam was still in progress. Having fought the system over the active-duty issue and won, I knew that I wouldn't be comfortable fiddling away the rest of my Navy career as a minor bureaucrat in Washington, D.C. I wanted to be where the action was and asked Wes to send me back to sea duty. Wes was still the detailer for aviation commanders, and the selection for promotion to captain technically removed me from his jurisdiction. But another technicality didn't faze Wes. He pulled strings, and I was subsequently ordered to the position of operations officer on the staff of Commander Carrier Division One (ComCarDiv One), whose home port was San Diego, California.[1]

I made two more deployments to WestPac and participated in tactical decisions relating to the air war over North Vietnam. In every

---

1. Wes McDonald's bending of the rules to help my case had no adverse effect on his own career. He went on to bigger and better things in the Navy and eventually retired as a four-star admiral.

recommendation I made concerning the employment of carrier aircraft, while ComCarDiv One was acting as Yankee Station commander, I tried very hard to remember what it had been like in the ready room, and what effect my opinion might have on the guys flying the tough combat missions over North Vietnam.

Following the CarDiv tour, I served on the staff of Commander First Fleet, where I was in charge of coordinating the readiness training of West Coast–based carriers and other ships preparing for Vietnam duty. On 1 August 1972, after twenty-six and a half years of service, I retired from active duty, shortly before our country's longest war came to a humiliating and inglorious end with the 27 January 1973 cease-fire agreement.

The ugliness and discontent generated by the Vietnam War has since faded, replaced by what has aptly been described as the long perspective of history. That perspective came to my attention one night almost sixteen years after the war was over. I was at the October 1988 Tailhook Association convention, an annual gathering of the active and retired people with the distinction of having made at least one arrested landing on board an aircraft carrier.

Late one night (or early one morning, I forget which) I attended a party hosted by the Pacific Fleet squadron that trained pilots to fly the A-6 Intruder, the Navy bomber whose name became a household word thanks to Steve Coonts's wonderful and moving novel *Flight of the Intruder*.

I met an earnest young newboy pilot. He was about twenty-five and had just reported for duty with the squadron. Curious about my artificial arm, he listened intently as I explained how it got that way. The young man blurted out: "Gosh, sir. The Vietnam War! That must have been *thirty* years ago!" Oblivious of the historical inaccuracy, but eager to share his newfound knowledge, the pilot excitedly grabbed a passing squadron mate, another young aviator, and gave me a flattering introduction.

"This man is a war hero," my young acquaintance said proudly.

The old Navy had met the future, and to me, that moment somehow made the loss of my arm seem worthwhile.

I came out of the Vietnam War with a physical impairment, but unlike many veterans of that conflict, I escaped without long-term emotional scars. However, for twenty-four years I was nagged by an unpleasant dream: *I am back on board* Oriskany, *trying to find my way to Ready Room Five so that I can rejoin my squadron. But I can't remember how to get there, and everyone is too busy to help me.*

In the summer of 1990 I went to Bremerton, Washington, for a reunion of the men of *Oriskany* and Air Wing 16. It was also our chance to say good-bye to the old ship. A memorial service was held on *Oriskany*'s flight deck, from which I had flown 163 combat missions. It was an emotional experience. Twenty-five years had elapsed since I had first landed aboard her. The forty-year-old ship, rust-streaked and seedy-looking from long inactivity in the mothball fleet, was at that time destined to be cut up for scrap.[2]

CAPT George "Moose" Lundy was there, still on active duty. After the service Moose and I went below. We sneaked past the forbidding yellow tapes intended to keep the casual visitor from going astray and paid a last, nostalgic visit to Ready Room Five. It was an unlit shambles, bearing little resemblance to the dynamic place we'd called home during the trauma of the Vietnam War.

But even in her sad condition, *Oriskany* worked her magic on me one last time. I'd finally found my way back to Ready Room Five. Moose Lundy was there as a stand-in for all the Saints I'd come to love during my tour with the squadron.

And the nightmares went away for good.

2. In 1991 Congress approved legislation that saved *Oriskany* from the cutting torch. Instead, she was to be sold to the Japanese for restoration as a floating memorial/museum named City of America.

Appendix

These songs were written for performance by "Four Wretched Amateurs and a Beginner," the 1965 *Oriskany* attack pilots' musical group.

"RIDIN' DOWN THE GLIDE SLOPE"
(Tune: "Ridin' Down the Canyon")

Ridin' down the glide slope, it's night, the meatball's low.
I read the ship's name on the ol' fantail.
The LSO is frantic, he's diving in the net.
In the tower, faces all turn pale.
Wave-off lights are blinkin', I figure something's wrong;
I add a little power and go 'round.
I tell you, folks, it's thrilling, ridin' down the groove
When the evening sun's gone down.

The glide slope is the theoretical angle a plane flies to a successful carrier landing. The meatball is the pilot's visual indication of his position in relation to the glide slope. The LSO is the landing signal officer, who is stationed on a platform at the aft port corner of the flight deck to monitor the pilots' carrier-landing techniques. A nearby safety net keeps the LSO from falling overboard should he need to suddenly jump off the platform to avoid being hit by a low-flying aircraft. A wave off, signaled by flashing red lights adjacent to the meatball, is the LSO's instruction to the pilot to abort a landing attempt.

233

"WINGMAN, HO CHI MINH, AND ME"
(Tune: "Little Brown Jug")

Ho Chi Minh, a nice ol' boy, lives in a place they call Hanoi.
He got missile, he got gun; boy-oh-boy do he have fun.

Chorus: Ha, ha, ha, you and me, li'l ol' wingman you'll agree.
Ha, ha, ha, just we three: wingman, Ho Chi Minh, and me.

Once we flew a recco route. Lordy, did that AA shoot.
Weather started closing in; we found ourselves on top of Vinh.

(Chorus)

With our Skyhawk day chores done, night road recco sure is
    fun.
Out we fly with lethal wares: two li'l bombs and sixteen flares.

(Chorus)

The old A-3 can't carry bombs, the admiral has too many
    qualms.
So they fly around, alas, above the ship just passing gas.

(Chorus)

An Alfa strike way up to Kep; staff man says the plan is "hep."
"Just fly low, you won't get hit." Staff man sure is full of shit.

(Chorus)

Strike leader's great, a nominee for Silver Star or D-F-C.
PacFleet gives a helping hand: downgraded to a reprimand!

(Chorus)

Yankee Station flying's swell: triple A, MiGs, and SAMs as well.
Occasion'ly I'm out of sorts, needing more clean skivvy shorts.

(Chorus)

At Dixie Station we bomb the Cong; never seem to stay there
    long.
No AA fire or MiGs, you see; happiness in In-Countree.

(Chorus)

Vinh, a city in central North Vietnam, was a regular hot spot for
antiaircraft fire. I was hit by AAA near Vinh. The A-3 Skywarrior, an

obsolescent twin-engine jet bomber of limited maneuverability, was not equipped with ejection seats for the crew. In 1965 it was decided that bombing missions in the AAA and SAM environment over North Vietnam were too hazardous for Skywarrior crews. Subsequently, the aircraft were equipped with large internal fuel tanks and performed yeoman service as aerial fueling stations for other carrier aircraft. "Downgraded to a reprimand" is a sarcastic reference to the rejection of CDR Harry Jenkins's award recommendation in 1965 (see chapter 5).

"THE FIGHTER BOYS"
(Tune: "The Thing")

The fighter boys were launching off the great flat boat one day,
And as they burner-ed in the blue, I heard the leader say:
"Now, wingman, pay attention and fly along with me.
When we get back to the great flat boat, you'll have a D-F-C."

Chorus: When you get back to the great flat boat,
    you'll have a D-F-C.

Down below the A-1 boys were loaded to the gills,
A-heading for a bombing jaunt back in the Annam hills.
They had no fear, they munched their lunch, their hearts were
    full of love,
Because the sleek Crusaders were flying up above.

Chorus: Yes, they were so happy with the fighters up above.

Out to the east from Hainan Isle, a Chinese Cay-det boy
Was on a "Faggot" training flight a-headed for Hanoi.
His navigation faulty, he wandered off of track.
"Oh, rook, some airpranes over there, perhaps they read me
    back."

Chorus: He joined those airplanes over there,
    so they could lead him back.

The reverie was broken, the news was quite a shock.
The fighter wingman said, "Hey lead, check your six o'clock."
The fighter lead had nerves of steel, his fortitude was true.
High o'er the Gulf of Tonkin, he knew just what to do.

Chorus: Yes, coolly, and with nerves of steel,
    he knew just what to do.

Crusaders fired their burners and shot up out of sight.
"Never mind the Spads," said lead, "I think they'll be all right.
We're heading south at one point five, we'll make it home, I
    think.
I hope they have the tanker up, so we can take a drink."

Chorus: Oh, surely, there's a tanker up, so they can take a
    drink.

The Chinese boy was nervous, 'cause his fuel was getting shy.
He felt so lost and lonely up in that hostile sky.
The fighter planes had left him, they'd put on quite a show;
So he tried to rendezvous with the A-1s down below.

Chorus: He tried to join the aged Spads a-chugging down below.

The A-1 guys, they panicked; they shouted, "Golly, jeez,"
And dove into a valley, flying ten feet o'er the trees.
They flailed around down near the ground, just trying to stay
    alive,
And accidentally shot the MiG right in his JP-5.

Chorus: Yes, 20 mike mike cannon got him in his JP-5.

The ready room was crowded as postflight tales were told.
Although the fighters stretched the truth, their manner it was
    bold.
"We yo-yoed up, we yo-yoed down, our tactics they were
    sound,
But we *had* to haul ass out of there, with all those MiGs
    around."

Chorus: Of course they hauled ass out of there with all those
    MiGs around!

"Faggot" was the code name for the Russian-built MiG-17 fighter.
"One point five" means Mach 1.5, one and a half times the speed of
sound. JP-5 is the designation of a fuel for jet aircraft.

Index

Manila, Republic of the Philippines, 1, 34, 195
Marcus Island, 30, 31, 33
Martin, Don, 23, 44, 118, 120, 138, 143, 147, 154, 180
MCBR (multiple carriage bomb rack), 61
Mekong River, 51, 70, 72
Memphis, Tennessee, 19, 20, 32
Merchant, Paul, 11, 32, 49, 58, 70, 77, 97, 108, 112, 125, 126, 128, 157, 220
Merry Point landing, 27
Miami, Florida, 208
Miles, John, 154, 159, 181, 204
Miller, Dale, 154, 203
Miller, Hank, 139
Mitchell, Fred, 153, 154, 161, 162, 178
Monsarrat, Nicholas, 167, 170
Morisette, Clem, 161, 165, 172, 180, 203
Munro, Pete, 145, 154, 164, 171
Mutiny on the Bounty, 47

Napalm, 68
NATOPS (Naval Air Training and OPerational Standardization), 27, 28, 30, 73, 112
Naval Aviation Safety Center, 204
Navy Commendation medal, 141
Navy Cross medal, 28, 141
Navy Surgeon General, 215, 217, 224
Nordby, Louie, 146, 154
Norman, Oklahoma, 16
North Island (San Diego, California), 25, 141, 206
North Vietnam, 2–5, 7, 11, 23, 38, 39, 42, 53–55, 57, 58, 59–61, 67–69, 80, 82, 84, 95, 96, 98, 99–101, 103, 109, 111, 112, 114, 115, 118, 122, 125, 132, 134, 150, 167, 170, 175, 176, 209, 229, 230, 233; Brandon Bay, 7; Cat Bai, 150; Da Cat Ba, 87; Dien Bien Phu, 67; Dong Hoi, 126, 127; "Dragon's Jaws," 102; Hai Duong, 122, 128, 130, 136, 175; Haiphong, 69, 80, 85–87, 91, 92, 94, 99, 100, 109, 113, 122, 128, 129, 150, 166, 176, 177; Ham Rong, 83, 102; Hanoi, 11, 42, 54–57, 66, 67, 69, 80–82, 84, 85, 88, 94, 99–101, 113, 121, 122, 128, 150, 170, 174–78; Ha Trung, 42,

44, 120; Hon Gay, 86, 87; Kep, 84, 85, 89, 91, 93–95, 100, 121, 151, 158, 169; Me Xa, 136, 137; Moc Chau, 54, 55, 57, 80; Nam Dinh, 56, 66, 67, 114, 122, 123, 176–78, 205; Ninh Binh, 114, 115, 175; Phuc Yen, 55, 56, 81, 150; Phu Ly, 114, 175–77; Qui Hou, 56, 57; Red River, 87, 113, 173, 176, 178; Song Lua River, 42; Song Ma River, 83, 101, 102; Son La, 80–83; Thanh Hoa, 57, 83, 99, 101–5, 113, 174, 177; Thanh Hoa bridge, 83, 102–4; Vinh, 3, 4, 56, 81, 82, 97, 99, 100, 104, 125, 183
NVn 502nd Regiment, 71

Oakes, Floyd, 154, 155, 162, 168
Oakland, California, naval hospital, 1, 118, 179, 197–99, 214, 217, 219, 220, 224
Oceana, Virginia, 19
Okinawa, 161
ORI (Operational Readiness Inspection), 23, 24, 26–28, 156, 157, 159

Palmdale, California, 143
Palmer, Fred, 177, 192
Pathet Lao, 2
Pearl Harbor, 26–28, 78, 155–57, 159
Pennington, Dick, 66
Pennington, Dr., 188, 189
Pensacola, Florida, 17
Personnel losses:
—KIA: Bisz, Ralph, 209; Bowling, Roy, 130; Brown, Donald, 82; McWhorter, Henry, 95; Powers, Dick, 122; Taylor, Jesse, 129
—Operational: Avore, Art, 74; Bell, Bob, 40; Kapner, Dan, 152; Miller, Dale, 203; Morisette, Clem, 203; Prezorski, Tom, 37; Spitzer, Tom, 203; Tardio, Ron, 203
—POW: Chapman, Harley, 122; Davis, Ed, 98; Jenkins, Harry, 127; Stockdale, Jim, 111
Peter Pan, 229
Peterson, Sonja, 205
Peter the Great Bay, 55
Phantom sensation, 2

ABOUT THE AUTHOR

Wynn F. Foster, retired Navy captain and career naval aviator, flew 238 combat missions during the Korean and Vietnam Wars before he "zigged when I should have zagged" in the latter conflict. After serving as a Navy aviation cadet late in World War II, Foster graduated from the University of Minnesota, was commissioned, and reentered the Navy in July 1949. Flying the F8F Bearcat, the F9F Panther, and the A-4 Skyhawk, he logged 600+ carrier landings aboard the USS *Wright, Kearsarge, Forrestal, Intrepid, Enterprise,* and *Oriskany.*

A native of Minnesota, Foster currently resides in Coronado, California. He is secretary and member of the board of directors of the Tailhook Association; a freelance writer and associate editor of *The Hook* magazine, the quarterly journal of carrier aviation; and vice president of Optimist International, a 170,000+ member organization of youth-oriented community-service clubs.

THE NAVAL INSTITUTE PRESS

CAPTAIN HOOK

*A Pilot's Tragedy and Triumph
in the Vietnam War*

Designed by Pamela Lewis Schnitter

Set in Garth Graphic and Futura Extrabold
on a Macintosh IIci and output
by BG Composition
Baltimore, Maryland

Printed on 60-lb. Glatfelter smooth natural B-16
and bound in Holliston Kingston Natural
by The Maple-Vail Book Manufacturing Group
York, Pennsylvania